TURIA

WOMEN IN ANTIQUITY

Series Editors: Ronnie Ancona and Sarah B. Pomeroy

This book series provides compact and accessible introductions to the life and historical times of women from the ancient world. Approaching ancient history and culture broadly, the series selects figures from the earliest of times to late antiquity.

TURIA

A ROMAN WOMAN'S CIVIL WAR

Josiah Osgood

OXFORD
UNIVERSITY PRESS

OXFORD
UNIVERSITY PRESS

Oxford University Press is a department of the
University of Oxford. It furthers the University's objective
of excellence in research, scholarship, and education
by publishing worldwide.

Oxford   New York
Auckland   Cape Town   Dar es Salaam   Hong Kong   Karachi
Kuala Lumpur   Madrid   Melbourne   Mexico City   Nairobi
New Delhi   Shanghai   Taipei   Toronto

With offices in
Argentina   Austria   Brazil   Chile   Czech Republic   France   Greece
Guatemala   Hungary   Italy   Japan   Poland   Portugal   Singapore
South Korea   Switzerland   Thailand   Turkey   Ukraine   Vietnam

Oxford is a registered trade mark of Oxford University Press
in the UK and certain other countries.

Published in the United States of America by
Oxford University Press
198 Madison Avenue, New York, NY 10016

© Oxford University Press 2014

Library of Congress Cataloging-in-Publication Data
Osgood, Josiah, 1974–
Turia : a Roman woman's Civil War / Josiah Osgood.
ISBN 978-0-19-983234-7 (cloth : acid-free paper)—
ISBN 978-0-19-983235-4 (paperback : acid-free paper)
1. Rome—History—Civil War, 49-45 B.C.—Biography.
2. Women—Rome—Biography.   3. Wives—Rome—Biography.   4. Laudatio Turiae.
5. Women—Rome—History.   6. Women and war—Rome—History.
7. War and society—Rome—History.   8. Marriage—Social aspects—Rome—History.
9. Rome—Social conditions—510-30 B.C.   I. Title.
DG266.O84   2014
937'.05092—dc23
[B]   2014016382

FRONTISPIECE CREDIT: Portrait of a young woman dated to the second half
of the first century BCE. Courtsey of Ny Carlsberg Glyptotek, Copenhagen.

In memoriam

Gordon Williams

Jeanne Williams, known as Jay

Contents

List of Illustrations, Tables, and Map

Figures

Tables

Map

Author's Note: Abbreviations used for the names of ancient authors, their works, and modern reference works are those of S. Hornblower and A. Spawforth, eds. (2012), *The Oxford Classical Dictionary*, 4th edition, Oxford.

Acknowledgments

Thanks must go first to Ronnie Ancona for inviting me to contribute a book to this series, and to Ronnie and Sarah Pomeroy for accepting my initial proposal. Stefan Vranka at Oxford University Press also was encouraging in the early stages and has been an excellent guide since. I thank him and an anonymous referee for their vetting of the manuscript, which led to a number of improvements. Sarah Pirovitz, also at the Press, greatly aided me as the book made its way into production, and I am most grateful to production editor Marc Schneider and copy editor James Titus for all their work in bringing the book to press.

At Georgetown University, my scholarly home, I thank members of the Classics Department including the chair, Charlie McNelis, and also Tommaso Astarita, Carole Sargent, and especially Maxine Weinstein for expert advice and helpful questions. Students in several of my classes usefully discussed my work with me. I owe a particularly large debt to Georgetown's Graduate School for the award of a senior faculty research fellowship that granted me a semester of leave.

Friends and family have been as supportive as ever, putting up with all the obsessiveness needed to get a book done. Susanna Braund's timely gift of Marcel Durry's *Éloge funèbre d'une matrone romaine*, one of my favorite works of classical scholarship, was most welcome. I doubt that I could have understood the individuals I write about in this book if I didn't have people I could count on. The Romans were right to prize the virtue of faithfulness, *fides*.

My greatest debts are acknowledged, all too inadequately, in the dedication. To Gordon Williams, whom I met as a student at Yale College in 1994 and worked with for years afterward, I owe education in Latin language and literature, and the sometimes surprising horizons that unfold therefrom, such as the nature of Roman law. Gordon's appetite for books on the widest range of subjects, his equally Gibbonian faith in humanity, and his freedom of mind forever changed how I think. Jay Williams, Gordon's wife, died only a few months after him in 2010, having taken good care of Gordon in his final days. To Gordon's students, Jay gave staunch support, and whatever success I have enjoyed professionally is owed as much to her. At the same time, her playful wit helped to raise an occasional, and much-needed, laugh at the enterprise of scholarship. Jay's generosity and sparkle live on as inspiration.

TURIA

Prologue

In 1863, a remarkable woman was brought back to life.[1] In October of
that year, the greatest of Rome's modern historians, Theodor Mommsen,
gave a lecture before the Prussian Academy of Sciences in Berlin that
reconstructed her dramatic story, beginning with the murder of her
father during the outbreak of civil war between Julius Caesar and
Pompey in 49 BC.[2] Fearlessly avenging his death, in the years that followed she stepped forward to protect the remaining members of her
family, including her sister, other kinswomen, and especially her husband, to whom she remained married for forty years until her death.
All of this, and more, could be known because her funeral speech—or
laudatio, to use the Roman term—given by her husband was subsequently inscribed on her tomb on large marble slabs, parts of which
began reemerging during the Renaissance.

By late antiquity, the tomb had been dismantled and the precious
marble put to new uses. Two hacked-off pieces functioned as coverings
for niches in the catacombs on the ancient Via Labicana just outside
Rome. In the seventeenth century they were identified and, by 1758, had
joined Cardinal Alessandro Albani's enormous collection of antiquities
housed at his splendid villa. Cemented back together, they were available for firsthand study in Mommsen's day, and to date remain in the
Villa Albani in Rome.

The text of two further pieces, though not the stones themselves, also
survived for Mommsen to examine through transcriptions made by an-
tiquarians in the early seventeenth century. One fragment (now known
as "Fragment A") had been plastered into the wall of an abbey north of
the ancient Theater of Marcellus, and before the abbey and the fragment

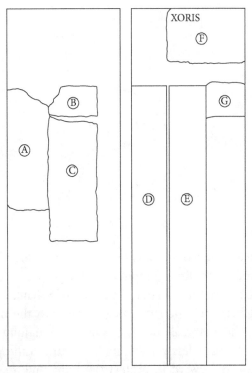

FIGURE 1. Schematic reconstruction drawing of the *laudatio*. The exact positions of Fragments A, B, and C in the left-hand column are uncertain, and the gap between Fragments F and G is an approximation.

with it were destroyed, several copies had been made, including one by G. M. Suarez, the librarian of Cardinal Barberini. The copy of the other fragment ("B"), also owed to Suarez, was said to have been made in the environs of the great tomb of Caecilia Metella on the Via Appia.

While scholars in the eighteenth century had already related the two sets of fragments to each other, Mommsen was able to go much further, thanks to a fresh discovery. By 1863, work was well underway on the historian's most heroic undertaking, a collection of *all* known inscriptions in Latin, including not just those on funerary monuments like the wife's, but also decrees, milestones, stamped bricks, and even graffiti on walls and pots.[3] Across the former Roman Empire, churches, museums, town-halls, antiquities collections, and libraries were scoured by an army of scholars in a manner reminiscent of the humanist hunt for literary texts several centuries earlier. Working at the then–Bibliothèque Impériale in Paris, one of Mommsen's young associates, Giovanni

Battista de Rossi, found in the papers of the Jesuit scholar Jacques Sirmond a transcription of forty incomplete lines of the *laudatio* made in Rome around AD 1600.[4] Where Sirmond viewed and copied the stone is unknown, but de Rossi recognized that the new fragment ("C") joined with Fragments A and B, and therefore rendered A and B much more comprehensible. Such talk of fragments and transcriptions may seem rather dusty, but it is important to recognize that de Rossi and Mommsen's detective work allowed a lost chapter in the wife's story to be recovered—a chapter, we shall see, that reveals the origins of her most important trait, her complete indomitability.

As luck would have it, none of the five fragments Mommsen had to work with mentioned either the wife's name or her husband's. Already in the eighteenth century, Philippe della Torre conjectured that she was Turia, the wife of Quintus Lucretius Vespillo, a high-ranking Senator who lived at the time of Rome's first emperor, Augustus; according to literary accounts, Lucretius' life was saved by Turia during the civil wars of that period.[5] Insisting that very few other couples could have had a story similar to that reported for Turia and Lucretius, Mommsen believed that della Torre's identification of the remarkable woman of the inscription with Turia must be correct.[6] But emphasizing discrepancies between the literary accounts and the *laudatio*, Dante Vaglieri in his 1898 publication of a new fragment of the inscription that had turned up ("F") cast doubt on Mommsen's view, doubt that has been shared by many since, though on somewhat different grounds (Fig. 2).[7] Because of the identification's uncertainty and also as a reminder of how much is still unknown on account of remaining gaps in the text, in the opening chapters of this book, I will refer to the "wife" and her "husband," and withhold from discussion the evidence for Lucretius and Turia in the literary sources.*

Even more than the couple's identification, it was the legal puzzles posed by the *laudatio* that excited Mommsen.[8] Through de Rossi's discovery, it became possible to set out most of the story of a bitter inheritance dispute that ensued after the murder of the wife's father, at the end of which she emerged triumphant. While the sources for Roman law, an area of increasing fascination for Mommsen in his scholarship, are relatively abundant, most date much later than the events of the inscription, refer to a somewhat different set of legal institutions, and may describe

---

* I retain "Turia" in the title of this book, however, to insure that those interested in the *Laudatio Turiae*, as the funerary speech is still conventionally called, may find the book more easily.

FIGURE 2. Fragment F of the *laudatio*. Museo Nazionale Romano, Rome, Italy. This piece was found by chance during sewer work in Rome in the late nineteenth century.

imaginary rather than real situations. The *laudatio*, therefore, offers both an opportunity, as Mommsen noted, and a challenge. Since he wrote, there have been numerous alternatives to his own precise views of what lay behind the inheritance dispute and how the wife prevailed; and a fresh consideration will be presented here.[9] All such discussions, though, underscore what Mommsen most insisted on, the vital importance of law in the lives of high-ranking Romans, including women.

However, then, one judges Mommsen's specific interpretations, his lecture—which in its published form included a new composite text with missing lines completed conjecturally—laid the foundation for all future study. Since 1863, though, two new pieces have emerged. One was the fragment published by Vaglieri in 1898, found on the Via Portuense, on the right bank of the Tiber River during sewage work; and the other ("G") was discovered in the depot of the Museo Nazionale Romano, January 1949, by the American classicist A. E. Gordon and his wife Joyce Gordon.[10] These reveal some vivid new details—how the wife used her jewelry to help her husband when he had to flee Italy, how she obtained a pardon for him, and how in his absence she defended his house from a gang. They also have provided information that has allowed a fuller reconstruction of the original appearance of the inscription.[11] The *laudatio*, it is now clear, originally appeared in two columns, headed by a larger title line, of which only the letters XORIS remain, from *uxoris*, meaning "wife" (Fig. 2). Each column was inscribed on a slab approximately 8.75 feet tall and 2.75 feet wide, each weighing perhaps around 1.5 tons. (This can be determined because the Gordons' fragment gave endings for the first nine lines of the Villa Albani fragments, allowing the width of each column to be determined; and on the reverse of the Portuense fragment survived a part of a gaming board that could be restored to full size, allowing approximation of the slab's height.)[12] The impressive size of this marble inscription complemented the husband's words of praise, as did also its beautiful execution. "Straight lines, letters consistent in shape, shading, and depth of cutting," rhapsodized A. E. Gordon; "the effect is harmonious and satisfying...a superior example of the stone-cutter's art."[13]

Inspired in part by the new discoveries and in part by the text already known, scholars in recent decades, in addition to working on the text itself, have continued to discuss problems dear to Mommsen.[14] New subjects have also opened up, especially how the wife's story illuminates the position of women in Roman society.[15] For the speech reveals, as Mommsen showed, not just how law affected women; it reveals, too, a Roman woman's ingenuity, her stamina, her willingness to fight. It reveals how Roman women could gain and control wealth, build networks, cultivate their reputations, and speak forcefully—to exert real power. As the civil wars that brought Augustus to power were unleashed on Roman society, women—long a force to be reckoned with in Rome's dynastic politics—gained greater power too. In the years that followed, Augustus and his legal experts struggled to recognize women's contribution to society, while also regulating their behavior in novel ways that provoked debate, a debate to which the husband's speech, along with his lavish inscription of it, makes a moving contribution. The *laudatio* casts some rare light, too, on challenges that women faced in their lives, civil war or no, including the pressure to have children, the difficulties of childbirth, and women's role in helping their families in bereavement.

In what follows, I attempt to reconstruct the wife's story more fully than it was in Mommsen's lecture, or in individual works of scholarship since, although these shall be key building blocks.[16] Some details in this reconstruction, the reader is warned, have to remain conjectural, given the present state of the *laudatio*; a full text, translation, and "Note on Chronology" are therefore included to allow for easy consultation of the evidence, and to suggest some other possibilities. But the attempt at reconstruction goes beyond guessing at what is missing. Throughout this book, subsidiary sketches are included of a number of the wife's contemporaries, such as Servilia, the lover of Julius Caesar who protected her own interests by pulling strings with the Roman Senate; Augustus' wife Livia, a refugee of the civil wars who fled Italy as a teenager with her two-year-old son in tow; and even the woman who built a marble arch that continues to draw visitors to her hometown in modern Croatia. By collecting the lives of similar historical actors (what historians call "prosopography"), a fuller portrait of the wife, and other high-ranking Roman women, is possible.

While much, including perhaps even the wife's name, may ultimately elude us, in trying to make sense of what we do know of her, through comparisons, we can understand better in particular the constraints placed on Roman women, the reasons for those constraints during that time (as well as in later times), and the ways in which women coped with them. A gulf between ancient and contemporary societies will be revealed, even as the story of the wife and her husband shall impress on us more insistently our shared humanity. To spend time with them not only deepens historical knowledge; the *laudatio* is also a superb literary reflection on what love can be.[17]

MAP 1. Italy, c. 50 BC.

1

Father's Death

When civil war broke out between Julius Caesar and Pompey in 49 BC, the wife was already engaged to her future husband. Shortly before their marriage was to take place, both of her parents were slain, "in the solitude of the countryside" according to a possible reconstruction of the text (1.3–4).[1] Because the opening twenty lines of the speech have not survived (where the husband would have discussed her family), little more can be said about the parents; it may even be, as we shall see later, that the husband talks loosely and that it was actually her father and stepmother who were killed, her mother having died previously.[2] What is clear is that by the time the crime occurred, the husband was gone; he would ultimately end up in Macedonia and the wife's brother-in-law, Cluvius, in Africa—two areas where opponents of Caesar gathered.[3] All plans for marriage had to be postponed, and revenge instead was required for the murder of her parents—without the help of her husband or Cluvius. But who were the assassins? Because the husband's speech is addressed directly to her, nowhere (it seems) did he find it important to reveal their identity. Was it, as Mommsen and many since have suspected, the family slaves?[4]

A full investigation into this mystery must begin with the situation in Italy in 49 BC.[5] On the first of January of that year, the Senate voted that Caesar should dismiss his army. Two tribunes vetoed the measure, but several days later, professing themselves to be in danger, the tribunes fled to Caesar in Ravenna. Caesar immediately crossed the Rubicon River, the provincial frontier, and began a rapid march southward, easily winning over the towns he passed through. With little hesitation, Pompey himself declared that the city of Rome must be evacuated, and he withdrew to Campania. His supporters, including Senators and equestrians (wealthy men who frequently served Senators as military officers and administrators), joined him, abruptly leaving Rome. Caesar continued to make public assurances of his peaceable intentions and spared Italy the plundering it expected. His insistence on mutual disarmament, though, was unacceptable to Pompey, who in March successfully made a risky crossing across the Adriatic in two waves from Brundisium. Pompey's plan—formulated well before January 49 BC, it has been argued—was to encircle Italy with ships and starve the peninsula into submission.[6] But already by the time he left for the Balkans, modifications had to be made; Sicily was abandoned to Caesar, and so Africa took on greater importance for Caesar's opponents.

While Caesar's initial takeover was smoother and more painless than many expected, there was still violence. Seizing the opportunity

TABLE 1 Roman Political History, 60–44 BC.

60	Caesar, Pompey, and Crassus form an alliance (the so-called "First Triumvirate")
59	Pompey marries Caesar's daughter, Julia
58	Clodius is tribune and drives Cicero into exile
57	Cicero returns to Rome from exile
54	Death of Julia
52	Milo kills Clodius (18 January); after his trial and conviction, he goes into exile
51	Cicero leaves Rome to govern Cilicia
49	Caesar crosses the Rubicon River, and war with Pompey breaks out; Pompey travels to Macedonia, and is joined by Cicero
48	Caesar travels to Macedonia; in his absence, the rising of Caelius occurs in Rome; Caelius and Milo, after trying to raise rebellion in Italy, are both killed; Pompey defeated at battle of Pharsalus and later murdered in Egypt
47	In Caesar's continued absence, Mark Antony is in control of Italy, clashing with Dolabella; Caesar returns to Rome and passes debt reform
46	Caesar defeats Pompeians in Africa; Cato kills himself
45	Caesar defeats Pompeians at Munda in Spain
44	Murder of Julius Caesar in Rome (15 March)

This table is based on the fuller chronology in Scullard (1982), pp. x–xxii.

furnished first by a distracted, and then a riven government, "great numbers of highwaymen," Suetonius writes in his biography of Augustus, "went about openly, armed as if to protect themselves, and travelers in the countryside—free and slave alike—were seized," and were then sold to landowners to staff the workhouses on their estates.[7] The problem was that hardly a soldier could be spared for policing, as at least sometimes happened before. Again from Suetonius, we happen to learn that Augustus' father was given a special assignment by the Senate in the late 60s BC to destroy a gang of runaway slaves operating in the territory around Thurii in southern Italy; the gang included followers of Spartacus, whose rebellion, officially anyway, had been crushed almost a decade before.[8] Many of these runaways were likely to have been herdsmen, armed so that they could protect their flocks from bandits and wolves in the lonely hills.[9]

Far from suppressing these dangerous bands, rival leaders in fact sought to use them. Pompey is said (admittedly by Caesar) to have recruited "slaves and shepherds," armed them, and made them cavalry.[10] More sinisterly, in 48 BC a frustrated politician, Marcus Caelius, tried to stir herdsmen, again in the territory of Thurii, to armed rebellion. His collaborator, Milo, put a gang of gladiators to work and also liberated slave barracks to launch raids. In one of his raids, Milo was killed by a stone thrown at him. Only some cavalry left by Caesar in southern Italy managed to put Caelius down.[11]

In understanding what life was like for the wife and her contemporaries, one must always keep this violence in mind. Traveling through the Italian countryside, or in the city of Rome, without armed protection would have been dangerous. Even before the civil war, a large bodyguard was standard.[12] It is therefore perfectly possible that a nameless gang such as those described by Suetonius could have been responsible for her parents' murder—while, say, the parents were journeying to one of their estates. But there are other possibilities, too; some perhaps more likely since, as the husband tells us (1.4–12), the wife was successful in avenging the crime, which would have been rather difficult if it was a nameless gang on the loose. If we assume for the moment that the crime did occur outside the city of Rome—or at least had its origins outside of Rome—another type of violence not uncommon in these years might have been to blame.

† † †

At the outbreak of the civil war, in a letter to his friend Atticus discussing the prospects, Cicero complains that those living in the towns and rural areas of Italy "cared for nothing but their fields, their farmsteads, their investments."[13] This was likely to have been true: in a world in which prestige depended on land owning, with relatively little significant economic production beyond agriculture and related activities, the acquisition of a rich and handsome estate was of the utmost importance. All might be sacrificed to this end, even potentially one's own family, through a marriage alliance undesired by the affianced themselves, for example, and even through worse means than that. It is several of Cicero's own earlier legal defenses that provide our best picture of this municipal life, for law—not to mention powerful patrons in Rome, like Cicero himself—was one of the weapons brandished in the ruthless battle for survival and success.

Most notorious are the affairs of Larinum, a town in a relatively poor region of central Italy, illuminated by Cicero's speech, *For Cluentius*.[14] Cicero's client belonged to one of the town's leading families, the Cluentii, who through marital alliances with another leading family, the Aurii, sought to consolidate their authority. Both were threatened, at least as Cicero portrays it, by an upstart, Oppianicus, who was married to Cluentius' aunt, until her death by poison, administered by Oppianicus himself (so Cicero says).[15] This is just one in a long catalogue of lurid crimes, of which two further specimens will suffice here; it matters less whether they happened exactly as Cicero reports than that he could report them rather matter-of-factly to a jury of high-ranking Romans.

One of Oppianicus' most patent schemes was directed against Asuvius, introduced by Cicero as a "wealthy young man of Larinum," which shows that his father was dead (otherwise, legally, Asuvius could have owned no property himself).[16] Asuvius set out for Rome accompanied by another man from Larinum, Avillius. Secretly employed by Oppianicus, Avillius was to engulf the youth in the city's fleshpots, which he did all too easily. While Asuvius was spending the night with a prostitute, Avillius—impersonating the young man—drew up a new will that favored Oppianicus. Asuvius afterward was taken to the sandpits outside the Esquiline Gates and murdered. The freedmen and friends of Asuvius would have brought Avillius and Oppianicus to justice, except that Oppianicus was able to bribe the investigating judicial official. The truth only came out years later, when Avillius himself along with others testified against Oppianicus.

While basking in this success, Oppianicus also had his sights on a far greater prize, the fortunes of the Cluentii and the Aurii.[17] He began with the Aurii. Their acting head was an old woman named Dinaea, mother by two marriages of one daughter and three sons, one of whom had disappeared during the Social War, when Rome briefly fought its Italian allies until deciding to grant them full citizenship. When news unexpectedly reached Dinaea some years later that her missing son was still alive, having been taken captive and put to work in a slave prison owned by a Senator, she summoned all of her relations, begging them to bring him back. Then falling ill, she drew up a will that named as principal heir her grandson, the son of her daughter Magia (through Magia's marriage to Oppianicus), but she also now left the long-missing Aurius 400,000 sesterces. Dinaea soon died (poisoned by Oppianicus, Cicero claims), Aurius was killed (on orders of Oppianicus), her will was further tampered with, and the vast Aurii inheritance passed to the Oppianici. So outraged was the town, though, that Oppianicus had to flee temporarily, returning only after he gained martial power over Larinum from the dictator Sulla. As for the wealth of the Cluentii, Oppianicus' hope was to gain it by murdering Cicero's client, who had not yet written his will and whose estate would pass to his mother, whom Oppianicus had married. Here Oppianicus failed, and when he subsequently died, it was alleged that Cluentius had poisoned him.

One should be cautious in accepting all that Cicero says; one should be equally cautious in dismissing it all as mere rhetoric. Ancient Italy, especially in an era of civil unrest, had its share of conmen, just as they can be found in the famous Paston letters that document English country life during the turbulent fifteenth century.[18] That correspondence introduces us to Thomas Daniel—an esquire of the royal household—who, in league with his sister Elizabeth, duped a man of all his lands; the victim was made to spend a romantic evening with Elizabeth, became engaged to her, and rashly turned his holdings over to a trust, only to discover that Elizabeth was already married. The Norfolk Pastons hoped to rely on Daniel's services when they became locked in a struggle with Lord Moleyns, after Moleyns with a posse of armed men had seized the Pastons' manor at Gresham (it had once belonged to the wife in the Moleyns family). As John Paston fought in London to uphold ownership, his young wife Margaret moved back onto a part of the property, and wrote her husband asking for crossbows, combat axes, and armored jackets to defend her small household. Moleyns sent a larger army—a thousand strong, John later claimed—and Margaret was ejected. With some effort, the Pastons regained Gresham, but they would go on to far more bitter struggles over other lands, inherited (or so they claimed) from their wealthy and childless patron, Sir John Fastolf, immortalized as Shakespeare's Falstaff.

As in fifteenth-century England, so in late Republican Roman society, neighboring estate-owners were often at war with another. The chaos of the Social War, followed by the first clash between Sulla and Marius, inaugurated a period of heightened violence, in which recourse was not just to personal crime and legal feuds, as seen in *For Cluentius*, but also fighting with small private armies.[19] At one point in Cluentius' defense, Cicero has to justify an attack made by the bailiffs of a Samnium property belonging to Cluentius, claiming that it was simply to defend Cluentius' "property and exclusive right of occupancy."[20] Herdsmen belonging to two men named Ancharius and Pacenus had (or so Cicero suggested) tried to seize Cluentius' holdings, or land that at any rate he controlled. Cicero elsewhere attacks the politician Clodius for seizing neighbors' property, not even through false accusations but "by the use of camps, armies, and military standards"; even such wealthy men as Publius Varius, who served as a juror in Rome, was driven from his property in Etruria, Cicero claimed.[21]

Worse still is the story of Marcus Tullius—probably no relation of his namesake, Cicero, but defended by Cicero in a partially preserved speech—for it involved bloodshed. Tullius had a farm, inherited from his father, in the territory of Thurii. When his neighbor, the Senator Gaius Claudius, sold his farm to Publius Fabius, Fabius began to covet a portion of Tullius' farm, the so-called "Popilian" field (named for a former owner), because it would join conveniently with his own holdings, which evidently proved less productive than Fabius had hoped. Failing to auction off his farm along with the Popilian field, which he illicitly threw in, Fabius then brought armed men onto what Cicero insists was Tullius' property, claimed it as his, and resolved with Tullius to settle the matter in court. But the next night, slaves of Fabius came back to the Popilian field, cut the throats of Tullius' slaves, and demolished the buildings on the land. One man escaping the massacre reported it to Tullius, who then made an appeal for help to his neighbors. Cicero, who appeared at least twice in court on behalf of Tullius, was concerned especially in his extant second speech with recovering damages for the murder of Tullius' slaves; Fabius' lawyer, Quinctius, evidently did not deny the basic facts of the situation at an earlier hearing.

As Cicero makes clear in *For Tullius* such was the violence in the Italian countryside that a new penalty was devised in 76 BC by the praetor Marcus Lucullus.[22] In earlier times, either simple or double compensation for wrongful damage to slaves or other property was sufficient because men's estates and their slave staffs, not to mention their covetousness, were all less; and very rarely, Cicero claims, would a man be killed. But by Lucullus' time, when "many slave gangs in remote fields and pasturelands were said to have been armed and carrying out murder," a fourfold award of damages now seemed appropriate—as a way to encourage men to settle their disputes legally rather than with (more) armed violence. Other related measures are known from around the same time and afterward, suggesting, unfortunately, that disturbances continued.[23]

In 49 BC, it could only have gotten worse, as magistrates would have little or no time at all for legal remedies. Rather than assuming, then, as Mommsen did in his discussion of the *laudatio*, that slaves belonging to the wife's parents were responsible for their murder, we have at least to consider the possibility of a plot by those with arguably a stronger motive, neighbors to their estates—or others who might have stood to benefit financially from their deaths. Could the parents have been assassinated on their estate, or even in Rome? Or did an attack by a neighbor's personal army, launched in an effort to claim property held by the parents, go astray?

† † †

The aftermath of the murder may offer more clues. According to the husband (1.7–9), by her strenuous efforts, his future wife fulfilled her duty to avenge her parents' death as effectively as if he had been there, receiving help only (so he states) from her sister. The guilty were punished. Were slaves implicated in the crime, this would have been all too easy. In the late Republican period, a master legally had the right to punish his own slaves, even to kill them, although this would change later.[24] If a master was killed by his slaves, it was even considered acceptable to kill every slave in the household; there was also a tradition of torturing the household to discover the truth. (The justification for all of this was that all slaves had a duty to come to their master's rescue, and none responsible for a master's death should be able to enjoy a testamentary manumission by a master he had murdered.) Well into imperial times, these practices were debated, suggesting that attacks by slaves on their owners did happen. A slave killing a man other than his master, by contrast, could be tried in Rome, and this would have been the legal recourse against a free Roman accused of homicide also, at least in some situations.[25]

Even if free Romans were implicated, though, there was another time-honored way of gaining vengeance, self-help.[26] This went well beyond many modern views of self-defense, as can be seen in remarks made by Cicero in his speech of defense for Milo (regarding the murder of Clodius in 52 BC): "If there are any circumstances in which a man is justly killed—and there are many—this one is not only just but unavoidable, when an onslaught of violence is driven back with violence."[27] A soldier, for example, is sexually molested by another and then takes his revenge in murder: justifiable, according to Cicero. And he then goes on: "When it comes to a bandit or a brigand lying in wait, can inflicting death be unjust? What, then, is the point of our bodyguards, our swords? Surely it should not be permitted to possess them, if it is absolutely forbidden to use them." A thief, especially one who came by night, could be apprehended and killed by a man with the aid of his neighbors, justly—in the eyes of the authors of Rome's early legal code, the Twelve Tables (dating ca. 450 BC), and doubtless in the eyes of many Romans in Cicero's day too.

With such a variety of forms of justice available, then, the wife's act of vengeance in itself does little to suggest the identity of the murderers—whether family slaves (as Mommsen thought), highwaymen, or agents of the neighbors. It is the inheritance dispute that followed that seems more suggestive. To understand it, some final, essential background on women's legal rights in Rome is necessary.[28] By historical standards, these were extraordinary: though formally excluded from political life, women by the late Republic were able to hold and dispose of property in their own name, even when married. To be sure, there were certain ways in which men might control women. Most importantly, so long as the male head of the family, the *paterfamilias*, was alive—this would usually be a woman's father, but could also be her paternal grandfather—the woman fell under his authority and could not own property herself; but exactly the same was true for her brothers (which is why we have to assume that the father of Oppianicus' victim, Asuvius, was no longer living). The Romans themselves recognized the distinctiveness of this so-called "paternal power" (*patria potestas*), but never abandoned it.

The same cannot be said for a second form of control, *manus*, the marital power that a husband exerted over his wife. Traditionally when a woman married, she passed out of her father's *potestas* into the "hand" (the literal meaning of *manus*) of her husband. At this point, any property that she had (or later came into) belonged to her husband (or to his *paterfamilias*). Marriage without *manus*, which allowed more easily for divorce, became the norm by the late Republic, although some Romans still favored the older custom. The union of Cluvius and the wife's sister happens to be one of the few known examples.

Especially important for understanding the wife's situation in 49 BC, after the death of her father, is the third form of control—guardianship.[29] If a woman's *paterfamilias* was deceased and she was not yet beyond the age of puberty, she would have a guardian (as would her brother). The guardian (*tutor*) would be named by the father in his will or, failing that, would typically be the nearest male relative on her father's side (these relatives were called "agnates"). After puberty, while her brother would now be entirely free, the woman—so long as she did not contract a marriage with *manus*—still would have a guardian. Traditionally this type of guardian also was the nearest male agnate, and he had in law a claim on his ward's estate if she died intestate; presumably because of this, the guardian had to give his permission for certain types of transactions his ward might make, including the alienation of some forms of property (including land) and making a will. Such agnatic guardianship, *tutela legitima*, might limit women to leaving their property only to certain male relatives, and, by the late Republic, was being circumvented through the naming of another man as guardian. Under the emperor Claudius, in the mid-first century AD, it was more or less completely eliminated and guardianship for adult women overall was essentially no more than a formality. The result was that unless she married with *manus*, a woman whose *paterfamilias* had died had virtually complete control over her own property.

This independence went hand in hand with other legal rights. In a civil case, a woman could petition for a hearing on her own behalf, although not on that of others. A woman could defend herself in court, although not others. Convention dictated that women should appear in courts—and in public more generally—only when they needed to, not necessarily because women were deemed weak (although some later jurists said that), but rather to protect them from male heckling and the like.[30] Thus ideally a woman would rely on a male advocate like Cicero to represent her, and Cicero indeed is known to have had several female clients.[31] But a woman could be made to stand trial (in both civil and criminal cases); and in trials initiated by other parties, she might have to serve as a witness. It was also considered entirely acceptable for women themselves to bring an accusation of criminal charge if, as the jurist Macer puts it, "they are pursuing injury to themselves or are obtaining satisfaction for the death of their relatives."[32]

The law, then, respected the almost sacred duty that Romans felt to avenge murdered kin, especially a parent. It was not for nothing that the young Augustus in 44 BC made so much of the initial failure by his rival Marcus Antonius (familiarly known, thanks to Shakespeare, as "Mark Antony") to have avenged the assassins of Augustus' (adoptive) father Caesar.[33] Even at the end of his long life, Augustus was parading his own response: "I drove into exile the murderers of my father, punishing their crime in legally established tribunals."[34] This was what the Romans called *pietas*. And while the husband could praise his wife in the *laudatio* for exactly this—perhaps thinking, at the back of his mind, of Augustus too—he makes it clear that it should have been he and Cluvius who saw to things.[35] Because civil war had broken out, she along with her sister had to take matters into their own hands, whether through the courts or the more traditional self-help, and they succeeded.

But the troubles continued. The father's will was contested by individuals claiming to be his kinsmen, on the grounds that it was improperly drafted. In particular, they said, he had with his wife contracted a *coemptio* (1.13–14). A *coemptio* (literally a "sale") was one of the mechanisms by which a wife entered into the *manus* of her husband. Now a consequence of this was that the wife herself would be one of the automatic heirs of her husband, should he die intestate; by law these heirs had to be explicitly included or excluded in a will, otherwise the will would be invalidated and the intestacy rules would ensue.[36] If, then, the father had contracted the *coemptio* after the writing of his will and failed to update the will accordingly, there might be some basis for the contest.[37] It is precisely this scenario that has suggested that he had remarried.

The bigger question, though, is why the claimants themselves would benefit from intestacy, and here *tutela legitima* rears its ugly head.[38] In intestacy, the wife should have inherited everything because her father's wife was dead, her sister had passed into the *manus* of Cluvius, and she had no other siblings. If she refused the inheritance, it would then go to the nearest agnate, and failing that, to relatives in the larger clan (*gens*) of her father (his *gentiles*). The problem was that, even if, as doubtless she would, the wife did claim the inheritance, she would pass into the guardianship of these *gentiles* too, and they would gain de facto control of all of her holdings. Her sister may never have gotten a single sesterce.

The situation is perfectly illustrated by a vivid comparison made by the poet Catullus.[39] Describing the love of his mythical heroine Laodamia, he says that it surpasses that of a grandfather, "weak with age," for a grandson newly born to an only daughter; the grandson, "found at long last to take his grandfather's wealth, has seen his name entered into the witnessed tablets, thus wiping out the unholy delight of a now derided member of the clan (*gentilis*)."[40] For reasons to be explained shortly, the father imagined by Catullus could not actually name his daughter as sole heir; she could inherit through intestacy, but then the wicked kinsman would pounce, refusing her the right to leave the property to any but him. But with the last-minute arrival of the grandson, disaster was averted. The new grandfather can now produce a valid will, the "witnessed tablets" Catullus mentions, which will securely exclude his unloved relative.

The unholy delight of the kinsman jolts us back into the world of Oppianicus. After the wife's parents' death, it would not be surprising if unscrupulous relatives, or even unrelated adventurers claiming to be relatives, stepped forward to oppose the will. "Romans," it has been observed, "were particularly litigious during estate settlements."[41] This was primarily because with the death of the *paterfamilias*, whose children after all could own nothing themselves, there was a rare opportunity for massive financial gain. So much so, of course, that it was thought that even murder would be a resort, to speed the process along. At a minimum, the wife's opponents were preying on her and her sister at a moment of great vulnerability: in grief for their loss, lacking male protectors. The sisters also had a husband and fiancé on the side opposite to that in control of Italy. But were the alleged kinsmen capable of worse? Could they have planned to murder the parents?

Such ruthlessness would be reminiscent not only of Oppianicus but also actors in Cicero's first great legal defense, *For Roscius*.[42] The case concerned the murder of Cicero's client's father, the owner of at least thirteen valuable estates, many along the Tiber River. Preferring to spend his time in Rome, the elder Roscius was killed one night on his way home from a party. While the prosecution claimed that his son, who had to manage the estates, was fearful of disinheritance and as so, murdered his father, Cicero points the blame instead at several kinsmen with whom the elder Roscius had a long-standing feud. With the connivance of a freedman of Sulla, there can be no doubt, they had managed to seize most of the Roscii holdings; and lest Cicero's client make trouble about it, Cicero alleges, they decided to eliminate him by the accusation of murder. Cicero strongly hints, but cannot actually prove, that these kinsmen were behind the elder Roscius' murder.[43] And with a hint too, rather than any proof, is where we are finally left with the parents' death. Perhaps the crime was planned by neighbors or distant relatives, or perhaps an altercation with such individuals—or their agents—somehow got out of hand. What can be said, more certainly, is that the wife's struggle provides an illustration complementary to that of Cicero's speech for Roscius, along with his other defenses, of what was at stake when a wealthy *paterfamilias* died.

† † †

It was precisely to protect against litigiousness, or worse, that Romans so carefully drafted their wills, for there was not a routine process of probate as such. Indeed Romans had no means at all of officially recording changes in land ownership, which, of course, was a further incentive to declare war on one's neighbors, especially at the critical time of the *paterfamilias'* death.[44] In drafting his will, though, the father of the wife faced a problem, in the background too of Catullus' memorable picture of the rapacious kinsman. In the second century BC, a law had been passed, the *lex Voconia*, which stipulated that persons in the highest census class could not institute women as heirs.[45] In a Roman will, one always named an heir or heirs, who were to split the bulk of the inheritance, while also fulfilling certain other obligations, such as discharging debts. One could name, in addition to heirs, legatees who would receive a simple bequest (a cash sum, for example). The *lex Voconia* seems to have aimed specifically to cut down on large fortunes passing to women, because it also stipulated that no legacy could be more than the amount the heirs took—thereby limiting women to at most one half of the estate. While reasons for this regulation are debated and may have had less to do with hurting women as such, rather than helping men involved in public life, it is clear that it was especially hard on daughters without brothers: their *paterfamilias* would have to institute as heir an outsider who got at least half of the estate.[46] Otherwise the father could die intestate, but for his daughter that meant, as we have seen, the odious *tutela legitima*.

Ways gradually were found to circumvent the law, as wealthy Romans—of which the father certainly was one—were expert in dodging the law: not necessarily breaking it (which was what more often the oppressed had to do), but finding loopholes.[47] One father of an only daughter, Cicero writes, was able to make her his heir simply by insisting that he had not properly registered in the census. Another tactic was to insert a clause in the will stipulating a wish for the whole estate to pass to an only daughter; this was open to challenge, but in his ethical writings Cicero suggests that it was the height of dishonor for the primary heir not to grant the wish. Another means still was a deathbed request to one's heir to pass the estate onto the woman in question.[48] With these last two methods, a father might institute his son-in-law as nominal heir, as we are told Julius Caesar did when his only daughter, Julia, married Pompey in 59 BC.[49] Caesar's thinking would presumably have been that, should he die, Pompey would not dare risk the ignominy of denying Julia Caesar's full patrimony. In the event, it never mattered because Julia died in childbirth in 54 BC—one of the circumstances that drove her father and widower husband fatally apart.

It seems likely that the wife's father resorted to a similar dodge. The precise contents of his will can never be known, but the husband does speak, perhaps casually, of himself and his wife as the father's "heirs" (1.13). It also seems clear that the father intended the wife's sister to inherit something, too. Presumably, then, the husband of the *laudatio* was instituted as heir, with the intention that he would share the inheritance with his wife—he was, after all, on the verge of marrying her. Ultimately, everyone must have hoped, the inheritance would then pass to one or more grandchildren (as in Catullus' simile). If the wife was to have, like her sister, a marriage with *manus*, her husband would hold all of the property anyway. And because the sister did have a marriage with *manus*, likely Cluvius himself was also named as an heir in the will, or otherwise a legatee. As for the wife's guardian, that would be her husband—a stopgap measure if she was ultimately to marry with *manus*.[50] The family's strategy of marrying with *manus* itself may have been, at least in part, a strategy to circumvent problems posed by the *lex Voconia*, although a potentially risky one, since it left the daughters rather at the mercy of their husbands. But when it came to only daughters in well-off families, there really were, legally speaking, no easy answers.

According to the husband, the wife through her persistence prevailed over the rival claimants, demonstrating they were not actually kinsmen. "Even if the will of your father had been broken," he states, "those who were bringing action had no such right [of guardianship], since they were not members of the same clan (*gens*)" (1.23–24). Whether the matter came to a formal hearing or whether she simply overwhelmed them with a show of strength cannot be known. Regardless, this was only a part of her victory; as the husband insists, while it was true that in intestacy the wife would have inherited everything anyway and could share it with her sister, it was important to her to "uphold the acts of [her] father" (1.20). Here, again, is *pietas*, for observing a man's final wishes, exactly as he left them, was also for Romans a sacred duty, transcending law, as Cicero's remarks on the *lex Voconia* suggest. And again there is an echo of the young Augustus, who struggled in the teeth of opposition in 44 BC to pay out the legacies to the people of Rome made in his father Caesar's will.[51]

"They gave way to your steadfastness and did not pursue the matter further," the husband concludes his discussion (1.25). "In having achieved this, you completed the defense that you had undertaken, all on your own, of respect for your father, devotion to your sister, and loyalty to us" (1.25–26). The origins of the struggle perhaps had nothing to do with the civil war that broke out in 49 BC, but the struggle itself played itself out after so many men, including the men in the wife's life, were away. The struggle, as it unfolded, almost certainly owed at least something to their absence: other lawsuits against female relations of the party out of favor are attested for Rome's civil wars.[52] But in the absence of male kinsmen, the wife was forced to act independently, and she learned important things about herself. She had the strength to avenge the death of her parents. She could manipulate the law to defend her own interests, as well as those of her sister. In the face of a terrible tragedy, she had her first taste of power and would rely on that feeling as new challenges came.

2

The Fiancé

Avenging her parents' murder and victorious in legal battle, the wife still had a problem. On her own and yet unable to marry her fiancé until his return—if he did return—she would have to consider her reputation; for a woman of her age and status to be living alone would have raised eyebrows in Rome. In an elaborate list that the husband gives of his wife's fine qualities, it is no accident that the first he mentions is her "sexual morality," *pudicitia* (1.30). This was a distinctly Roman concept—the Greeks had no equivalent—and it was felt important for the community's wellbeing.[1] Men were supposed to exhibit it as well as women, but for woman *pudicitia* was more important and achieved in different ways. While a man might sleep with a prostitute (for example), a woman could only sleep with her husband. There was some grounds, of course, for this double standard, at least within marriage: men desired a guarantee of the legitimacy of their children, the future citizens of Rome, which only strict fidelity by their women could provide.[2] A woman's *pudicitia*, though, embraced many other traits and was sought for its own sake; in the honor-driven society that was Rome, it was a part of her honor.[3] She should not make unnecessary appearances in public, hence the ban on her serving as a legal advocate for others. If she did appear, she should appear only with certain people and should walk a certain way, talk a certain way, dress a certain way: the husband himself mentions specifically in his list the wife's "unassuming appearance and sober attire" (1.31), but these, in a way, were aspects of *pudicitia*. Dress, though, one may add, is always in society a useful way of sending a message about oneself (Fig. 3).

    Pudicitia can sometimes almost be seen in action, as for example in a letter of Cicero to his friend Fabius Gallus, who wished to buy a house

FIGURE 3. Marble statue of Viciria Archas, a woman from Herculaneum, of mid-Augustan date. Museo Nazionale Archeologico, Naples, Italy. The elaborate mantle she wears suggests her sexual morality, and indeed scholars call her pose (seen in many other examples) the "pudicitia type."

next to Cicero's on the Palatine that belonged to a certain Crassus, but was occupied by Crassus' sister Licinia.[4] Licinia's husband was away in Spain, and so Cicero sent his daughter Tullia to speak to her about the matter; for if Cicero had gone himself, it could have compromised Licinia's *pudicitia*. Lest this convention seem utterly restrictive, it could be opportunely invoked by women, as the sequel to the story shows. Licinia told Tullia that "she did not dare move when her husband was away...and without his knowledge" and thus avoided the hassle of any further discussion with the Ciceros, not to mention the sale of her brother's property where she was so comfortably residing.

Yet *pudicitia* did most certainly have a restrictive side to it, which also can be seen in action. Augustus, his biographer Suetonius tells us, forbade his daughter Julia and also his granddaughters from the company of strangers, even once writing to a handsome young man, Vinicius, "that he had acted indiscreetly in coming to pay his respects to Augustus' daughter at Baiae."[5] A resort town on the Bay of Naples, Baiae was renowned for its natural hot springs, as well as its beaches, bathhouses, and boating parties. *Pudicitia* notwithstanding, men and women partied with abandon there, at the "seashore which was no friend to girls' modesty" as a contemporary love poet puts it.[6] It was no surprise that the especially puritanical Augustus, obsessed with his family's reputation, kept a close watch on Julia, as she vacationed at one of the properties he owned there. The loose behavior of some led to strict rules for others.

To protect her own *pudicitia*, the wife might have lived with her sister, but as Cluvius was also away, she found the even neater solution of moving in with her soon mother-in-law, to await the husband's return. By doing so, she was able to keep an eye out for the older woman, and she did so well. "You took care of my mother as well as you did your own parents and saw to her security as you did for your own people," proclaims the husband, at the culminating point in his cataloguing of her virtues (1.32–33). It all seems tame enough, but he was probably referring to the next dramatic chapter of life, which only was revealed for us after Dante Vaglieri published the Via Portuense fragment of the *laudatio* in 1898.[7] Though a rather small piece, this new discovery shows that the wife was plunged directly into the political unrest that ultimately broke out in Italy itself during the civil war years. Fortified by her earlier successes, she would again muster the strength to stave off threats to herself, her fiancé, his mother, and the hoped-for marriage.

† † †

As Pompey and Caesar prepared to leave Italy, and then left along with their allies, life for those who remained behind was to prove difficult.[8] It was not simply that robbery and murder were on the rise throughout the countryside; these were feared now even in the city of Rome itself. Also dreaded was the official confiscation of land, or less official plundering, by whichever side prevailed.[9] Writing to his wife Terentia in January of 49 BC, Cicero already expressed concern that Caesar might give Rome over to pillaging—which did not happen.[10] Later, though, as Caesar's ultimate victory came into sight, Cicero, Terentia, and their friends expressed a more realistic concern that as a Pompeian who had left Italy, Cicero might lose his own estates, and she might lose hers.[11]

But then for a time, as Caesar became ensnared in a war between Cleopatra of Egypt and her siblings, it looked as if the Pompeians might prevail—but *after* Cicero had abandoned their cause.[12] Cicero in the end was spared, but seizure of properties of those who went down fighting against Caesar did ultimately occur, including the extensive portfolio of Pompey himself, perhaps worth a staggering 200 million sesterces. During the prolonged liquidation, Caesar's onetime mistress Servilia, among others, was said to have picked up some fantastic bargains.[13]

To complicate everything, including the sale of confiscated property, there was a liquidity crisis, something Romans had experienced in years prior, and also a nearly unprecedented shortage of coin itself.[14] Fear drove coin along with other portable valuables, such as silver plate, underground—sometimes literally, into buried hordes. Yet more coin than ever was needed, primarily to pay the increased number of men under arms. "Soldiers and money," as Caesar liked to say: the two went together.[15] In 49 BC, Caesar tried selling off some of the haul in gold he had taken from Gaul, but in flooding the market so quickly, he discovered a basic law of economics: the gold became devalued in relation to silver and other baser metals, and he only got half its normal value.

In a desire to gain coin and also out of fear of the fate of debtors, loans started to be called in, which had further devastating consequences. In Rome one could pay for large transactions, by issuing (or transferring) a promissory note; these IOUs effectively were a type of money, a useful alternative to coin.[16] But with the fear of confiscations, few would want to accept such notes, putting yet more pressure on the desire for coin. Even settling loans with tangible assets such as land was difficult, because land itself was fetching relatively little in cash—especially with the rush to market after the calling in of loans. From wealthy landowners on down to the lower classes of Rome, many found themselves either illiquid or on the verge of bankruptcy altogether. As credit dried up, the economy threatened to grind to a halt.

This financial crisis took a toll on individuals' domestic lives—including, we shall see, the wife—and it was also responsible for major developments in public life. Caesar himself in 49 BC attempted a first solution by two measures.[17] To help with the liquidity crisis, he ordered that all property should be valued by assessors at prewar prices, and that creditors should accept estates so valued on the assumption that prices would be restored soon. To help even more directly with the shortage of coin, he forbade the holding of more than 60,000 sesterces in silver or gold (claiming that he was reviving an already existing law). When it was suggested that rewards should be offered to slaves who informed against their masters, Caesar refused.

By the following year, the new urban praetor, Trebonius, an old ally of Caesar, commenced with the assessments. Another Caesarian, Caelius Rufus, angry that he had not himself obtained the senior praetorship, sensed political opportunity: many of the ordinary city dwellers, up to their ears in debt to landlords, loan sharks, and others, had been clamoring for more extensive reform.[18] First attempting to take up appeals against Caesar's assessors, Caelius then pledged directly to help all those in debt and also promised a suspension of rent payments. Putting on the mantle of the late Clodius, he gained a following that he was ready to turn on Trebonius. After a riot in the Forum, the consul Servilius, who by this point had his own forces, passed a decree against Caelius and barred him from further official duties and attendance at the Senate. Caelius decided to set out for Campania, to join Annius Milo, who was launching his own rebellion.

In the 50s BC, Milo had fought a gang war in the streets of Rome against Clodius, culminating in the murder of Clodius just outside the city in 52 BC, in the aftermath of which Milo was prosecuted, convicted, and forced into exile.[19] Caesar did not permit Milo's return along with other political exiles in 49 BC, presumably in an effort to keep Clodius' still fiercely loyal partisans on his own side, but Milo returned anyway and began gathering large forces, including his former gladiators, armed herdsmen, and the desperate poor.[20] Breaking open slave barracks, he ravaged the rich Campanian countryside, forcing the consul Servilius to declare war on him. Defying Servilius, Caelius fled to Milo, who by this point was driven from Campania to central Italy and killed before Caelius could reach him. Caelius, who tried to bring the southern Italian shepherds over to his side, himself perished after he failed to win over through bribes some cavalry of Caesar posted there.

In the East as all of this was happening, Caesar was forced to invoke his dictatorial powers and sent Antony to Rome as his "Master of the Horse": Rome would effectively be under martial law.[21] Antony's primary task may, in fact, have been to win back over the supporters of Caelius and Milo to Caesar's side, but in the face of new appeals to the city masses, especially by the tribune Dolabella, he ended up having to play up the military aspects of his position.[22] Born a patrician, Dolabella like Clodius before him became a plebeian through adoption so that he could hold the tribunate, a position that he used as a platform to launch a radical program of complete cancellation of debts in arrears, probably including unpaid rent.[23] Already furnished with his own troops inside Rome, Antony clashed violently with him, even for a time fighting over control of the Forum. Arson, theft, and murder rained on Rome, with the situation only assuaged by Caesar's return in 47 BC.

What women in particular faced through all of this can already be imagined, but is richly documented through Cicero's correspondence with Terentia and also his friend Atticus. Women, the letters make clear, had to cope not just with the lack of security, but also the threat of confiscations and the difficulties of the financial crisis. There was also the agony of not knowing which side would prevail and the dilemma of how, or even whether, to support the men in their lives, especially those on the Pompeian side, which had lost control of Italy itself and increasingly looked likely to be the losers in the war altogether. Hard choices had to be made. Terentia's story is worth sketching out here because it helps to expose the difficulties that the wife herself would have faced.[24]

† † †

The civil war that broke out in 49 BC was not in fact the first disaster that Terentia and her husband had to live through. We must start eight years prior, when Cicero was driven into exile by Clodius on the grounds that he, as consul in 63 BC, had executed without trial several of the Catilinarian conspirators.[25] After Cicero's departure, mobs were unleashed on his Palatine house, which, along with his other property, was confiscated and sold for the benefit of the state. Through a middleman, Clodius obtained the ravaged mansion and built on it a shrine to Liberty, an act ideological and practical at once, because Clodius could rally his supporters here.[26]

Cicero wrote to Terentia while still in Italy: "Should I ask you to come, a sick woman, physically and mentally worn out? Shall I not ask you? Am I, then, to live without you?"[27] The writer's desperate emotional state is clear, but what he goes onto say—like the rest of this and the other letters to her—reveals much about Terentia too, even though her side of the correspondence does not survive: "If there is any hope of my return, you must strengthen it and help the cause." Obviously Cicero believed that she could be of great assistance in reversing Clodius' banishment, even as she also had to take full charge of their teenage daughter and young son, and also worry about the fate of her dowry. Technically this belonged to Cicero and so could be confiscated, but there might be some room for appeal.[28] (Additionally, by having Cicero informally manumit slaves that constituted some of the dotal property, there might be a way to dodge any penalties.)

In the face of these worries, Terentia immediately sprang into action, working for Cicero's return. Moving in at least for a time with her half-sister, the Vestal virgin Fabia, she along with her daughter Tullia wore mourning garments—a visible protest and a way to elicit sympathy.[29] It would have been seen by those visiting the women and when they went out publicly, which Cicero writes they did only rarely (here is the ideal of *pudicitia* again).[30] With help from her husband, Piso, Tullia went down on her knees before the consul—exploiting her pitiful young age, as Terentia could not.[31] But Terentia, it can be inferred, solicited the support of other politicians; "I have thanked the individuals you wished me to," Cicero notes, "and written that it was you who informed me."[32] In the campaign to bring back Cicero, Terentia clearly was serving as a power-broker, calling in favors owed and indebting herself and her husband to others for the future.

There were other ways for Terentia to help. She supported the children financially, even though this was Cicero's responsibility, and seems even to have been willing to use her resources to help Cicero himself (theirs was a marriage without *manus*, and so she held separate property).[33] In response to the latter, Cicero protested: "Terentia, dear, what is this you write to me about selling your block of houses? What, oh what, for heaven's sake is to become of me?"[34] Her money had to be saved, he thought, for their children. She sent Cicero detailed updates on developments in Rome.[35] She wrote him words of encouragement, and at the same time, kept him in the dark of what happened to her: "The considerate Publius Valerius wrote to me—I wept bitterly as I read—of how you were escorted from the Temple of Vesta to the Tabula Valeria. Really, dear Terentia, the light of my life, my darling…to think that you should be harassed like this!"[36] Evidently, Clodius had ordered Terentia to appear at his tribunal and, to humiliate not only her but also Cicero, treated her insultingly.

The letters Cicero wrote to Terentia from exile, some of the most moving in all his correspondence, highlight his wife's tenacity and his own weakness. "I see that you are taking upon yourself every hardship," Cicero himself acknowledges; and he latter adds: "Many write letters and everybody tells me of your unbelievable bravery and strength, of how you are worn out by no trials, mental or physical."[37] "I cannot write further," he claims in the same letter, "so strong is my crying, and I wouldn't wish to reduce you to the same grief."[38] Hundreds of miles away, Cicero even imagines that he can see Terentia, a sustaining vision, but one that also induces the fear that his weeping exhausts her.[39] Published like the rest of his correspondence only after Cicero's death, these letters are a fine monument to the vital love they felt for one another: "Take care of yourself and be assured that there is nothing more dear to me than you, nor ever has been."[40]

A sad contrast is provided by the letters Cicero wrote to Terentia during their next great crisis, his voluntary absence from her during the struggle between Caesar and Pompey.[41] Successfully restored in 57 BC, Cicero had been sent in 51 BC to serve as governor of the province of Cilicia. To many, civil war already seemed a possibility, and there could be little doubt that if it did break out, Cicero would join the side of Pompey. This had to have weighed on the minds of Terentia and Tullia as they considered, in Cicero's absence, whom Tullia should marry after she had recently been divorced by her second husband, Crassipes, perhaps because of a lack of success at having a child.[42] Various candidates were considered, including, on the suggestion of Caelius—who had been apprenticed to Cicero years earlier and remained friendly, despite his renegade streak—another character we have also met already, Dolabella.[43] Cicero was perhaps not so opposed to a match with Dolabella as he is generally thought to have been, but had to be guarded in what he wrote to friends because Dolabella was engaged in a controversial prosecution.[44] In fact, Cicero seems separately to have been trying to curry favor with Dolabella, as this would give him a connection with a favorite of Caesar.[45] Likely the same consideration weighed on Caelius' mind, and impressed Terentia and Tullia, too. For them, already having lived through the bitter year of Cicero's exile, Dolabella, as charming as he was, must also have represented something of an insurance policy.

After the war broke out, Tullia and Terentia initially stayed in Rome. Cicero—back in Italy, but apart from them—wrote asking them to reflect on whether they should remain; while Dolabella did offer them security, "what concerns me," he said, "is that I see that all the good men have left Rome and they have their women with them."[46] If Terentia could be Cicero's representative in Rome when he was in exile, so she would be now; for her even simply to live in Rome, Cicero felt, could undermine his position, by reflecting sympathy for the opposite side. "Look at what other women of your rank are doing," Cicero wrote, but doubtless other considerations as well weighed on the women's minds—the danger of food shortage, for example.[47] For a time, they did actually leave the City, but against Cicero's objections they returned, still continuing to agonize over what Cicero should do. Tullia begged Cicero not to leave with the Pompeians; Caelius urged him to save himself, but he refused and left for Greece.[48]

During his absence again, Terentia had to assume greater control of his and the family's finances, with the help of her steward Philotimus.[49] The key difference from the year of exile, though, was the financial crisis, which made the task nearly impossible. One problem was how to keep Cicero himself comfortable during his time away; another, even harder, was how to raise money to pay the dowry to Dolabella, which was due in three yearly installments. At the same time, Dolabella himself, absorbed totally by his own political scheming, seems to have failed to provide for his wife even the most basic needs. (This, too, after Tullia's first pregnancy with Dolabella ended in a premature delivery, with the child dying shortly afterward.) In letters from this time, Cicero repeatedly expresses worry about his finances.[50] Liquidating some of his own property proved impossible. Even an attempt so sell valuable silverware, textiles, and furniture failed; they at least could be set aside, Cicero wrote, "so that they escape the looming destruction."[51] Fear of confiscation, whether by Caesarians or vindictive Pompeians, was the ever-present worry for the Ciceros, so much so that Terentia finally determined to rewrite her will.[52] This was a source of pain, for to protect her children, Terentia would have to disinherit not only Cicero but also the children themselves, for so long as he remained alive, any inheritance to them would belong to Cicero as their *paterfamilias*. The only solution was to name a friend as heir, Atticus for example.

Adding to their stress was anxiety about Cicero's own wellbeing and increasing fear about his son-in-law, who of course was on the other side.[53] Even as Dolabella neglected Tullia, Terentia and Cicero had to keep scraping together large sums of money to pay him; it almost seemed as if Dolabella's own debts were engulfing the whole family. There were other problems with him too: his radical politics—which extended to erecting a statue of the old family enemy Clodius—violent behavior, adultery. Yet all of that notwithstanding, it seemed too risky to go through with a divorce. "What weight he has, politically, I don't know," Cicero wrote Terentia at one point, "nor how stirred up the mob is. If we have to fear his rage, don't do a thing."[54]

It was in part through Dolabella's efforts that Cicero had been allowed to return to southern Italy in late 48 BC, where he had to wait some time for a full pardon from Caesar before he could travel to Rome itself.[55] The pardon finally did come, but it was not enough to save Cicero's marriage. Letters to Terentia herself do little to illuminate what exactly went wrong, and even those to Atticus have only a few clues.[56] The problems, at least superficially, concerned money. Asked by Atticus to send Cicero a bill of exchange for 12,000 sesterces, she sent one for only 10,000, with a note that this was what was owed. "What can top this?" Cicero wrote. "When she snitches such a small sum from a small sum to begin with, you grasp what she has been up to when the stakes are very high."[57] But other correspondence at this time reveals Cicero's desperation to secure a remittance of only 30,000 sesterces; and the banker who was to remit it initially could only credit Cicero 12,000.[58] Terentia may well have been justified to take care about the 2000 sesterces she felt was hers.

Constant worry about money, as well as about Tullia's wellbeing, not to mention the stresses of the civil war, clearly had taken a toll. For Terentia, too, Cicero's choice to leave Italy, when neutrality most likely would have been possible, may have been grating. Cicero's biographer Plutarch preserves what appears to be contemporary gossip, to the effect that the breakdown in the marriage stemmed from Terentia's neglect of her husband in his absence, including efforts to rob him.[59] The letters do virtually nothing to back this up, nor do they document in any detail the actual unfolding of the divorce. But perhaps after all, they do provide, implicitly anyway, something of an explanation for what happened. On the eve of his reunion with Terentia in 47 BC, Cicero wrote in the last extant letter to her as follows: "I think I shall be coming to the Tusculan house either on the Nones or the day after. Have everything there ready. There will probably be many with me and I think I shall be staying for some time there. Have a tub put in the bath if there is not one. And take care of everything else needed for health and subsistence. Goodbye."[60] The brusque words, such a contrast with his outpourings from ten years earlier, are devastating. Cicero has lost all feeling for his wife.[61]

† † †

Engaged to a Pompeian, though not yet married, the wife in 49 BC was in a situation not dissimilar to Terentia's. Like Terentia, she was concerned to help her fiancé materially as he prepared to head East at the start of the year. The gold and pearls she had in her possession ("sober attire" notwithstanding), she handed over to him. The pearls are a detail worth noticing, as they are a pointer to very substantial wealth.[62] Chiefly imported to Rome from the Indian Ocean, they were sold mainly on Rome's luxury shopping street, the Via Sacra, at high prices (it was only the likes of Augustus' wife, Livia, who could have a full-time pearl-setter on her staff). Julius Caesar aimed to restrict their display as a part of his (failed) sumptuary legislation; Augustus dedicated pearls, along with other gems and gold, in the Capitoline temple of Jupiter, so valuable were they considered.[63]

In part, the wife used her jewelry because this was a form of wealth that a woman had at hand. One could cite juristic texts dealing with the legacy of women's jewelry to show this or also those great moments in

FIGURE 4. Marble funerary monument for an imperial freedman (T. Flavius Pinitus) and his freedwoman (Flavia Alcimenis) to whom he was likely married, dating late first century AD. S. Paolo fuori le Mura, Rome, Italy. Though Roman women owned jewelry such as the earrings and pearls seen here, it was rarely shown in publicly displayed sculpture: Fejfer (2008), pp. 345–347.

FIGURE 5. Portrait of a Roman woman in mosaic from Pompeii, likely of Augustan date. Museo Nazionale Archeologico, Naples, Italy. The mosaic recalls a mostly lost world of panel paintings of real Roman women: Dunbabin (1999), pp. 48–49 Jewelry, fine textiles, and an elegant hairstyle proclaim this woman's status.

Rome's early history when the city's matrons gave up their gold to support a war effort, but more vivid still is a moment from the trial of Caelius in 56 BC for various acts of violence.[64] During this it was alleged that Caelius had borrowed gold from Clodius' sister, Clodia, ostensibly to cover the cost of games he needed to give, but really to procure a murder. Cicero, in his defense of Caelius, can present Clodia not only taking gold from a safe but also stripping a statue of Venus of jewelry—said to have been the gifts of her various lovers.[65] (This was not a woman well known for her *pudicitia*; in the same speech Cicero describes her pleasure-gardens on the Tiber River, sited so that she could pick up young men swimming by, and her diaphanous dresses were apparently notorious.[66]) The other reason the wife reached into her own jewelry box though was of course the desperate currency shortage. True, she did also manage to find and send some coin itself, and with that, slaves and provisions, somehow managing to thwart the "enemy guards" (2.5a), perhaps those encircling Brundisium in the early part of 49 BC, before the Pompeians actually sailed across the Adriatic.[67] By this time, too, Cluvius likely had departed for Africa, which was seized by the republican Attius Varus, who had governed the province several years earlier.[68]

For the wife, angst-ridden months—like those Terentia endured—must have followed. There was in 48 BC a more spectacular challenge too. A house belonging to the husband came under attack by a gang associated with its former owner, none other than Milo, having returned and attempting to foment revolution. After his conviction (in multiple courts), Milo had lost all of his holdings in Italy, including a country villa along the Tiber and at least two houses in Rome, one a particularly grand residence on the northwestern part of the Palatine; all were auctioned off, with the proceeds going primarily to pay Milo's creditors.[69] The husband clearly bought at least one of the properties, likely the Palatine mansion. Although Milo himself did not in the end make it to Rome in 48 BC, his old band, presumably on his instructions and perhaps Caelius' too, must have attempted to take the house, for, just as Cicero's house represented Cicero's standing, so did Milo's, especially his major house on the Palatine.[70]

Now it may be that the wife, along with her future mother-in-law, were not actually residing in this house, but it fell to the wife to take care of it, just as she was taking care of her mother-in-law.[71] Twice before the mansion had come under assault by Clodius' thugs, the second time in the aftermath of that man's murder. On that occasion, the attack was "successfully driven off by arrows."[72] The first time was in 57 BC and is described in a contemporary letter of Cicero:

> On 12 November Clodius was trying so hard to storm and burn down Milo's house, the one on the Cermalus [part of the Palatine], that around eleven in the morning in full view he brought with him men with shields and drawn swords, and others with lighted firebrands. He himself took up the house of Publius Sulla as his base camp for the assault. Then from Milo's other house, the Anniana, out led Quintus Flaccus some ferocious men and killed off the most notorious members in all of Clodius' gang.[73]

Just as in the last years of the republic, houses had become more ostentatiously decorated to glamorize their owners, so competition between politicians could descend into attacks on one another's properties.[74] The *laudatio* supplies precious evidence of the continuity of that trend into the early 40s BC, as a battle raged for the control of Rome.[75]

"You defended our house," the husband says with pride (2.11a), but not making clear how—could it have been arrows again? Had she—and other women left behind—armed their slaves? What is evident is that orchestrating such a defense was an utterly untypical role for a woman, only to be explained by "the opportunities offered by civil war" to Milo's gang (2.10a). Like the wife's alleged relatives earlier, they were hoping to take advantage of her (and her future mother-in-law). But the woman who had avenged herself on her father's murder and scotched a run on his estate was not to be overwhelmed now.

Supplying her husband in flight, defending his interests in his absence: to these great services the wife added a *coup de grâce* when she helped gain forgiveness for her fiancé so that he could return to Italy, marry, and begin a shared life with her. Her chance came perhaps as early as the immediate aftermath of Pompey's death at Pharsalus in 48 BC, but likelier sometime afterward, as men, including Cicero in southern Italy, and a number of others in Greece, awaited Caesar's return from Egypt, at which point he issued a number of full pardons.[76] The scrappy state of the *laudatio* (2.6a–8a) frustrates a perfect understanding, but enough words survive to suggest what happened: the wife's "courage" (we can gather) inspired her to make a plea for her fiancé, and as a result of "the clemency of those against whom produced your words," he was protected.[77] The plural of "those" makes it clear that it was to more than Caesar alone she spoke.

Most likely, in fact, it was not even to Caesar initially, if at all, that she spoke—"with strength" as the husband puts it (2.8a)—as a further episode from Terentia's story suggests. Convention dictated that a high-ranking woman eager to solicit a favor from a man should speak to his wife or to other female relatives first. So, for example, when Cicero's friend Sestius was away from Rome and wished to have his provincial assignment modified, his wife lobbied Terentia, who, in turn, lobbied Cicero.[78] And so too, Mark Antony claimed that his mother Julia (hoping to bury her husband, Antony's stepfather Cornelius Lentulus, after his execution by Cicero in 63 BC) went to Terentia for help.[79] Terentia herself, upon Cicero's return to Italy after his withdrawal from the civil war, sought help by going to Volumnia, the mistress of Antony.[80] A one-time slave and actress, this woman had specialized in the risqué genre of mime, which blended acting with singing and dancing, all done with no masks and often little clothing either.[81] Her stage name was Cytheris (after the island that was in mythology the birthplace of Venus), but off the stage too "Cytheris" was no less seductive. Her patron, the sybaritic Volumnius Eutrapelus (his extra Greek name "Eutrapelus" means "cheeky"), clearly countenanced an affair with Caesar's right-hand man because it gave him access to power. For a time, Antony could hardly be separated from the woman: Cicero complains in a letter to Atticus about how the man traveled around Italy with her in a litter with the curtains drawn open.[82] Antony's mother was also a part of the entourage, Cicero later added, showing how little her son respected *pudicitia*.[83]

"Volumnia," Cicero wrote Terentia at the start of 47 BC, "ought to have been more considerate to you than she was and could have done what she did with greater care and caution."[84] Just what she did do is suggested by a separate letter to Atticus, explaining that Caesar, because he had heard that various Pompeians were returning to Italy with the intention of going to Rome, was banning all from Italy except those whose cases he had heard.[85] Antony published a decree to that effect, exempting Cicero and one other by name. This was publicity Cicero did not care for, but of course he did continue to exploit the exemption, until Caesar's full pardon. One may guess that the wife secured something along these lines for her fiancé, going, like Terentia, to Volumnia— and perhaps ultimately to Antony too, or Caesar's trusted agents Balbus and Oppius. This would explain how the husband was "shielded" by the "clemency of those against whom you produced your words" (2.7a). The full and formal pardon presumably came later—after Caesar secured victory in the Egyptian war—and perhaps was mentioned in the lacuna between Vaglieri's fragment and the start of the Villa Albani fragments.

† † †

However it happened, the wife's fiancé was allowed to return, and the couple was soon married. One can easily imagine that for all the misery of the last couple of years, their early days together were most special ones, far different than they would have been had they married a few years earlier and civil war not broken out. A foundation, built on trust, was already established, and made for what the husband describes as a very strong marriage throughout—admittedly as he was looking back late in life. "Rare are marriages as long as ours—marriages ended by death, not cut short by divorce," he initially comments; "it was granted

to us that ours lasted into its forty-first year without any wrongdoing"
(1.27–28). It is hard not to think of Cicero and Terentia's marriage here,
which did end in divorce; and as the husband becomes more specific
about why his marriage flourished, one cannot be surprised that he has
a great deal to say about money. So obsessed were high-ranking Romans
with preserving, if not increasing, their property, that finances were a
stumbling block for full marital harmony.

In principle, this should not have been so, as there was a clear set of
rules to follow.[86] If the marriage was with *manus*, all that was the wife's
became the husband's. If not, then there was supposed to be strict sepa-
ration of property, with wife and husband keeping separate inventories
of their holdings; they were not even supposed to give gifts to one another, beyond a modest birthday present or the like. A bride would bring
to her new husband a dowry, provided by her *paterfamilias* or (if he
were dead) other relatives or herself, which became the husband's for
the duration of the marriage, though income from it was often intended
to support the wife (and any children she had). Strictly written contracts
specified what would happen to the dowry upon dissolution of the marriage; in a divorce, generally speaking, it was recoverable by the wife,
because it was believed that women needed to have property sufficient
to maintain their status. Segregation of property theoretically facilitated
divorce, which the husband or the wife equally could initiate—important because the leading families of Rome, who developed the civil law,
came to conceive of marriage, at least in part, as a tool for making alliances that might not be lasting.

Married couples, then, did not have a joint estate. Even if in practice
they inevitably shared the use of their resources with one another, "in
the background we hear sounded always the note of separateness."[87] It is
in the background of the *laudatio* too. Ultimately the wife and her husband had a marriage with *manus*, as Cluvius and his wife did, but this
seems only to have been a decision made later, for reasons we shall see.[88]
During and immediately after the civil war, it surely would have seemed
safer for each to maintain ownership of their patrimonies. Yet even with
separate patrimonies, there were ways to protect one another's interests,
and this is what the husband suggests that he and his wife did from the
start, such was their trust for one another.

"Through careful management together we kept intact all of your
fortune, as it was handed down from your parents," the husband begins
(1.37). Assuming that the marriage was initially without *manus*, at a

minimum the husband would have had control of part of the wife's patrimony in the form of dowry. But since he refers to "all" of her inheritance, the implication is that he helped to oversee the successful management of not just her dowry, but also her entire portfolio. In part he could have done this in his (likely) role as her legal guardian.[89] In part he could have handled any important business that arose in the management of the properties (any litigation, for example). Furthermore, we are explicitly told (1.45–51) that he helped to maintain her and her sister's patrimony when they wished to use some of it to help some female relatives. These kinswomen—their precise identity is unknown—were brought up by the wife and her husband and naturally required ample dowries when it was time to marry. The only way to raise the sums was to liquidate some holdings or (perhaps likelier, under normal circumstances) to transfer the income-bearing holdings directly. The husband along with Cluvius refused to allow their wives to touch their estates, and instead themselves made a gift of the dowries. Not only was this an honorable act in Roman eyes, it is a perfect example of the legal dodges so beloved of wealthy Romans because it allowed the husband a way to make a gift to his wife, thanking her for all her support in the years of trouble, including the sacrifice of her jewelry, some of which may have been family heirlooms.[90]

The wife, while benefitting from her husband's generosity on this occasion, had her own contributions to make to his financial wellbeing. For one thing, of course, by battling off the challenge to her father's will, she saved the inheritance that he stood to benefit from, whether directly as an heir or indirectly through her.[91] For another, she could fulfill a traditional role for a Roman wife, that of *custos*, the "watchwoman" of her husband's property.[92] Some charming stories survive to illustrate the ideal. Antony's mother Julia, already met in this chapter in the grim aftermath of her second husband's death and touring with Volumnia Cytheris, is on record for helping her first husband too, Antony's father.[93] Not a man of much property himself, but prone to liberality, he, along with the rest of the household, was kept under close watch by Julia. A friend came to him one day, asking for help, and to oblige, Antony called a slave to bring in a silver bowl filled with water, as if to shave, but then gave the bowl to his friend. "When a thorough search was then being made among the slaves," writes Plutarch, the source of this story, "seeing that his wife was angry and wished to examine them one by one, Antony confessed what he had done and begged for her forgiveness." Even more homespun is the story of Cicero's mother.[94] When writing to

Cicero's secretary Tiro, Cicero's brother, Quintus, asks for a letter to be sent even if there was no news; the empty letter would show that he was not being cheated of correspondence, just as Marcus and Quintus' mother would seal empty wine bottles to make sure nobody was drinking unauthorized. The unfortunate slaves seem to be hovering in the background here too.[95]

Quaint as these stories may seem, they point to some important realities. As in many other preindustrial societies, in Rome the household was the major economic unit. For the wealthy, it could easily include dozens, even hundreds, of slaves and other dependents beyond the family members themselves, all of whom needed to be fed, clothed, housed—and supervised.[96] Stewards like Terentia's Philotimus helped with this, but heads of households themselves might take a direct hand in things. Atticus' friend Cornelius Nepos felt it appropriate to devote a section of his biography to his friend's skill in domestic management; although a wealthy equestrian who lived in keeping with his status, Atticus ran his estates so efficiently that he could boast that his out-of-pocket expenses came to no more than 3000 sesterces per month (he had the accounts to prove it).[97] He would hardly have faulted Terentia for rectifying an error of 2000 sesterces! As an equestrian who stayed out of the Senate, Atticus had time for this management, and, as we shall later see, his story is suggestive for the identity of the couple in the *laudatio*. But even a Senator such as Crassus ran a household of which the complexity would rival that of a reasonably large company today.[98] In households where the male head might be away on public business (or on personal business), it would have been common for a woman to run things.[99] Even when her husband was present, it was expected that she would oversee certain tasks, such as the very labor-intensive wool working required to produce clothing for the entire household.[100]

In the preserved *laudatio*, the husband makes a final comment that may be relevant to his wife's concern for his financial interests. "Through careful management we kept intact all of your fortune, as it was handed down from your parents," he says, and then continues: "there was no effort on your part to acquire what you had handed over in its entirety to me" (1.37–38). Underlying this may be an implication that some wives aimed—or at least were thought to have aimed—to shift the holdings that constituted their dowry, during the course of the marriage. They might do so by exchanging an asset in the dowry for something else. For example, a wife could purchase a farm with cash, at a moment when her husband needed the liquid asset.[101] She gained an income-bearing vehicle, and if the farm in question abutted others in her possession, it simultaneously increased the value of her own holdings.

All such talk may seem rather a letdown after the stirring tale of what the wife did for her fiancé during the civil war. The husband himself recognizes as much when he interrupts his praise of her wifely virtues: "... you have countless other things in common with all married women who keep up a good reputation. The qualities that I assert you have belong to you alone; very few other women have lived in times similar enough so as to endure such things and perform such deeds as Fortune has taken care to make rare for women" (1.33–36). Still, he seems to recognize that while the wife's heroic loyalty to him during the civil war helped to lay a foundation, it was their continuing concern for one another that made their marriage last. That concern went well beyond financial affairs, but finances presented a tangible sign for it. "We shared the duties in such a way that I stood as protector of your fortune, while you kept a watch over mine," the husband says, with pleasing symmetry (1.39).

As Rome settled down to Caesar's dictatorship, the wife and husband's own shared future was brightening. Little could they have known that just a few years later the husband would be put in grave danger, again. In a far more hideous way, the wife, along with other women of rank, once more would have their love and loyalty tested, going far beyond the ordinary test that sharing (or separating) finances presented. And, before all was over, the husband was to find himself tested too. When, in a terrible crisis, the wife offered to divorce him, his heart burst: "for you to be able in any way to conceive the thought...when you had remained utterly faithful to me, at the time I was exiled and practically dead!" (2.42–43).

3

At the Tribunal of Lepidus

Julius Caesar, it could be said, had won the war against Pompey, but he lost the peace. Returning to Rome from the East in 47 BC, he left the following year to fight reorganized Republican forces in Africa; and the year after that, he was called to Spain to suppress guerilla attacks of Pompey's two surviving sons.[1] By early 44 BC, he was readying himself for a major campaign in the East. Just at this time, he was renamed "Dictator for Life," demonstrating that the restored republic many Senators fervently were hoping for was not to be. Life in Rome would remain, much as it had been for the last five years, in the hands of his subordinates. That, along with the new heights of arrogance Caesar had been found to ascend, was too much for some. Perhaps as many as sixty men, led by the famous Marcus Brutus, the less-familiar Decimus Brutus, and Cassius, banded together and took his life at a meeting of the Senate on the Ides of March in 44 BC.[2]

Further proof that Caesar had failed to attain any kind of political consensus was furnished by the chaotic eighteen months that followed, among the most tortuous in all of Roman history.[3] The upper hand lay initially with Antony, who was serving as consul in 44 BC. After the assassination, he arranged for the dictatorship to be abolished and agreed to amnesty for the assassins, but also presided over a funeral that whipped the people of Rome into frenzy. The two Brutuses, Cassius, and the others had to leave. Antony no doubt hoped to achieve personal supremacy of some kind, but a wrench was thrown in his plans by young Octavius, the primary heir of Caesar's will, who began calling himself "Caesar" (to avoid confusion, modern historians often prefer "Octavian").[4] Coming to Rome and putting pressure on Antony, Octavian—the future

TABLE 2 Roman Political History, 44–40 BC.

44	Murder of Julius Caesar (15 March); Octavian comes to Rome, challenges Antony, and by December, allies himself with Cicero; assassins of Caesar are driven from Rome, and Marcus Brutus and Cassius go East
43	Antony besieges Decimus Brutus at Mutina, but is defeated; Octavian marches on Rome and is made consul (19 August); Antony joins Lepidus in Gaul, and they then form an alliance with Octavian, ratified as the triumvirate; Proscriptions are launched (late November) and Cicero murdered (7 December); Sextus Pompey offers refuge to proscribed on Sicily
42	Women's taxation protest in the Forum in Rome; at Philippi (in Macedonia), Brutus and Cassius are defeated by the army of Antony and Octavian; Lepidus in charge of Rome; Octavian returns to Rome, late in the year and initiates a policy of partial clemency
41	Perusine War in Italy (Octavian vs. Fulvia and Lucius Antony); in the East, Mark Antony meets Cleopatra and travels to Alexandria for the winter
40	Lucius Antony is defeated by Octavian at Perusia; Antony's mother, Julia, travels from Sextus Pompey to Antony; the death of Fulvia; peace between Mark Antony and Octavian confirmed at Brundisium (October); Mark Antony and Octavia marry

This table is based on the fuller chronologies in Scullard (1982), pp. x–xxii, Crook, et al. (1994), pp. 780–98, and Bowman, et al. (1996), pp. 995–1005.

Augustus—secured support from Caesar's financiers, his veterans, and the city-dwellers of Rome and was able late in 44 BC to form an alliance with Cicero.

Antony, meanwhile to secure his position, had command of Cisalpine Gaul, strategically located just over the border with Italy, transferred to him and went to take over the troops there, held by Decimus Brutus. Antony put Decimus under siege at Modena (ancient Mutina), and in response, the Senate sent an army to help Decimus, under the command of the two consuls of 43 BC along with Octavian. Caesar's heir and avenger thus was marching to liberate one of Caesar's assassins, and one of the most treacherous assassins at that, for Decimus Brutus had been a personal favorite of Caesar. (The other Brutus and Cassius had left Italy altogether and gone East, ultimately to amass large treasuries and armies.) Antony was forced to abandon Modena and then proceeded to Transalpine Gaul, where he hoped to gain the support of armies under the Caesarian generals Lepidus and Plancus. Having been the most powerful man in Rome a year earlier, Antony was now declared a public enemy.

Into this turmoil and that which followed, Rome's high-ranking women were to be swept, even more than they had been in the earlier struggle between Caesar and Pompey. Many would prove themselves to be as formidable as ever, or more so, the wife among them, as we shall see. Another who did so—and whose story illustrates the world in which the wife lived—was Servilia, among the greatest of the female politicians of her generation. To speak of "politicians," we shall see, is no distortion: women formally may have been excluded from political life, but in the years after Caesar's death, they helped to conduct government business and also to put pressure on the government, defending not just the interests of their menfolk—as they always did—but their own, while also at times trying to put a stop to civil war. As they had before, they acted behind the scenes; but they also now had to operate more overtly, and in doing so, they raised questions about the traditional division of the sexes.

† † †

As a member of one of Rome's most distinguished patrician families, Servilia could claim descent from no less than Servilius Ahala, who legend held saved his country when he killed a would-be tyrant with a dagger hidden beneath his arm (*Ahala* in Latin means "armpit").[5] Her own father, Servilius Caepio, had died during the Social War, lured into an enemy ambush, before having attained the consulship.[6] Her brother died in 67 BC, leaving no sons, and not having attained even the praetorship.[7] She may have had another brother, or half-brother, but if so, he, too, left no sons, and enjoyed little political success.[8] Certainly by 44 BC, and probably for years prior, she was effectively head of the family.[9] It was up to her to perpetuate the glory of the ancient Servilii, who had experienced many ups and downs over the centuries.[10] While of course Servilia could not hold political office herself, by pursuing dynastic power, she was typical of her class, female or male. Her contemporary, Julius Caesar, similarly worked to restore the distinction of the Julii, a clan that could claim descent from Rome's founder Aeneas and his mother Venus, but had left little mark on history for generations.[11]

TABLE 3 Servilia's Family.

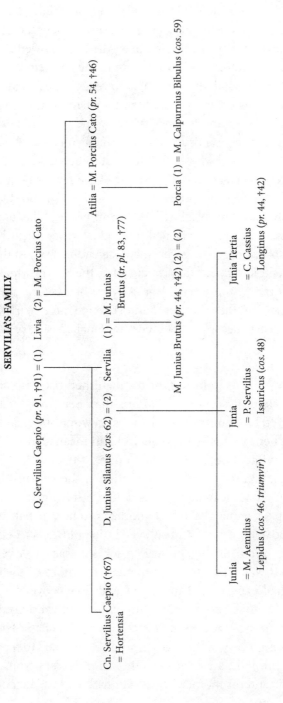

SERVILIA'S FAMILY

Q. Servilius Caepio (*pr.* 91, †91) = (1) Livia (2) = M. Porcius Cato

Cn. Servilius Caepio (†67)
= Hortensia

D. Junius Silanus (*cos.* 62) = (2) Servilia (1) = M. Junius
Brutus (*tr. pl.* 83, †77)

Atilia = M. Porcius Cato (*pr.* 54, †46)

M. Junius Brutus (*pr.* 44, †42) (2) = (2) Porcia (1) = M. Calpurnius Bibulus (*cos.* 59)

Junia
= M. Aemilius
Lepidus (*cos.* 46, *triumvir*)

Junia
= P. Servilius
Isauricus (*cos.* 48)

Junia Tertia
= C. Cassius
Longinus (*pr.* 44, †42)

Note: This family tree is based on Table II in Syme (1986). Men's most senior magistracies are indicated in parentheses, along with dates of death (marked †).

Servilia's greatest asset was her own son Marcus Brutus, the child of her first husband, the tribune of 83 BC who had joined the attempted coup against the Sullan order after Sulla's death in 78 BC and was put under siege (also at Modena) by Pompey. Though he surrendered, he was killed by Pompey, whom young Brutus grew up to hate.[12] Servilia subsequently remarried and had three daughters, all of whom were married out to members of other highly prominent families.[13] None of these children bore the name of the Servilii, but by 59 BC at the latest, Brutus had been adopted into the clan and was, as Cicero puts it, to "renew and enhance the memory of two most illustrious families"—the Junii Bruti and the Servilii Caepiones.[14] Coins issued by Brutus when he was a junior treasury official paid tribute to both clans.[15] Even the name that Brutus now officially went by, Quintus Servilius Caepio Brutus, managed to proclaim the glory of his father and his mother's lineage at once.[16]

When the civil war between Caesar and Pompey broke out, Brutus, with some misgivings, threw in his lot with the Pompeians.[17] On the eve of battle, Plutarch writes, Caesar gave strict orders to his officers not to lay a finger on Brutus—"as a favor to Servilia."[18] She and Caesar had, earlier in life, been lovers.[19] Nor was this the only time Servilia's influence was reputed to have saved her son. Years earlier, in Caesar's first consulship, Brutus was implicated in an alleged conspiracy against his father's murderer, Pompey, but his name was dropped when Caesar called on the informer a second time to state his allegations.[20] "It was plain," Cicero joked to Atticus, "that a night, and a nighttime entreaty, had intervened."[21]

After Pharsalus, Brutus accepted Caesar's pardon, refusing to follow his uncle Cato to Africa.[22] But Cato, after his suicide in 46 BC, came—especially as Caesar's autocracy developed—to embody the idea of the republic, just as Brutus' own legendary ancestors did. On Brutus' request, Cicero wrote a eulogy of Cato, and this book, at least in part, precipitated a crisis in Brutus' own conscience.[23] Married to the patrician Claudia, he divorced her in 45 BC for Cato's daughter, Porcia—a perfect illustration of the impossibility of separating the personal and the political in the lives of Rome's nobles.[24] Servilia evidently was dismayed.[25] But so the road was paved to Brutus' involvement in the Ides of March.

In the aftermath, Servilia would again do all she could to save her son and the rest of her family, which included Cassius, married to her third daughter Tertia.[26] In working to protect them, she was exactly like the wife of the *laudatio*. The only difference was that Servilia could draw on her better-developed mastery of backstairs politics—something that she shared with her dear friend, the equestrian Atticus, whose well-attested career helps to make sense of hers.[27] Through the connections he cultivated with a galaxy of prominent Romans, among them Senators, Atticus was able to influence government decisions. In 51 BC, for example, he helped to get the terms of Cicero's governorship adjusted to Cicero's benefit by writing directly to the consul.[28] In turn, Atticus himself used Senators to protect his own interests, especially his financial empire, which stretched from Italy across the Adriatic, to Greece and beyond.[29] Servilia may not have had so extensive an empire herself, but in 44 BC, she too operated behind the scenes, in defense of kin.

On the fifth of June that year, Brutus and Cassius were voted the task of transporting grain to Rome from the provinces, in an effort by Antony to get them out of the way.[30] Three days later, a council was held at Anzio (ancient Antium) to discuss their response. Not only was Servilia there (along with Tertia and Brutus' wife, not to mention Brutus and Cassius themselves), she presided over the whole meeting, as Cicero, also present, wrote to Atticus.[31] Cicero had prepared his advice in advance and shared it now: the grain commission should be accepted. The martial Cassius dissented—he preferred to go to Greece—while Brutus hoped that he himself might be able to return to Rome. A discussion of their past mistakes followed, and as Cicero warmed to the theme, Servilia cut him off. "Well!" she said, "I've never heard anyone say such a thing before!"[32] Cicero then held his tongue, Brutus was persuaded to stay away from Rome—he was not to be allowed to make his father's mistake—and Cassius assented to lay low for the time being, after Servilia promised that she would get the grain commission removed from the Senate decree.[33]

Several months after the conference, their position still untenable in Italy, Cassius did leave, and Brutus too, not for the provinces assigned to them, but areas more suited for military recruitment and fundraising.[34] A rapprochement with Antony seemed more out of reach than ever. Challenges only mounted when Cicero made his pact with Caesar's heir. Servilia kept a close watch on developments in the East, relayed news from Italy to her son, and sought to protect his and Cassius' interests in Rome itself.[35] Against her wishes, Cicero moved in February of 43 BC that Cassius should be entrusted with a powerful command against Cicero's old son-in-law, the Caesarian Dolabella, who had seized control of the Roman Far East.[36] According to Cicero, Servilia's fear was that the consul Pansa might take umbrage.[37] Pansa, a voice of moderation at this time, himself attacked Cicero's proposal at a public meeting by mentioning that Cassius' mother (name unknown) was opposed to Cicero's making it. More than one of the women of tyrannicides, it seems, was eager to keep her family out of harm. Cicero was none too pleased, dismissing Servilia herself as a "nervous lady" (*mulier timida*).

As Antony's fortunes ebbed by late spring of 43 BC, Brutus and Cassius were in a much stronger position. But in the rapidly shifting political landscape, Servilia soon had a new problem to contend with. On 30 June, another of her sons-in-law, Lepidus, was declared a public enemy, after he and his army in Gaul had gone over to Antony and abandoned the Senate.[38] This suddenly put Servilia's daughter and grandchildren, resident in Rome, at the greatest risk of Senatorial reprisals.[39] Antony's wife, Fulvia, had already been harassed in the courts, and there was a threat that her children would be declared enemies.[40] Servilia's daughter could only expect the same.

"On 25 July," Cicero wrote to Brutus, "that most clever and careful mother of yours, whose every care starts and ends with you, asked me to come see her. And I did so straightaway, as I was bound to."[41] When he arrived, Cicero found other prominent men there. Again Servilia presided, and she ran the meeting as if it were a session of the Senate—and she the presiding consul! On the agenda: Should Brutus now be sent for, and was this in his best interests? Cicero writes that he stated what he had been urging Brutus for some time now, that he should come back, with his army, "to rescue the tottering republic." This evidently was not the view of Servilia, who (Cicero indicates) was writing Brutus separately. A civil war between Brutus, on the one side, and Antony and Lepidus, on the other, was bound to hurt her family. Whatever her exact thoughts, Cicero does reveal that he had pleaded for the interests of her grandchildren in the Senate, "as I believe you will from your mother's letters have been able to learn."[42] So we see her influencing deliberations in the Senate, just as Atticus did.

The last we hear of Servilia is from Atticus' biographer Nepos, writing after Brutus' defeat at the battle of Philippi in 42 BC: "Atticus even took care of Brutus' mother Servilia, no less after Brutus' death than while she was in her prime."[43] Brutus, in the end, like Cassius, could not compromise and fell fighting for the republic. So in addition to her father, her first husband, and her half-brother Cato, Servilia lost her son and son-in-law. It was a staggering sequence of premature deaths, but not accidental: she was at the heart of a nexus of some of Rome's proudest families, the men of which would sooner die than surrender their freedom. But she could not entirely share their views.[44] Though a generation younger and almost certainly of a different heritage, the wife of the *laudatio* shared Servilia's distrust of civil war and, as we shall now see, also embraced the caution that some men dismissed as timidity.

† † †

Lepidus' surrender to Antony in the summer of 43 BC was followed by yet another volte face, the one dreaded by Brutus and Atticus: Octavian decided to turn on Cicero and the Senate, knowing that Cicero's plan all along was to discard him. Soldiers came to Rome in early July to petition the Senate to allow Octavian to seek the consulship, even though he was only nineteen years old. The request was denied, and so he marched on the City and had himself elected anyway (on 19 August). With his new colleague, he pushed into law a condemnation of Caesar's assassins, who were tried and found guilty *en masse*. Then he went back North to meet with Antony and Lepidus, and after two days of negotiations, the three agreed to form a triumvirate, a board of three that would rule Rome for a five-year term.[45] The triumvirs had the right to appoint all urban magistrates, and the rule of the provinces would be divided among themselves. Their immediate priority was to regain control from Brutus and Cassius in the East. To keep soldiers loyal to their side, they announced that veterans of Caesar, upon discharge, would receive land confiscated from eighteen of Italy's richest towns.

Their other major decision was made public upon their return to Rome in November: they would hold a proscription.[46] At the end of his civil war with Marius and Marius' followers, Sulla had published a list of names of high-ranking citizens who were declared outlaws; if caught within Italy, they would be killed, and all of their property was forfeit to the state. Now the triumvirs repeated this dreadful practice, but at the start of a major civil war, rather than at the end. Ostensibly their targets were those who had plotted against Caesar and those who were plotting against the triumvirs themselves, Cicero included. Thus could opponents be easily removed, from Italy at least. The triumvirs were also hoping, by the use of some revolutionary terror, to cow those who remained. And they were hoping to fundraise for the war effort.

The procedure was devilishly simple. According to an edict issued by the triumvirs, the head of anyone on the list would be rewarded with a large sum of cash—or, for a slave who turned in his master, cash and also his freedom.[47] Informers who supplied valuable information also were to be rewarded. At the same time, those who helped the proscribed were to be proscribed themselves, and any private property could be searched for fugitives. The proscriptions, then, affected not just those men whose names were put on the list: those around them faced the dilemma of either helping the proscribed, at great risk to themselves, or collaborating with the triumvirs. For some—maltreated slaves, for example, or quarreling neighbors—the proscriptions even afforded an opportunity to settle old scores.

Among those proscribed, we learn from the *laudatio,* was the husband. Was it for political reasons? Had his old Pompeian sympathies been stirred up? The much better guess is that the triumvirs were targeting his wealth, perhaps the Palatine mansion of Milo in particular—which could not only be sold, but also kept for one of the triumvirs themselves, or given to a faithful partisan.[48] The historian Appian, who provides the fullest and most copiously researched account of the proscriptions, remarks that there came a point when "a person was proscribed because he had a fine villa or house in town."[49] And Atticus' friend, a harmless poet named Julius Calidus, was proscribed in absentia simply "because of his massive holdings in Africa."[50]

Decades later, the husband could summon up a vivid recollection of these events:

> Why should I now divulge our private and hidden plans and
> our secret conversations? How I was saved by your plans when
> I was provoked by unexpected news to court immediate and
> imminent danger; how you did not allow me to tempt fate in
> a rash way; how you made me think more calmly and prepared
> a secure hiding place for me; how you made your sister and
> her husband, Gaius Cluvius, partners in your plans to save me,
> at a risk shared between all of you: it would be an endless task,
> if I tried to touch on all of this (2.4–10).

That the "news" of his proscription was unexpected is a further indication that it was motivated by his wealth rather than politics. The result, certainly, was that unlike in 49 BC, he and his wife had no time whatever to make plans. His own solution, it seems, was to attempt an escape from Italy, most likely to Sicily, "then the most dependable place of refuge for those who had been proscribed," as one ancient writer puts it.[51] Pompey's last surviving son, Sextus, was already based there, using a fleet to cut Italy off from its overseas grain supplies, and he could now gain further advantage through sheltering prominent political refugees.[52] One of those who made it was Lentulus Cruscellio. After his departure, his wife Sulpicia was eager to follow him, but was held in close custody by her mother; "nonetheless she reached him by secretly running away with two maids and two male slaves, having dressed herself up as a slave."[53]

The wife of the *laudatio* had a cooler plan than this. In a situation reminiscent of Servilia's summit at Anzio in June of 44 BC, though with even greater urgency, she thrashed the options over with him; and like Servilia, she carried the day, persuading her husband, and anyone else there, that his safety was most important and that she could secure it. To join, or rejoin, the Pompeians was in her view too risky. Relying on her established network of her sister and Cluvius, she would put her husband into hiding. Where? Appian's history contains stories of a number of other attempts to hide the proscribed, for shorter or longer periods, in chests, in tombs, in country houses, even in a cesspit and an oven.[54] Amidst his tales comes one of the two literary accounts of Turia, whom Mommsen believed was the wife of the *laudatio*: she hid her husband in the attic of their house.[55]

The identification will only be considered later; here it is important to note what Appian's stories of the proscriptions, taken as a whole, show, beyond possible hiding places. After the proscriptions were over, it was of great interest to record what happened to the proscribed. Remarkable escapes, near brushes with death, and of course the betrayal by members of one's household all made for gripping reading. Yet the genre can only have developed in the first place because of the dilemmas faced by Roman society during the proscriptions, and the divergent choices made.[56] Already in the reign of Tiberius, over a hundred years before Appian wrote, Valerius Maximus can furnish examples of the remarkable fidelity and treachery of men's wives during the proscriptions. As an illustration of fidelity, he too tells of Turia and the risk she took upon herself.[57] For treachery, he cites the wife of Vettius Salassus: in hiding, he was turned in to the authorities by his wife.[58]

It is stories of treachery like this that provide the context for the husband's praise of his wife's loyalty and bravery. Not only did she *not* have to save him, she might as easily have turned him in, under the compulsion of the triumvirs' proscription edict. But she, her sister, and

Cluvius—all were willing, as he puts it, to take on a "shared risk." Cluvius, if caught, clearly could have been proscribed. No women, however, seem ultimately to have suffered that; not even the triumvirs would sink that low. Appian recounts how the wife of Ligarius, after her husband was betrayed by a slave-girl, turned herself in but was ignored, as a result of which she then starved herself to death.[59] Still there were other ways the triumvirs could make trouble for women. Women could be harassed in the courts, with no man daring to represent them.[60] The dowries of the wives of the proscribed could be withheld. Allegedly these were to be protected, and the triumvirs also announced that male children would receive a tenth of their proscribed father's property, and female children a twentieth; but, according to our source for this, the promises were rarely kept.[61]

† † †

So it was that when the husband found himself proscribed, the wife acted quickly. Coming up with a plan to save her husband, enlisting allies in it, persuading him of its merit, and carrying it out successfully, she showed all the resourcefulness of her earlier years. But her efforts did not stop here.

In early 42 BC, Antony, followed by Octavian, crossed the Adriatic to confront the armies of Brutus and Cassius. Cassius took his life at the end of their first major encounter, Brutus after their second—both at Philippi, in Macedonia—and the triumvirs' victory was sealed. Basking in success, Antony then went East to regain control of the provinces there while Octavian was given the hateful task of returning to Italy to settle discharged veterans on confiscated lands. There was great trepidation as he made his way back, and reports that Octavian had fallen ill were distrusted: he was planning some worse mischief, people felt.[62] Perceiving this hostility, and suspicious that Lepidus, the triumvir left in charge of Rome, might try to exploit the situation for his own ends, Octavian had to take measures to regain control of the situation. Recovering at Brundisium, he wrote to the Senate assuring its members that he would act clemently, exactly as his father Julius Caesar had.[63] One way to show this was to pardon some of the proscribed, and it was this that gave the wife her opportunity. Getting in touch with Octavian, and (no doubt) reminding him of the chance to echo his father's clemency to her husband, she obtained an edict of restoration.[64]

Before her husband could return to Rome itself, though, the wife also sought the consent of Lepidus. It may be that Octavian himself required her to obtain this consent, in keeping with the agreement the triumvirs made with one another in the fall of 43 BC; more likely she herself did not dare bring the husband out of hiding until she had full assurance that he would be safe.[65] Lepidus was the man in charge of Rome and had legions to back him up. Yet, the *laudatio* makes clear, he refused, at least initially, to give his approval—suggesting indeed that in some way the young Caesar's edict did not show respect for his colleague. Convention dictated that the wife now approach a female relation of Lepidus (perhaps his wife, Junia, Servilia's daughter).[66] Evidently this was not feasible, or else it obtained no result; she would approach Lepidus at his public tribunal.

There, too, he was not to be budged. Confronted by the wife, Lepidus refused to acknowledge the edict, and the wife was forced to go down on her knees before him. At this point, the husband says (2.15–18), she was dragged away from the tribunal and carried off; her "body covered with bruises." Yet "most strenuously" she kept reminding Lepidus of "Caesar's edict, with its rejoicing over my restoration...Although you had to endure Lepidus' insulting words and cruel wounds," he continues, "you kept on putting forward your case in the open so that the person responsible for my trials would be publicly disgraced." Writing so many years later, after the disgrace and death of Lepidus, and not having been present himself, the husband may, understandably, provide an exaggerated account of what occurred. It may be that Lepidus simply ordered his lictors to escort the wife from the tribunal; laying hands on her even in this way would have seemed reprehensible enough.[67]

But as the husband himself makes clear, the wife did not allow herself purely to be a victim. Her decision to go to the tribunal in the first place along with the way she conducted herself there was a political ploy. She was aiming to discredit Lepidus in the eyes of the public, in such a way that he would have finally to relent, or else his authority would be undermined. In lashing out at her, he fell for her bait—perhaps even more than she could have hoped for. Not only would her husband be restored, she had managed visibly to disgrace one of the most powerful men in Rome.

The wife quite likely had the idea for staging such a confrontation because it had been used, successfully, by the most prominent matrons of Rome in prior months. When the proscriptions began, Antony's mother Julia was shocked to discover that her own brother had been put on the list (on the grounds that he had voted Antony a public enemy earlier in the year), and she took him into her own house.[68] Stopping the bounty hunters when they appeared there, she then stormed into the Forum, where Antony was presiding at his tribunal. "*Imperator*," she is reported to have said, "I inform you that I have taken Lucius into my house, still have him there, and will have him there, until you kill both of us together, since it has been decreed that the same penalties apply to those who have taken in the proscribed." It is unlikely that her precise words were recorded, but they are not essential for understanding what was going on in this well-attested episode.[69] Julia could have perfectly well and easily approached her son in private. She approached him publicly so that she could put him in the wrong, emphasizing that he was not acting as a son to her, even though *she* was acting as a sister to her brother. And not only that: by approaching him publicly, she was able to gain sympathy from a crowd of onlookers.[70]

In the face of her challenge, Antony relented, and Julia's brother was pardoned. This was a patrician woman of great political acumen, and a woman with a political agenda that demonstrably went beyond protecting her brother. Like Servilia, she was well familiar with civil unrest: her father was killed during the war between Marius and Sulla and her second husband put to death in the Catilinarian conspiracy.[71] If Rome could be spared more bloodshed, it should be. In 40 BC, as civil war between Octavian and (a still absent) Antony threatened to break out and engulf Italy itself, she traveled to Sextus Pompey and then took an offer of help from Sextus to her son.[72] But when Octavian then became more serious about a reconciliation with Antony, she helped to broker the final pact they made. Italy was spared.

Julia was involved in another episode in which the high-ranking women of Rome, collectively, challenged the rule of the triumvirs. Almost immediately, it became clear that the proscriptions would not succeed in bringing in the profits hoped for, not only because of the flood of properties on the market, but also because few buyers, understandably, were willing to step forward in the face of such flagrant disrespect for property rights. In consequence at the start of 42 BC, an array of new taxes was announced, including a levy on the wealthiest women of Rome.[73] A list appeared with 1400 names; those on it would have their property valued and an assessment determined by the triumvirs. It was in essence a proscription without the threat of murder. Still, it was a potentially devastating policy: not only would women lose the assessment made on them, but in raising the cash to make their payment, they might have to liquidate property at aberrantly low prices.

Those matrons affected—including quite possibly the wife of the *laudatio* and the earlier heroine of this chapter, Servilia—appealed first to the womenfolk of the triumvirs, we are told, that is to Julia, to Antony's wife, Fulvia, and to Octavian's sister, Octavia.[74] Unsuccessful in this—Fulvia allegedly turned them away at the door—and with no male protectors willing to step forward, they then decided on a public protest. They would march *en masse* into the Forum and lodge a complaint at the triumviral tribunal, voiced by their chosen representative, Hortensia, the daughter of a great orator, sister of one of the proscribed, and one-time sister-in-law of Servilia.[75] After she delivered her remarks, the triumvirs ordered the lictors to clear the women away, and the crowd began to boo. The lictors were then called off, and the triumvirs said they would defer the question. The following day a notice went up, stating that only 400 women of the very greatest wealth would be taxed, on a simple percentage basis. The matrons had scored at least a partial victory.

On one level, their behavior simply grew out of episodes such as Terentia's and Tullia's public appearance in mourning during Cicero's exile in 58 BC.[76] But it was more than that, more than backstairs politics in the style of Servilia. It also harkened back to an earlier demonstration staged by the high-ranking women of Rome, in 195 BC.[77] In this year, two tribunes proposed repeal of the Oppian law, a measure introduced during the great Hannibalic War that severely restricted the availability of luxury items to women, including the amount of gold they could own. When two other, more conservative tribunes threatened to obstruct the repeal, the women blocked the Forum, made appeals to men passing by, and then besieged the houses of the two opponents, who finally withdrew their planned vetoes.

What we are dealing with, in the triumviral period, was not just a protest, like Terentia's, but civil disobedience: the contravention of law and custom in an open flouting of authority. The oldest record in world literature of such disobedience, it has been noted by David Daube in a remarkable book on the subject, is in the Book of Exodus, where the Hebrew midwives refuse to carry out Pharaoh's order to slaughter the firstborn sons.[78] And, Daube goes on to observe, "a woman is the main figure also in the Greek prototype of civil disobedience: Antigone."[79] In

Sophocles' play, she insists on defying the edict of Creon, the king of Thebes, that forbade anyone to bury the body of her brother. Why in both cultures should women be associated with civil disobedience? They were "largely outside the power structure," Daube suggests, neither having the training for a physical struggle nor enjoying formal inclusion in political processes; they were also likelier to take a more personal view of matters.[80] Women resist, these stories are saying, but they can only do so nonviolently.

Obviously there is something of a parallel here with Rome: civil disobedience was more viable for Roman women than the civil war of men. And yet, Daube asserts, the Roman women involved in civil disobedience, whether those in 195 BC or in 42 BC, are not the true counterparts of the Hebrew midwives.[81] Roman women of rank, as we have seen, *were* very much a part of the power structure, and in many respects held values close to those of men of rank. They were hardly the most downtrodden, and indeed the great majority of men in Rome's hierarchical society were in many ways more downtrodden than they.

Moreover, the matrons in 42 BC—or, for that matter, Terentia earlier— were not merely sticking up for loved ones in a time of civil unrest, important as that was. Like those in 195 BC, they were also fighting to preserve their own wealth, the status bestowed on them by their wealth, and the influence that came from their status. A copy of the speech Hortensia gave after the women appeared before the triumvirs' tribunal was known in later times and may form the basis of some stirring words Appian assigns to her in his history.[82] In these she emphasizes not only how women's status depends on their wealth, but also that there is an important division between women and men. Women do not serve in public office or in military commands; they do not conduct civil war; and therefore, they should not be required to pay taxes that fund civil war.

Similar ideas can be found in words certainly written closer to 42 BC—in Livy's account of the debate over the Oppian law. In a speech assigned to one of the reforming tribunes, we find the argument that "Neither magistracies nor priesthoods nor triumphs nor decorations nor gifts nor the spoils of war can be granted to women. Elegance of appearance, adornment, finery: these are the decorations of women, in these they delight and take pride, this was what our ancestors called the woman's world."[83] Terentia, Servilia, and the wife of the *laudatio* might not have put it exactly that way; for them, the ability to hold and control their own property went beyond their personal appearance. But when we ask why high-ranking women such as these accepted their formal segregation from political life, surely part of the answer must be that, as they saw it, they had an implicit contract with men. Women would not involve themselves formally in public life; but in exchange, men were not to restrict their access to property, or to deny them the affections they felt as family members.

That such a notion existed is suggested by the women's response to the proscriptions and the taxation plan of 42 BC; it also could be guessed at by the way women of means in later historical periods have accepted their exclusion from political and military life. In eighteenth-century Britain, for example, it has been argued that, at least in some levels of society, women and men alike saw their world as one of "separate spheres": men inhabited the public domain, while women's realm was domestic; and women would stay out of men's affairs, provided that men in turned respected women's "moral influence."[84] The terms of this contract are not exactly parallel to what we find in Rome, in part because Roman women, even those married, enjoyed on average more independence in the wife's day than eighteenth-century British women. What seems apposite, though, is the sense that at least in some respects women were a distinctive group within the polity and therefore were entitled to differentiated treatment, entailing restrictions but also, crucially, rights.

Yet just as it has been argued that in eighteenth-century Britain, the very assertion of "separate spheres" suggests that in some ways these spheres were very much under threat (otherwise there would be little need to reassert them as vigorously as they were, or to reinvent them), so too were traditional gender roles in triumviral Rome blurring.[85] Hortensia and her colleagues may ultimately have been conservatives, far more eager to defend their traditional rights than to seek any new ones; but in asserting their rights so visibly, they were acting unconventionally. Women, including the wife, were acting not just behind the scenes, but in public. And the men, meanwhile, were themselves dragging the women into the public, through their own policies, including their novel plan for taxation.

Ultimately, though, there was to be no true social revolution, for the simple reason that modesty was still too much a part of women's reputation to lead to a complete breakdown in gender roles. This is best shown by the fate of a final female politician to be considered from these years, Antony's wife Fulvia.

† † †

Fulvia makes her spectacular entrance into recorded history in 52 BC when, after the death of her first husband Clodius, she put his corpse on display in his house and grieved in such a way as to incite the crowd of Clodius' supporters.[86] Snatching the body, they took it into the Forum, hosted a rally against Clodius' murderer Milo, and then held an improvised funeral, the cremation for which got out of hand and engulfed the Senate house in flames. More riots followed, and Fulvia did her part again when she, along with her mother, was the last to give testimony at Milo's trial, shedding tears that moved all those in attendance.[87] Fulvia, it has been suggested, could command the loyalty of the Clodian clientele, and it is not surprising to see her married next to Curio, one of the tribunes who fled to Caesar in 49 BC on the eve of civil war, and then, finally, to Antony, probably exactly when he was challenged by Dolabella for control of Rome.[88]

Fulvia was as loyal as any wife after the Ides of March. Appearing with Antony in October of 44 BC at Brundisium, when he was receiving troops transferred there from Macedonia, she vigorously defended his interests after his departure for northern Italy.[89] With Antony's mother, Julia, she canvassed Senators to support him in January of 43 BC, dressing in mourning and bringing her young son from Antony along; and this was not just behind the scenes, but in open daylight, as the Senators made their way to the Senate, and then outside the doors of the Senate house.[90] Riding out the threat posed to her by Antony's foes that summer, the following year when Octavian returned to Italy from Philippi, she was still defending her absent husband's interests. She appeared with her

FIGURE 6. Gold coin of the moneyer Numonius Vaala, issued 41 BC (*RRC* 514.1). The bust on the obverse is Victory (as the wings show) but art historians have suggested that the woman's distinctive features, including a contemporary hairstyle, are meant to evoke Fulvia.

children before the returning army, insisting that her husband receive full credit for his essential part in the soldiers' bounty.[91]

Evidently successful in this, Fulvia then faced a different challenge. Her husband's younger brother, Lucius, was one of the consuls in 41 BC. While initially cooperating with Fulvia in her efforts to support her husband, he then, startlingly, took up the cause of the dispossessed. According to one version of events, Fulvia was critical initially, but then, at least to a degree, put her weight behind Lucius and ostentatiously fled Rome with her children, for whom she claimed to be in fear.[92] Whatever Lucius' own ambitions may have been, it seems that Fulvia was hoping that she could seize the opportunity to topple Octavian completely.[93] This would be the ultimate gift for her husband upon his return home.

To be sure, another version of events is recorded, according to which Fulvia was in charge of Lucius from the start, even to the extent that he was only able to celebrate a triumph at the start of 41 BC through her permission.[94] She and Lucius, this same version holds, were acting solely to obtain power for themselves: the defense of Antony's interests was a pretense. Lucius began raising an army, and Fulvia too. Making her headquarters at Praeneste, she conducted deliberations there with Senators and sent orders to checkpoints across the peninsula; she even put on a sword herself, gave the watchword to the troops, and harangued them.

Certainly relations between Octavian on the one hand, and Lucius and Fulvia on the other broke down. Octavian broke off his marriage with Fulvia's daughter, Clodia (contracted in 43 BC to help secure the triumvirate), rudely claiming that he had not even touched the girl.[95] By the end of 41 BC, Lucius was trapped with the army he raised at the old Etruscan city of Perusia, hoping—as Fulvia was too—that generals loyal to Antony in northern Italy and Gaul would rally to his side.[96] They failed to do so. Lucius was driven from Perusia, and Fulvia at this point fled along with her children, as did Antony's mother, Julia, who went to Sextus Pompey in Sicily.[97] After the defeat of one son and her daughter-in-law, and with peninsular Italy now in Octavian's grip, Julia had to take measures to repair the family's fortunes: with an alliance between Antony and Sextus, Octavian might be toppled yet. Or Octavian could be forced to reconcile with Antony peacefully.

Fulvia, meanwhile, after meeting her husband in Greece, soon fell ill; Antony had to leave her for Italy, and news subsequently reached him there that his wife had died.[98] It was just at this point that, prompted in part by his mother Julia, who proved perfectly willing to double-cross Sextus Pompey, Antony came back from the brink with Octavian, saving Italy from a war between them.[99] Patching things up, to the extent that Antony now married Octavian's own beloved sister Octavia, both found it all too convenient to blame everything that had gone wrong the year before on the dead Fulvia.[100] Hence, almost certainly, the version of events that attributed the whole struggle to her and to her desire to gird on the sword and all. The far likelier reality was that Fulvia had done her very best to defend her husband's interests—which, of course, were not unconnected to her own and those of her children. Indeed, a good deal of her doings may well have had Antony's support. Yet, all that now had to be swept under the carpet, which is why disinterring the truth about Fulvia proves so difficult.

The condemnation of Fulvia's memory was useful not only in 40 BC, but in years afterward as well. Early imperial writers give a sense of what was said. "Fulvia, the wife of Antony, who had nothing womanly about except her body, was disturbing everything by armed insurrection," Velleius Paterculus writes.[101] And here is Plutarch: "a woman who took no interest in spinning or housekeeping, nor thought it worthwhile to rule a husband not involved in public life; her wish was to rule a ruler and command a commander."[102] Much had gone badly wrong in Rome from 44 BC, especially during the proscriptions. The triumvirs, it seemed, had waged war not just on Caesar's assassins, but on Roman society

FIGURE 7. Gold coin of Antony, issued 38 BC (*RRC* 533.3a). On the reverse is depicted Octavia. The paired portraits, showing similar features, proclaim "the harmony of the couple," on which peace for the Roman world depended: Wood (1999), p. 46.

itself. Through covert resistance and overt disobedience, women had protected themselves, their menfolk, and even at times their country. In doing so, they had become more involved in public life than was usual. To be sure, in besieging the Senate house or traveling to army camps, Fulvia may have gone to an extreme that ended up undermining her own influence; this was one step too many beyond Servilia-style politics. But it is also true that in casting her as the demon of early triumviral Rome—goading Antony, strapping on the sword, and shutting the door on the other matrons—men and women too found a way to assert that the worse was now over, that traditional gender roles might return.

But in fact there could be no going back, at least not completely. Women during these years, including the wife, had made too much of a mark. However psychologically satisfying the portrait of Fulvia was, the challenge remaining, in the years ahead, was to find ways to recognize women, especially the survivors, for what they had done. The *laudatio*, along with its lavish reproduction in marble, was one answer to the question.

4

Children Hoped For

After the husband's year or so underground, he and his wife were able to move on with their lives; they were not to be affected, not directly anyway, by the civil war that persisted for a decade more. The wife now turned her attention, according to the *laudatio*, to what she had been unable to do during the mayhem of their first years of marriage: giving her husband children. All told, he says, Fortune had been favorable to them as a couple, but on this score, the goddess was determined to frustrate their wishes. Naturally the wife showed all of her characteristic indomitability: "What you planned . . . and what you attempted! Perhaps in some other women this would be remarkable and worth commemorating, but in you it is nothing at all to marvel at, compared to your virtues" (2.28–30). And when these attempts failed, being who she was, she steeled herself for a more extreme solution yet.

Unlike the trials that came before, their childlessness seems a purely domestic problem. As we shall see, it was one probably more common in ancient Rome than has generally been acknowledged, both in extant ancient writings and in modern scholarship. Infertility, and even more miscarriages and infant mortality, took such a toll that many a couple had their hopes to reproduce thwarted. The *laudatio* casts some precious rays of light on this largely hidden social problem and its implications for women.

But the wife's final solution, we shall also see, does need to be set against the backdrop of Rome in the early 20s BC. By then, Antony was dead, Lepidus was under house arrest, and Octavian had gained sole power. As the husband himself puts it, an age of peace was dawning; he then immediately admits, "We did, it is true, desire children, whom for some time circumstances refused us" (2.26–27). The association of thoughts here is hardly casual. It springs from the ambitions that Octavian harbored for Roman society and its regeneration after nearly twenty years of civil war. While there was great relief that hostilities had (so it seemed) finally ceased, survivors were anxious for there to be no relapse; neither could they easily forget their losses and the sacrifices that had been made. How best to move forward with one's own life? In escapist art? Or a cultivation of domesticity? Even when sympathetic to Octavian, as the husband was, despite his earlier proscription, individuals held a range of answers. This debate, too, had profound implications for the lives of Roman women at all levels of society.

Civil war, then, might have been over, but the challenges the wife faced were not. Her own advancing age, longstanding Roman ideals, and new political pressures all came bearing down on her. With all of her old strength and spirit shining through, she rose to meet these new challenges, and in doing so achieved more distinction yet. It did not take civil war for the wife to show her extraordinary courage and generosity.

† † †

Marriage in Rome was, as a traditional formula put it, "for the sake of begetting children."[1] The words, perhaps originating in the wedding ceremony, were used in a variety of contexts, including an oath that the elected censors required men to take. As the censors (and others too) saw it, in marrying and having children one was doing one's patriotic duty.[2] It was not only a great blessing to be fruitful in marriage, but an honor worthy of public recognition. In a funeral speech for Lucius Caecilius Metellus, a general in the First Punic War, his son counted among the ten "greatest and finest things which wise men spend their lives pursuing...to leave behind many children."[3] A later member of the clan, Metellus Macedonicus, was said to have been blessed by Fortune from the day of his birth to his final breath: he was born in Rome, had noble parents, and—to pass over much else—Fortune had granted him "a wife famous for her sexual morality (*pudicitia*) and fecundity," and so he could die amid the embraces of his children.[4] By his death, three sons had reached the consulship, another the praetorship, and his three daughters were given out in marriage and had children of their own.

Women of exceptional fertility were themselves singled out, like Cornelia, mother of the Gracchi brothers and ten others, or Claudia Fortunata, commemorated in her epitaph also as a mother of twelve.[5]

In the Augustan age, large families were recognized too. In 4 BC, a humble man of Fiesole came to offer sacrifice on the Capitoline in Rome with eight children, twenty-seven grandchildren, and eighteen great-grandchildren, and the visit made it into the official public gazette.[6]

The corollary of all this was that fertility was looked for (as much as was possible) in candidates for a bride.[7] The physician Soranus, employing the familiar formula, explains: "Since women are usually married for the sake of children and succession, and not for mere enjoyment, and since it is utterly absurd to make inquiries about the excellence of their lineage and the abundance of their means but to leave unexamined whether they can conceive or not, it is only right for us to give an account of the matter in question."[8] He goes onto discuss age (women fourteen years of age to forty years are fit for conception) along with other physical characteristics (such as fleshiness).[9] Age certainly would have been a primary criterion in the eyes of men looking for a bride, and also a woman's general health and appearance. Also to be considered was the woman's family history and, if she had been previously married, her own reproductive history.

Soranus does not discuss how to assess the fertility of men, and modern scholars have sometimes said that women alone were held responsible for the fertility of their marriages.[10] In proclaiming "what you planned...and what you attempted" in the face of childlessness, the husband himself seems to take such a view in the *laudatio*. Certainly divorces initiated by husbands on the grounds of their wives' inability to bear children are known, and the reverse not.[11] But in actuality, medical and scientific writers, going back to the Greeks, did sometimes locate the cause of sterility in the male rather than the female.[12]

The late Republican poet Lucretius, reacting (to be sure) against commonly held views, insists that the problem can lie with men.[13] Women sterile in a previous marriage are known, Lucretius says, to have procreated with a new mate. Lucretius also dwells on the idea that some partners are simply reproductively incompatible, and in later times, Pliny the Elder cites no less an example of this than Octavian and his wife of over fifty years, Livia, each of whom had children with an earlier spouse but not each other—a situation that the speaker of the *laudatio* may have had in mind as he gave his speech.[14]

Biologically speaking, though, complete sterility in a couple, each in the respective peak reproductive years, is relatively uncommon.[15] Far more common in Roman society—and not necessarily sharply distinguished—was childlessness, caused by high rates of miscarriage and infant mortality.[16] As historical demographers constantly remind us, death was a constant presence in people's lives, afflicting not just the old, but the young, and especially the very young, making large families like that of the humble freedman (eight children, twenty-seven grandchildren) indeed exceptional. According to another source, Octavian and Livia did in fact have a child, who died prematurely.[17] Cicero's daughter Tullia apparently achieved her first pregnancy to term, or close to term, only with her third husband, Dolabella: the child was delivered two months premature, Cicero wrote to Atticus; the little boy was very weak, and he died soon after.[18] From Dolabella, another child followed a couple of years later, and this child too died in infancy, around the same time as Tullia herself (apparently from complications from childbirth).[19] Pliny the Younger—to give just one more example—was childless after his first two marriages, and his third wife, Calpurnia, miscarried after her first pregnancy.[20] "The gods will provide us children," Pliny wrote Calpurnia's grandfather; "her fertility, though it has been ascertained with all too little happiness, has made our hopes surer."[21]

Pliny's mention of the "gods" here is typical. Writer after writer blames divine will for childlessness.[22] The husband of the *laudatio*, in attributing his and his wife's childlessness to a personified Fortune, was not alone. In another letter, Pliny says that his friend, the biographer Suetonius, has been denied children through "the spitefulness of Fortune."[23] The poet Martial describes childlessness as "what Fortune forbids from happening," while also celebrating a successful union with these words: "Give thanks to the gods that she [Claudia Rufina] has been fertile and born children for her virtuous husband!"[24]

In his account of sterility, Lucretius reacts strongly against the idea that the gods are to blame for it, decrying the men as they were "dolefully sprinkling the gods' altars with much blood and making burnt offerings on them, in order to make their wives pregnant with copious seed."[25] He reacts against the idea because it was so widely held. Attributing reproductive success to capricious deities was a convenient mechanism for coping with a common problem: probably something like 20 percent of Roman fathers ultimately had no heir, female or male.[26] This was the fate of the husband of the *laudatio*—not necessarily, though, because of his or the wife's natural sterility. Nothing he says precludes the statistically likelier scenario of miscarriage, even repeated miscarriages, or the death of infant children. A possible indication (though hardly firm proof) of this latter possibility is that it was only at a more advanced age that the wife despaired of her ability to have children. If when the civil war between Caesar and Pompey broke out, she was around twenty years old—a plausible age for her to marry—by 28 BC, she would be around forty.[27] That was the year often associated in ancient thought with the end of female fecundity, and this could be the source of the wife's alarm, rather than an entrenched belief that she was infertile per se.[28]

The *laudatio* brings to the fore a problem that lurks in the background of Roman writing, and shows most fully its implications for women. While not necessarily blamed entirely for childlessness, they had fewer years of fertility than men, and this put pressure on them if they failed to deliver healthy children who could reach maturity. The husband is vague, but likely the wife, in the run up to her more extreme solution, coped initially as other women did throughout Greek and Roman antiquity, by medical treatments and by appeals to the gods. In the many references he makes to women's health in his encyclopedia, Pliny the Elder suggests that curing barrenness and promoting conception were paramount concerns for women.[29] Special foods or other substances were recommended; ointments and suppositories were prescribed; even bathing in the waters of a town in Campania was said to heal barrenness.[30] Certain substances were recommended for preventing miscarriage, and the use of amulets was prescribed too.[31] Newborns were also said to be protected by amulets—for example, branches of coral tied around their necks.[32]

The second avenue for the childless was religion. At sanctuaries this might be associated directly with medicine, but this need not have been, since virtually any god could be thought a healer.[33] But there were also rites thought specifically to promote fertility, such as the famous Lupercalia, held each year in February.[34] The association of Luperci gathered at the cave where Romulus and Remus had been reared by the she-wolf; a goat and dog were sacrificed, and the Luperci were then provided with loincloths cut from the hide of the sacrificial goat along with whips, to be used as they ran through Rome, otherwise naked, hitting those they met. Women struck, it was thought, would become pregnant—through the symbolic penetration—and so offered their hands or backs to the Luperci.

Certain deities were also associated specifically with women's reproduction, such as the goddess Natio, thought to watch over women in childbirth, or Juno Lucina, also a protectress of those in labor.[35] Men prayed to Juno Lucina too, and indeed (as Lucretius suggests) probably made prayers to any number of deities for children, just as women did.

A different solution still was for the man without success in having children to divorce and remarry. Historical tradition credited a third century consul, Carvilius Ruga, as setting the precedent, when he ended his marriage because his wife, owing to a physical defect, could bear no children; despite loving her, he felt his oath to the censors to marry "for the sake of begetting children" was more important, or so he said anyway.[36] Others followed, such as the dictator Sulla. He aroused criticism, though, because while he did cite his wife's sterility as grounds for divorce, he remarried within a few days, suggesting his motive was different.[37] This implies that divorce on the grounds of a wife's sterility seems in principle to have become accepted, but was not widely deemed essential (despite any oaths to the censors). As we shall later see, divorce flew in the face of an ancient ideal that the marriage bond should be for life.[38]

"You were despairing of your fertility and pained over my childlessness," the husband says; "so that I would not, by keeping you in marriage, have to put aside any hope of having children...you mentioned the word 'divorce'" (2.31–33). For her (rather than him) to do so was unconventional, but her plan did not even stop there. The wife would yield their house "to another woman's fertility"—the fertility of a woman she would go out and find for him (2.33). So far as the wife was concerned, the children whom this (no doubt younger) woman bore would be regarded as if they were the wife's own, meaning she would support them financially; she would not insist on taking her property away with her as legally she could in a divorce, but it would remain in the husband's control, still managed by her, if he wished. She would now fulfill the duties of "sister or mother-in-law," guiding the (young) bride with her greater experience, which by this point likely included helping her kinswomen in the early days of their marriages (2.39). All of the wife's trademark virtues are here in this extraordinary proposal: not just the selflessness and willingness to sacrifice, but the lawyer-like attention to the financial details.

It was now the husband's chance to pass a test of his faithfulness. Thankfully, he did, as he says in some of the most heartbreaking lines of his whole speech:

> I must say that I became so enraged that I lost my mind; I was
> so horrified at your designs that it was very hard to regain my

composure. To plan for a divorce between us before Fate gave its decree to us—for you to be able in any way to conceive the thought that you would cease to be my wife, while I was still alive, when you had remained utterly faithful to me, at the time I was exiled and practically dead! (2.40–43)

His feelings, in all their raw beauty, are not just described. They are conveyed too by his inability to move on in his speech. "What desire or need to have children, could have been so great for me, that I could have broken faith?" he asks. "But why say more?" (2.44–45). But then he summarizes her plan all over again, this time though emphasizing the nobility that inspired it.

Just as the bitterest moment of the husband's life was with his wife's experience at the tribunal of Lepidus, so her anguish over failing to give him heirs palpably pained him, at the time and years later. His natural desire for children and her advancing age certainly were factors in this second crisis; but also relevant was the moral and political climate of Rome in the years after the husband emerged from hiding.

† † †

The reconciliation between Antony and Octavian made in 40 BC with the assistance of Antony's mother, Julia, had not brought much stability.[39] Disgruntled over being shut out of the final negotiations, Sextus Pompey resumed his attacks on the coast of Italy. Grain ships from overseas were blocked, food shortages grew acute, and a riot occurred in Rome, during which Octavian was nearly stoned to death. The triumvirs were forced to come to terms with Sextus. While this rapprochement too proved short lived, both sides made one agreement of lasting importance: all of the proscribed, aside from Julius Caesar's assassins, were now welcome to return to Italy. Among them was an erstwhile Caesarian, Tiberius Claudius Nero, who had fled with his wife Livia Drusilla.[40] She is one of the best-known Roman women of these years, and her life story perfectly encapsulates the final transition from republican to monarchical government in Rome.[41] Parts of it shall be told here, and parts later in this book, as a way of understanding better the experience of the wife of the *laudatio*.

Livia was descended from the highest aristocracy in Rome. She was the peer of Servilia or Antony's mother Julia, but a generation younger. Her father, born a patrician Claudius, but later adopted into the prominent family of Livius Drusus, had, like Cato after Thapsus, taken his

TABLE 4 Roman Political History, 39–27 BC.

39	Attacks by Sextus Pompey on Italy; pact of Misenum between Sextus, Antony, and Octavian results in amnesty for proscribed (except for Caesar's assassins); Livia returns to Italy
38	Marriage of Livia and Octavian (January)
37	Antony and Cleopatra reunited
36	Sextus Pompey defeated by Agrippa and Octavian at Naulochus in Sicily; Lepidus ousted from triumvirate and placed under house arrest; Antony's failure in campaign against Parthia
35	Livia and Octavia awarded statues, freedom from guardianship, tribunician sacrosanctity; death of Sextus Pompey
34	Antony's recognition of Cleopatra and her children in ceremony at Alexandria
32	Divorce of Antony and Octavia; oath of loyalty sworn by Italy to Octavian and a declaration of war on Cleopatra
31	Antony and Cleopatra defeated at Actium (2 September)
30	Deaths of Antony and Cleopatra in Alexandria; annexation of Egypt by Rome
29	Octavian returns to Rome and celebrates his triple triumph (August)
28	Octavian's program of temple restoration; attempts to pass early version of marriage law
27	Octavian relinquishes control of some provinces and gains honors from the Senate, including the name "Augustus"; Augustus leaves for Gaul and Spain

This table is based on the fuller chronologies in Scullard (1982), pp. x–xxii, and Bowman, et al. (1996), pp. 995–1005.

own life in the aftermath of Philippi, rather than surrender.[42] Her equally aristocratic husband—also a patrician Claudius—was more compromising, and agreed, despite some republican sympathies, to serve as praetor in 42 BC.[43] But he then fought Octavian during the awful war at Perusia, and afterward proscribed, he had to flee Italy.[44] Still only a teenager, Livia made a harrowing flight to southern Italy, with her two-year-old son, the future emperor Tiberius, so that the family could cross together to Sicily.[45] While Sextus Pompey's sister greeted Livia warmly, Tiberius was less pleased with the reception he got from Sextus; the couple went East with Antony's mother, Julia, and took refuge in the ancient city of Sparta, where the Claudii had long been patrons.[46] In the tales of loyal wives, Livia's story had a most

FIGURE 8. Marble bust of Livia Drusilla from Ephesus. Ephesus Archeological Museum, Selçuk, Turkey.

prominent place: such was her support for her husband that she even underwent a voluntary exile.

The return of such distinguished refugees offered Octavian, now mainly based in Italy (while Antony was in the East), an opportunity to gain valuable support. Livia, not only young, beautiful, brave, and intelligent, but also well connected to the surviving republican nobility, quickly figured into his plans.[47] It posed little problem for Octavian to divorce his wife Scribonia, whom he had married hastily in 40 BC to try to forge an alliance with Scribonia's relative Sextus Pompey.[48] The bigger obstacle was Claudius Nero, with whom Livia was now pregnant a second time. Nero gave his consent, as did Livia, recognizing that this alliance was the best way for them to repair their fortunes, and for their (first) son to have any chance at a future.[49] Still, to divorce during pregnancy and become betrothed defied convention, so much so that

Octavian anxiously consulted with Rome's pontifical college to gain clearance. With their blessing in the fall of 39 BC, he and Livia were betrothed, Livia's son Drusus was born on 14 January of the following year, and then just three days later the new marriage was solemnized.[50]

The pontifical ruling gave backing to the irregular union, but the couple relied on a further strategy.[51] After her betrothal, it later became widely known, Livia was out riding in a carriage when an eagle dropped a hen of remarkable whiteness into her lap; in the hen's beak was a laurel branch bearing berries.[52] The soothsayers were consulted and ordered that the bird and her chicks should be preserved and the laurel branch planted. This was done at a country estate of Livia's on the Tiber, dubbed "The Poultry." There a grove grew; when Octavian later celebrated a triumph, his laurel branch was drawn from here, as was the wreath of laurel he wore on his head.[53] The omen and the perpetuation of its memory in the grove not only sanctioned the union, but linked it to the everlasting peace and victory that evergreen laurel symbolized. In art of the Augustan age—temples, altars, cameos, coins, and more—laurel became ubiquitous; laurel was even planted on either side of the entrance to Octavian's house.[54]

Recollection of the omen in the years to come allowed Octavian to acknowledge the value in which he held Livia and her piety. By extension, he was showing respect for all of the *matronae* of Rome, renowned for their devotion to the gods.[55] This was important for the triumvir, especially after the proscriptions and taxation plan that Hortensia and her peers had protested, a plan that had offended so many. Meanwhile, Livia herself could serve as an ambassador to women who had opposed the triumvirs, not least because she had been one of them—for all we know, even joining the protest back in 42 BC.[56] Thus in 36 BC, after a major victory off the Sicilian coast over Sextus Pompey, among various honors voted to Octavian was the right of wearing a laurel crown on all occasions and also "of giving a feast with his wife and children on the anniversary of the day on which he had won his victory, which was to be forever a day of thanksgiving."[57]

By convention, other Senators in attendance would bring their families to the yearly gatherings. At the festivities, women would not only bask in their recognition, but talk with one another, reminded by Livia of the improvement in their fortunes since the dark days—when the out-of-line Fulvia had tried to be in charge. Even those not at the banquets could be taken in by Livia's dramatic story. Tongues might have wagged about her scandalous betrothal to Octavian, the costume parties at which they were said to have dressed up like the Olympian gods.[58] Now she was playing a quite different part: she was the wife of the perpetual victor, able to supply him with laurel crowns from the verdant grove that showed the gods' continuing favor to her. The role was utterly traditional and novel at once.

Not coincidentally, Octavian's sister Octavia, married to Antony since 40 BC, was to preside at commemorative banquets with her husband at the Temple of Concord, after the final defeat and death of Sextus in the East in 35 BC.[59] In that year, too, Octavia and Livia were rewarded three other major honors: public statues, the right of administering their own affairs without a guardian, and the same security and inviolability that the tribunes of the people enjoyed.[60] These distinctions—based in part on those customarily awarded to the Vestal Virgins—need to be seen in the context of Antony's developing relationship with the Egyptian queen Cleopatra, another woman whose story had a major impact on events.[61]

After meeting Cleopatra on her resplendent barge in Tarsus in 41 BC, Antony was inspired to visit her in Alexandria the next winter.[62] Twin children were born to the queen, but the couple did not meet again until 37 BC (resulting in another child, a son).[63] From this point, their fortunes were closely interwoven: after Antony's spectacular failure in his Parthian campaign of 36 BC, Cleopatra arrived on the scene with crucial resources.[64] Octavia herself also set out, from Rome, with supplies and troops, and while Antony took the gift, he sent Octavia back to Rome.[65] Meanwhile, he presided over a spectacular ceremony in Alexandria that recognized not only to Cleopatra, but her children with him—the price, surely, for the help she was giving him.[66]

Octavian drew a sharp contrast between Antony's apparently uncaring treatment of Octavia and his burgeoning love for Cleopatra—a worse woman even than Fulvia, because she was foreign—showing that the value in which a respectable wife was held could matter a great deal in the eyes of the Roman public, men as well as women.[67] How different was Octavian's respect for Octavia, not to mention for his own Roman wife Livia! Meanwhile, other divergences between the two triumvirs were highlighted. Whereas Antony lost against the Parthians and dallied with Cleopatra (so it was said), Octavian was fighting successfully across the Adriatic to defend Italy from marauding tribes based there;

FIGURE 9. Marble bust of Cleopatra, probably from Italy. Antikensammlung, Staatliche Museen, Berlin, Germany.

whereas it was Antony who was now partying in Alexandria, Octavian and his associates, especially his indispensable right-hand man Agrippa, were rebuilding the city of Rome; and their soldiers were being used to restore security through the Italian countryside.[68] The final push to win over Italy firmly to Octavian's side came in 32 BC, with more ferocious attacks on Antony (culminating in a divorce from Octavia); the swearing of a mass oath of loyalty to Octavian; and a declaration of war on Cleopatra.[69] She and Antony were trapped the following year in the bay of Actium, off the coast of Greece, and after losing in a naval battle, escaped to Egypt, where they were defeated, each taking their own lives.[70]

The factors in Octavian's success had been several: his cultivation of political allies in Italy, his increasing mastery of public relations, Agrippa's superb generalship, and Antony's miscalculations. While

Antony had retained powerful backers in Rome, including a number of Senators who in 32 BC fled to him in the East, by 30 BC, the majority in the Senate, and of Roman society, had come to accept, if not embrace, Octavian.[71] The couple in the *laudatio* should be counted in this larger group. The removal of Lepidus into a sort of permanent house arrest in 36 BC, after he had tried to cross Octavian, would have given them a specific satisfaction.[72] The respect accorded to Livia, Livia's own willingness to support publicly her husband, and the incorporation of *matronae* into celebrations of Octavian's successes also were part of the wife's experience in the years after the proscriptions, and provided further grounds for her to reconcile with the man who had earlier been responsible for great danger to her husband. If Livia could forgive Octavian, perhaps the wife of the *laudatio* could too.

† † †

Octavian returned to Rome only in August of 29 BC, to the greatest of fanfares. Over three days, he celebrated his military victories—in Illyricum across the Adriatic; in the Actium campaign; and in Egypt, which had been made part of the Roman Empire, furnishing an enormous booty.[73] Some was on display in the triumphal procession, along with an effigy of Cleopatra herself, showing her pale in death, her arm punctured by twin asps.[74] Egyptian wealth helped fund generous handouts to the people of Rome and to thousands of discharged veterans, and also lavish games to mark the opening of the new Temple of the Divine Julius constructed at one end of the Roman Forum; gladiators were brought from Dacia, and for the beast hunts, a rhinoceros and hippopotamus.[75]

Italy was awash in money, not only through Octavian's handouts, but also tax relief and massive spending on the public works and on lands designated for veteran settlement. Real estate prices soared and interest rates dropped in tandem.[76] The rich improved their villas, mansions in Rome were decorated with elegant wall paintings that evoked the masterpieces of Greek art, and even more ordinary folk could delight in attractive new red-gloss tableware, decorated with dancers, Cupids, and scenes of lovemaking.[77] Couples in Rome again were meeting up in Pompey's portico, or the new portico of the Danaids built by Octavian on the Palatine, admiring, along with each other, the masterpieces of Greek art that he and Agrippa were determined to display to the public.[78] In private, for the well off, there were parties with fine wines, delicacies to savor, almost heavenly perfumes, and the most alluring

FIGURE 10. Painting of seated Venus from Cubiculum B (a bedroom) of the Villa under the Farnesina in Rome dating c. 20 BC. Museo Nazionale Romano, Rome, Italy. The depiction of Venus on a golden throne recalls classical Greek art.

entertainers, including actors, mimes, and prostitutes.[79] "Now it is time to drink, now the time to stamp the ground with unfettered feet!" sang the poet Horace.[80] "Before it was sacrilege to bring out the Caecuban from the ancestral cellars, while the queen was making a mad plan to destroy the Capitol and bring death upon the empire."

It was around 29 BC that another young poet, Propertius, released his first book of verse, *Cynthia*, which evoked this lifestyle in a confessional style of poetry not irrelevant, we shall see, for understanding the *laudatio*.[81] Cynthia, the reader learns from the opening poem, has ensnared Propertius, "never before touched by love," and the poems that follow share the extraordinary highs and lows of his relationship with her.[82] In the second poem, Cynthia's beauty is celebrated. It lies not in the latest hairstyle, diaphanous silks, or fragrances that were all the rage.

FIGURE 11. Painting of erotic scene from Cubiculum B (a bedroom) of the Villa under the Farnesina in Rome, dating c. 20 BC. Museo Nazionale Romano, Rome, Italy. Preliminaries to lovemaking.

It lies, as also for the heroines of mythology one could admire in contemporary wall paintings, in her naked form—and as Propertius says this, one has to suspect he is only trying to seduce her once again. In a later poem, we see Cynthia dallying in the louche resort of Baiae. Propertius hopes she is only playing with a toy boat or swimming, rather than hearing the "seductive whispers" of a rival, as she lies at rest "on a beach that can keep its secrets."[83] For all such hardships, the life of love is not one Propertius would trade for any other: an early poem effectively draws a contrast between the poet and his friend Tullus, who is traveling overseas for military service with his uncle. "I was not born to be fit for glory," Propertius announces, "fit for war: love is the military service the fates wish me to endure."[84]

Readers have long debated who exactly this Cynthia is.[85] One ancient source says that she in fact is a stand-in for an (apparently high-ranking) Roman woman, Hostia (the pseudonym being a nod to respectability, since the love would have been out of wedlock).[86] Some have seen her as a high-class prostitute. Others still think she is purely a

FIGURE 12. Arretine bowl in terracotta by M. Perennius Tigranes, dating
c. 25 BC. Ashmolean Museum, Oxford, United Kingdom. The lovemaking.

protean fiction, as imaginary as the mythological heroines of Greek and
Roman paintings. But what does seem clear is that she is not easily envisioned as Propertius' actual wife.

Marriage, after all, was "for the sake of begetting children." Or for
the sake of allying families. For men of Propertius' status, erotic pleasure
was more easily to be envisioned with a prostitute, or a mistress like
Antony's Volumnia Cytheris, the actress who so scandalized Cicero, and
who is said to have been the inspiration for the poems of an immediate
predecessor of Propertius, Cornelius Gallus.[87] Erotic pleasure could, it
is true, be imagined with another man's wife, a widow, or a divorcée.
Pudicitia notwithstanding, some high-ranking women were increas-
ingly hard to distinguish from the likes of Cytheris, so alluring were they
in their dress, conversation, even ability to dance and sing.[88] Quite possibly given as teenagers in marriages designed to foster political alliances, they themselves might only have had a chance for real erotic

pleasure through an extramarital affair.[89] Such affairs were not infrequent, moralizing ancient historians and orators assure us, but one does not need to take their word alone for it.[90]

While serving as provincial governor in 50 BC, Cicero shared with Atticus some gossip about a certain Vedius Pollio.[91] Vedius came to call on Cicero with an extraordinary entourage, including a troupe of slaves, a pack of wild asses, and large horse-drawn carriages, on one of which rode a baboon. Lodging with a freedman of Pompey, Pollio had left behind some of his baggage. The freedman died, an inventory was made of all the property, and among Pollio's holdings were found "five small pictures of distinguished women," including one of Servilia's daughters, married to Lepidus, "who puts up with this sort of thing lightly." All of the matrons, it seems, had been lovers of Vedius and shared paintings with him, and for Lepidus's wife, Vedius was not her only paramour, if Cicero's comment is to be trusted (cf. Fig. 5).[92] The son of one-time slaves, Vedius rose to great prominence around the time of Actium. Helping Octavian in financial affairs, be became fantastically rich himself, the owner of a massive estate in Rome as well as a spectacular villa on the Bay of Naples that went by the Greek name *Pausilypon* (meaning "Free from Cares," or *Sans souci*).[93]

Propertius mocks enterprising types like Vedius in his poetry, exactly because their wealth might outmatch his own affections, as well as his poetic tributes, in the heart, or mind, of Cynthia.[94] But the lifestyle envisioned in Propertius' poetry bore a resemblance to that of Vedius, and whatever Cynthia's status, the poems themselves were, along with the wines, paintings, and other luxuries, a prop for those seeking escape after the terrible civil wars. To at least some members of a new generation, the lifestyle of Vedius and his ladies looked more appealing than ever. This did not all go unnoticed by Octavian. In 28 and 27 BC, he was crucially rearticulating his political position, by professing to return control of the Roman world to the Senate and the people's assemblies—by "restoring the republic," as the husband of the *laudatio* says admiringly.[95] In exchange for this, he received elevated but not explicitly monarchical honors—above all, the new name of "Augustus" (meaning "revered one").

Simultaneously Augustus was embarked on a conspicuous religious revival and could announce that he had restored no fewer than eighty-two temples in the year 28 BC alone, the year in which he also dedicated a massive new Temple of Apollo on the Palatine Hill.[96] In what had long been the address of Rome's most exclusive families, Augustus had been buying up properties to create a palace for himself in the manner of a Hellenistic king.[97] But after the victory over Sextus Pompey, as part of the gradual makeover of his image, he set these aside for the Greek deity, whose traditional associations with culture made him a perfect icon in the more placid art of Augustan Rome.[98] Silver statues of Octavian were melted down, and the money used to dedicate golden tripods for the new Augustan sanctuary, advertising the triumph of piety over the reckless individualism of the era of the triumvirs.[99] *Pietas* was, along with valor, clemency, and justice, one of the virtues inscribed on a golden shield set up by the Senate for Augustus in 27 BC.[100]

It was not only that Augustus wished to distance himself from the excesses witnessed during the civil war; he was also suggesting now that civil war had been caused by such moral failure.[101] Horace in one of his *Odes*, addressing a rich man who builds extravagant villas, urges that "whoever shall wish to get rid of godless slaughter and the madness of civil war...let him dare to rein in unbridled wantonness."[102] To repent of the civil wars, the poet continues, is to offer up Rome's treasures to the Capitoline sanctuary—an act that unmistakably evokes Augustus. Such thinking stemmed from traditional habits of thought in Rome—the health of the community was linked to the health of the state, and traditionally censors concerned themselves with individuals' morality—but it also conveniently focused attention off Octavian's own misdeeds by making civil war a *societal* problem.

In another ode, Horace proclaims that civil war will only be expiated through temple building and restoration.[103] Rome's troubles began in the home, with young women thinking of nothing but sex. "Soon, while her husband is in his cups, she seeks out younger men as lovers; but she does not choose one to whom she may give forbidden pleasures hastily with the lamps removed." No, the vivid account continues: "Right in the open with her husband's full knowledge she gets up when asked, whether it is a salesman who summons her or the captain of a Spanish ship...."

Yet a different ode still holds out a more hopeful picture: Augustus, returning victorious from a long campaign in Spain in the summer of 24 BC, is to be greeted by his wife, "rejoicing in her one and only husband," having made a sacrifice to the just gods.[104] Joining her will be Octavia, "sister of our distinguished leader," and with them other married women, the mothers of Rome's soldiers, and also the young wives of the soldiers, girls who might marry them, and the soldiers' younger brothers. Horace, too, will join in giving thanks, at a private celebration at home: "I shall not fear insurrection or death in domestic violence, so long as Caesar holds the world under his sway."

As already in the decade before, Augustus' family in this poem serves too as an emblem of traditional Roman values, values thought to have made Rome strong and that also could make Rome strong again: piety to the gods, devotion to the *patria*, and also commitment to the family. Women might not have served as soldiers, but, Horace is suggesting, they had their own unique contribution to make by bearing sons to be soldiers (sons like Octavia's Marcellus, and Livia's Tiberius, both of whom served in Spain) and daughters to be those soldiers' wives.[105] For this they could be recognized, but it was recognition, after all, of their most traditional role.

† † †

This celebration of women as mothers cannot have made things any easier for the wife—and gives context to the husband's insistence on her worth to him.[106] But very likely, there was more specific pressure on her than that. Despite recent views to the contrary, it seems clear, as scholars had long maintained, that in tandem with his political settlement and religious revival, Octavian embarked on a formal program of moral reform in 28 BC, proposing the precursor to a law concerning marriage and the birthrate, which he did successfully pass in 18 BC.[107] The main evidence is a poem from Propertius' second book, a sequel to *Cynthia* released in the mid-20s BC, which tells of a law that might have parted the poet from his beloved.[108]

This was a law, Propertius makes clear, of Octavian, a law intended to force Propertius to marry legitimately, in order to provide manpower for Rome. "How should I furnish sons for my country's triumphs? No soldier will there be of my blood!" the poet defiantly says. Fortunately, though, the law was withdrawn from consideration before it was actually passed. In the face of protests from high-ranking Romans, who did not wish to have Octavian meddling in their private affairs—protests echoed by Propertius himself in his poem—the plan was temporarily abandoned.[109] For Octavian, building consensus was imperative, and a focus on immediate enhancement of Rome's military glory proved politically more advantageous, hence the major war in Spain, as well as campaigns to the south of Egypt and in Arabia.

The legislation that was passed in 18 BC was modified in some respects in AD 9, and legal sources speak of the measures in tandem, making it hard to know exactly what was specified by the earlier law.[110]

By the Julian marriage law of 18 BC, it does seem clear, the unmarried could not inherit from those other than relatives up to a certain degree, and childlessness in married couples might also have been so penalized (after AD 9, penalties on the married but childless were definitely lighter than those on the unmarried).[111] It may further have been stated in the Julian law that husbands and wives could only inherit one-tenth from each other, unless they had children; the birth of three children who survived to be named gave full capacity.[112] This "right of three children" brought other privileges: priority in government appointments for men, and for women, freedom from legal guardianship.

These rewards and penalties suggest that Augustus was most concerned about encouraging reproduction among the upper classes, although the law did apply to all Roman citizens and had consequences for them.[113] Also targeting the upper classes was another measure of 18 BC that criminalized, for the first time in Roman history, adultery, that is sex with a married woman, as well as sex with any unmarried free woman (prostitutes, actresses, and several other categories aside).[114] The legislation was substantially harder on women, as it completely regulated their sexual lives, in essence compelling *pudicitia* rather than leaving it a matter of choice.

We cannot be sure what, exactly, was proposed in 28 BC, but something along the lines of the later Julian law, or the Julian law as modified by the Papian law, seems a very good guess.[115] If so, in 28 BC, the wife quite possibly had a further motive to contemplate divorce and find a fertile young bride for her husband. If he failed to have children, he might have stood to lose valuable legacies and inheritances and—what must have seemed even more outrageous—nine-tenths of his wife's patrimony could have been lost. By divorcing him, in contrast, she could simply give him all of her property outright, an utterly generous act. The husband would hear none of it, and like Propertius, he could soon breathe a sigh of relief anyway. But what about in 18 BC, when the marriage law was actually passed?

True to themselves and to their class, they could rely on a dodge to circumvent one of the worse penalties of the marriage law, the ban on inheriting more than a fraction of each other's estates.[116] It is no surprise that once the marriage law was passed, and again after it was modified by the later measure of 9 AD, a number of dodges were tried. Some men betrothed themselves to immature girls, since betrothal exempted them from penalties on the unmarried.[117] Some married just in advance of receiving a major legacy, and then divorced.[118] Some adopted children for brief periods at critical moments in their career, to game the law's requirements.[119] Heirs were charged to disburse money to those who could not legally inherit (a trick also relied on by those circumventing the Voconian law).[120]

The loopholes were closed by subsequent legislation, as was another: the childless entering upon a marriage with *manus*. If a wife married her husband with *manus*, all of her property became his, even after her death, while if he died, she could inherit his whole estate through intestacy, since she was within his power and thus became an automatic heir. The main evidence that this dodge was relied on is a Senate decree of the mid-first century AD that banned it.[121] But the *laudatio* itself seems also to provide an example of the practice, or at least recognition of its value.[122] It may well be that already by 18 BC the couple had made theirs a marriage with *manus*, for as we saw, this provided a good way around the *lex Voconia*; if so, in 18 BC they simply would have seen added value in their choice. Our major legal sources were compiled centuries after the age of Augustus, when marriage with *manus* was essentially obsolete. The *laudatio*, though, along with the Senate decree just mentioned, helps suggest that it may have been a more vital institution in the age of Augustus than has generally been thought, especially appreciated by those who had faith in the durability of their marriages.

So it was that for our resourceful couple the Julian marriage law probably had little impact on their lives. But the Julian law, the first attempt at legislation ten years earlier, and the prominent promotion of childbearing throughout these years did not leave them altogether unaffected. For all his seeming traditionalism, and even in the face of his own childlessness with Livia, Augustus through his legislation downplayed the ideal of the eternal marriage bond and emphasized the value of bearing children at all costs, a burden that fell much harder on women than men. In insisting that he and his wife fervently hoped for children, and that she would do anything possible to see that he did have children, the husband of the *laudatio* pays respect to Augustus' view for the regeneration of Roman society. But if divorce is to be the answer, they part company—or at least the husband parts company with Augustus the lawmaker. The husband was hardly like the narrator of Propertius' love poems in lifestyle, but he had as much reason to resent the intrusions of the lawmaker. "You alone give pleasure to me; Cynthia, may I alone please you," proclaims Propertius; "this love will be worth more to me than the name of father."[123] And the husband: "What desire or need to have children could have been so great for me, that I could have broken faith, and traded certainty for uncertainty?" (2.44–45). Each is emphatic about the choices he has made in life.

The husband dismissed his wife's proposal to divorce out of hand, and they would stay married until her death. Still, the proposal remains a key event for assessing her life, and the lives of Roman women. In a perverse way, it shows again her independence, her resourcefulness, and her confidence in managing her own, as well as her husband's, properties. It complements her earlier heroism in the civil wars. While her exploits then could be paralleled by the deeds of other women (Terentia, Hortensia, Julia, and more), we have little other evidence about how other women acted in the face of a childless marriage. Did Livia, for example, offer to divorce Augustus? What the wife's actions do underscore, though, is the unique pressures placed on women—pressures made worse by Augustus' legislation. Whereas the censors of old had (at least at times) fulminated about men's need to marry and have children, the new law with its ongoing penalties and rewards was as firmly aimed at women as it was at men.[124]

5

Preparing for Death

Nothing is known of the couple's life until the final crisis they had to face, the wife's last illness and death, about twenty years after she broached divorce. "Fate decreed that you should precede me," the husband says succinctly, and with a typically Roman attitude (2.54).[1] In the face of all too prevalent illness, striking down those of every age, there was great insistence not just on death's inevitability, but also its unpredictability. The Fates gave every mortal a preordained span, maybe long, maybe not. As one woman is made to reassure us in her own epitaph: "I do not want you to grieve for my end, friend; this quickly completed life was what Fate gave me."[2] Typical, too, in the *laudatio* is the husband's failure to mention what exactly the cause of the wife's death was. For many Romans, any notion of an afterlife was shadowy at best (although ghosts do feature in some literary texts). It was better to recall the dead as they had been in life, rather than to linger on their death, unless the death was itself heroic.[3]

And when one could prepare for death, as the wife did, the ideal was to focus not on preparations for the next world, but on sealing one's legacy among the living.[4] Has the will been kept up to date? Are the survivors taken care of? The wife herself, it shall come as no surprise, anticipated her husband's overwhelming grief at losing her and tried as hard as she could to preempt his suffering. So even as she faced her own extinction, she put her husband first, just as she had when she offered divorce, and once more, her extraordinary service to him extended beyond the civil war. Although this last good deed was clearly the culmination of many that came before, it would not have surprised the couple's contemporaries: women in ancient Rome of many different social backgrounds and across generations had the job of helping their families in bereavement. The *laudatio* gives a glimpse of this major contribution.

† † †

Because she was married with *manus* and her property was technically in the ownership of her husband, a will was not important for the wife.[5] Nonetheless her husband, in almost the last words of the *laudatio,* promises: "I have treated your final wishes (*mandata*) as law; whatever further it is free for me to do, I shall" (2.68). Romans approaching death, or even on their deathbeds, would impress upon their survivors wishes—in Latin, *mandata*—which, though separate from a will, there was an almost a sacred obligation to carry out.[6] One might make specifications about one's funeral, or the decoration of one's tomb. One might also include in one's *mandata* requests that an heir honor relatives, friends, and slaves with cash bequests, tokens of appreciation, or manumission. *Mandata,* as we saw, were one way those with only daughters tried to circumvent the *lex Voconia.*[7] Propertius, a poet fascinated with death, frequently imagines expiring characters, or the ghosts of the very recently dead, giving their final words—and in them, *mandata*. Cynthia implores Propertius: "Let Parthenie my nurse lack for nothing in her palsied old age…and let not my darling Latris…hold a mirror for a new mistress."[8] Cynthia's childhood caretaker is to be looked after, and the slave who tended to her appearance was to be freed (women's cosmeticians are known, through epitaphs, to have been freed not infrequently).[9] It is easy to imagine the wife making such wishes, or giving instructions on the disposal of certain heirlooms, such as her jewelry.

But she said more than this to her husband. An important clue about her preparations for death comes when the husband says that, despite his sorrow, "I for my part will steer my feelings to your views.…" The text then breaks off for a few words, and resumes with discussion of "all your opinions and precepts" (2.55–56). This is something separate from *mandata,* words rather designed to help the husband, preemptively, to cope with his loss.

Because Romans—including, it would seem, the husband—typically did not harbor a very robust vision of an afterlife, a great comforter for them in the face of death was philosophy.[10] Already the Hellenistic philosopher Crantor had written an influential work *On Grief,* and this spawned a whole tradition of consolatory literature, often for Romans in the shape of letters, which hammered at the idea that death was inevitable, but not evil.[11] In one such letter, addressed to a Titius who had probably lost at least one son in an epidemic, Cicero acknowledged the repetitiveness of the genre:

> There is, however, that especially well known form of
> consolation that we ought always to have on our lips and in
> our minds: we must remember that we are men, born on the
> condition that our life lies open for all the darts of Fortune; we
> must not protest that it is on these terms that we live; we must
> not bear so hard those misfortunes which we cannot avoid
> through any amount of prudence; and we must by recalling the
> experiences of others reflect that it is nothing new that has
> happened to us.[12]

Cicero proceeds to give arguments specifically relevant to Titius as a man of affairs. Because he lives in the public eye, Titius must maintain his customary dignity and therefore not grieve unduly. And a little reflection should convince him that his sorrow is passing: "The fact is, if there has never been a woman so weak-minded that she did not, after losing her children, at last put an end to her mourning, then certainly we ought by using our reason to apply in advance what the passage of time will bring."[13] The implied prejudice is that women are normally more susceptible to grief than men.

Yet despite that prejudice, it is not the least bit fanciful to imagine that the wife of the *laudatio,* held up by her husband again and again for her reasonableness, had some acquaintance with and appreciation for philosophy, whether through consultation with practicing philosophers or reading philosophical treatises. Women of her rank were, it is true, less favored than men educationally.[14] They would be given instruction in reading, writing, and the higher study of literature—but not, as men were, rhetoric. The result was that we do find adult women engaged with poetry, reading it and sometimes writing it.[15] And they are also known to have studied philosophy. Cicero's wealthy friend and correspondent, Caerellia, is the classic example; eager to obtain a copy of Cicero's philosophical work *On the Ends of Good and Evil*, she had slaves of Atticus sneak her a copy before it was ready for circulation. While rebuking Atticus, Cicero forgave Caerellia, because he says she had "an extraordinary passion for philosophy."[16] Sadly, Cicero's correspondence with her, known in the early Empire, is now lost.[17]

For women (as for men), philosophy was especially helpful in "cop[ing] with the blows of Fortune."[18] In a consolatory work addressed to a woman, Marcia, Seneca draws a contrast between Augustus' sister, Octavia, who gave into grief completely when her son died, closing her ears to every form of consolation, and Livia, who dealt with the loss of her son Drusus more easily by seeking out the philosopher Areus.[19] Areus, as Seneca describes him, did not just load Livia down with undiluted Greek philosophy; he also urged her, in a very practical, very Roman way, to take consolation from allowing herself to listen to the praises of her dead son, as Octavia would not. This was result-oriented philosophy, even a form of therapy really. As Seneca said in another consolatory work, addressed to another woman, his own mother, "And so I lead you to that place where all who are fleeing Fortune must seek refuge, to study of philosophy. It will heal your wounds, it will get rid of all your sadness."[20]

A close reading of the final part of the *laudatio* shows that the wife had given her husband some guidance for his impending bereavement—including, presumably, at least some of the now highly traditional consolatory themes, but also some more formal arguments that he could respond to, and did (at least in his funeral speech).[21] As we shall shortly see, it is a very good guess that she urged upon him the Stoic view that feelings of anguish, while seemingly natural, in fact derive from judgments that we can, and should, control. Whatever the precise contents of her advice, she insisted on his promising to heed it. "I...will steer my feelings to your views," he bravely states (2.55). But he then later admits: "I cannot abide my promise" (2.62).

For all of the remarkability of the woman of the *laudatio*, the scene of a dying, or even newly dead, wife giving her husband consolation is not an unfamiliar one in the Roman imagination; other examples will add depth to the situation that we can just make out from the husband's words. Propertius envisions the Roman matron Cornelia asking, just after her death and cremation, various things of her husband, Paullus, and also reminding him of the inexorability of death, and the futility of grieving: "the black door [to Hades] is open to no prayers...the ways are firm with unbending adamant."[22] He must take consolation from her life. The poet Statius envisions Priscilla dying in the embrace of her husband, but not without uttering these comforting words: "Part of my soul that shall survive me, oh that I may leave for you the years which cruel Atropos [one of the Fates] snatches away from me! Spare your tears,

I beg you, do not beat your breast in savage mourning...."[23] While she dies younger than was expected, at least she points out "the order of death is upheld," meaning that she was the elder partner in the marriage. Fate, all knew, could have been more capricious.

Probably most affecting, though, is the monument set up in the early first century AD by a former slave of a freedman of the emperor Tiberius, for himself and for his slave-wife, also subsequently freed.[24] Claudia Homonoea is made, on the front of the monument, to speak Greek verses: "I, the talkative and cheerful swallow Homonoea, lie here, leaving behind tears for Atimetus. To him I was dear since I was little. But unexpected ill fortune cut off this great friendship." Latin verses on the left side of the monument, also attributed to Homonoea, reiterate the familiar idea that she was seized by "hateful Fate." On the right, Atimetus is made to converse with her. "If cruel Fate allowed lives to be exchanged...," he says, "whatever time is owed still to my life I would have gladly exchanged for you, dear Homonoea." But Fate is inexorable, and all he can do is hope for immediate death. She then replies with the familiar consolatory themes: "Tears are of no use nor can Fate be moved. I have lived my life; this one end rules all." It must have been at least in part thoughts like these that the wife shared with her husband, as she prepared for death in the fine Roman fashion, focusing on those around her.

To be sure, the verses on Homonoea's tomb, like the poems of Propertius and Statius, are imaginary works. And it may be better to argue that in fact the *laudatio* helps us understand these (more) imaginary works, more than the reverse. It was, as we shall see, women's task more than men's to help their families through a time of bereavement (even if not every wife was well versed in philosophy). For a wife to predecease her husband, then, was an awful blow—just the kind of tragedy that a poet, whether the lofty Propertius or the writer behind Homonoea's tomb, could make the most of.

†　†　†

About the wife's final moments, the husband says nothing. One hopes that they occurred under the best circumstances possible, at home, with the husband present to catch—as Roman custom required—her final breath with a kiss.[25] However her passing occurred, and his promise to her notwithstanding, naturally it was still a shock for him. When delivering the *laudatio*, his emotions were still raw, and included the feeling of guilt at surviving her—the classic response of a survivor, well familiar to Romans as the verses from Claudia Homonoea's monument among many other texts shows.[26] As the husband says toward the end of his speech: "I wish that each of our lifespans had allowed our marriage to continue until I, the older spouse, had been carried off—which would have been more just" (2.51–52). Yet—a sign of how much he felt this—he had already voiced almost the same thought earlier, when discussing the length of their marriage:

> Rare are marriages as long as ours—marriages ended by death,
> not cut short by divorce. It was granted to us that ours lasted
> into its forty-first year without any wrongdoing. I wish that our
> long-enduring union had been altered by something happening
> to me, not you; it would have been more just for the elder
> partner to yield to fate. (1.27–29)

The wish expressed here was exactly that of Claudia Homonoea's husband, and it is not an unfamiliar one in Roman epitaphs.[27] Less typical of epitaphs, though, is the husband's final remark, yet another expression of guilt: "The conclusion of this speech will be that you deserved everything but it was not granted to me to give everything to you" (2.67–68).

The truth was, as the husband points out, that he was the likelier one to have died first in the marriage, simply because he was older. Since they were married fully for forty years, and the wife was probably around twenty at the start of the civil war between Caesar and Pompey in 49 BC, she should have been in her early 60s when she died.[28] In keeping with the Roman pattern of upper-class marriage, he was likelier to have been at least ten years older, perhaps more still—especially if, as is just possible, she was his second wife.[29] Men tended to marry later, and they remarried, making the widow a more common figure than the widower.[30]

It was therefore more typical for middle-aged and older women to bury their husbands, rather than the reverse, and women took a greater role in the rituals of burial and grieving.[31] It was usually a woman who pressed the last kiss on the lips of the dying, who bathed the dead body and anointed it with scented oils, and organized the lying in state of the body in the family house and the ensuing funeral. It was usually a woman too who collected the remains of the dead at the pyre after cremation. During the lying in state, the funeral, and formal mourning that followed, the custom was for women to grieve more visibly than men—or for the women to hire female mourners—thus helping the family to channel all of its sorrow. Fulvia, we saw, used the convention to political advantage.[32]

In facing the prospect of her death, the husband knew now that he would have to see to all of this without his wife; the situation was, as he saw it, almost like that of a parent burying a child. What is more, he also lacked the customary consolers for a man in his position. Despite the wife's very best efforts at preparing for death, the husband can say: "You consigned me to grief through longing for you, and you left no children to comfort me in my misery" (2.54–55). The ideal, for a Roman man such as him, was to be like old Metellus Macedonicus, whom Fortune had smiled on from birth, giving him among so many other blessings a brood of children and grandchildren. Passing into extreme old age, Metellus, we are told, died "a tranquil sort of death amid the kisses and embraces" of this brood, and "his sons and sons-in-law carried him through Rome on their shoulders and placed him on his pyre."[33] What a sad contrast with the husband, left to bury his wife alone! If only he had died first, he says, perhaps not entirely unselfishly; she could have performed the last rites and, because they had married with *manus*, would have succeeded him as a "substitute daughter."

Also overwhelming the husband at the moment of his wife's death was the inescapable fact that for all her efforts in advance, she was no longer around him to help with the crisis of her death, or anything that came thereafter: "When I think of how you foresaw and warded off all of the dangers that befell me, I am shattered in misfortune" (2.61–62). Always she could make the best of an awful situation, turning disasters into some sort of advantage. When her parents died, she showed her loyalty to them through vengeance; in the defense of her father's will, she showed loyalty to him again, and "devotion to your sister, and loyalty to us" (1.26); to her destitute female relatives, she showed "devotion and generosity" (1.50); and so on. The husband hopes to take inspiration from this example, as a supplement to her philosophical advice; "instructed by your deeds, I shall stand up to Fortune" (2.59). But then to think of her leads him immediately back to despair: "I am shattered in misfortune and I cannot abide by my promise" (2.61–62). "I seem kept alive for longing and grief" (2.66).

"A natural sorrow jerks away my power of self-control (*constantia*); I am overwhelmed by sadness," he declares, pointing to another aspect of his situation (2.63). He was judging himself not just against her record and her last words to him, but also against the widely recognized duty for a man of his rank to retain self-control, *constantia*, at all times, even ideally in bereavement.[34] A brave face was required, as Cicero had written Titius. Julius Caesar famously lived up to the ideal, resuming command in Gaul only three days after he learned of the death of his daughter; as again Cicero wrote, to his brother Quintus, one of Caesar's officers, "I had great pleasure from your letter about the brave dignity Caesar showed in his time of acute grief."[35] The one-time Caesarian Asinius Pollio, whose upholding of old Roman standards at times almost verged on parody, went further: he boasted that he had gone out to dine the day his son died, and gave public speeches three days later.[36] Still, this was *constantia*, the essence of which was that normal aristocratic dignity had to be retained under not just any, but all circumstances. It was one basis for the traditional ruling class's claim for power. Even the wife displayed *constantia*, the husband says, when she refused to back down when an attempt was made on her father's estate (1.25).

A further sign of the importance of this ideal for high-ranking Romans was that self-control during bereavement became one of the virtues that Augustus and his family, female members as well as male, sought to exemplify.[37] Octavia's total breakdown, admittedly, was not exemplary, but Livia, for all that she was shaken by the loss of her son Drusus, showed more restraint. In the words of a poet, it was her duty to distinguish herself from the ordinary: "Fortune set you high and ordered you to uphold a position of honor."[38] When, in 20 AD, Tiberius lost his adopted son Germanicus, he, along with Livia, refrained from grieving in public. Interestingly, though, the people of Rome, devoted to Germanicus and his wife, Agrippina, grew angry at Tiberius and Livia for *not* appearing publicly, leading Tiberius to issue a rebuke. "Mourning and the comforts of grieving had been suitable when the pain was still fresh," Tacitus has him say; "but now their [the Romans'] spirits must be stiffened again, just as once Divine Julius—after he lost his only daughter—and divine Augustus—after his grandsons were snatched away—had suppressed their sadness."[39] The Senate, in a subsequent decree, made sure to praise the imperial family, including Tiberius and Livia, for showing the proper amount of grief throughout the episode.[40]

This remarkable incident suggests—something that is not surprising—that a range of views existed on what counted as suitable grieving, even for Rome's ruling class. If the husband broke down after his wife's death, admitted it in his *laudatio*, and left a written record of his despair for posterity, he was not the only one. A very good parallel, in fact, is Cicero himself, who, soon after he wrote to Titius, had to face the loss of his beloved only daughter Tullia, a blow he hardly coped with as briskly as he suggested Titius could with his loss.[41]

Tullia died in February of 45 BC at Cicero's villa at Tusculum, where Cicero could not bear to stay, so reminded was he of his loss.[42] He also declined to stay at his main residence in Rome, lest he have to put on a good face for all the visitors who would come to see him there. He retreated to a property of Atticus outside Rome for about two weeks, reading everything he could find "by anybody on assuaging grief."[43] (Atticus, adept in Epicurean philosophy and the owner of a well-stocked library, surely had many or all of the relevant titles.)[44] At the start of March, Cicero then left for Astura, on the coast of Italy, where he had a lodge with a good view of the sea.[45]

FIGURE 13. Bronze bust of a young Roman man, dating c. 30 BC. Hermitage, St. Petersburg, Russia. The man's beard indicates that he is in mourning, as does the artist's sensitive rendering of grief.

"I go without talking to anyone in this lonely place," he wrote Atticus, in a letter of tellingly short phrases. "In the morning I hide myself in a dense, thorny woodland, and I do not emerge before evening. After yourself, being alone is my best friend. In this state all of my conversation is with my books. But fits of crying interrupt it. I fight them back as best I can. But so far it has not been a fair fight."[46] When he could, he worked on "an endeavor that I imagine no one before me has," a consolation addressed to himself, which he planned to share with Atticus when completed; in it he gathered together the different arguments that he had found in his reading in Atticus' library.[47] The effort of writing provided some distraction. It was the only way Cicero knew, he says, "to restore my outward appearance but not my inner self."[48]

He writes this because he knew that he was not living up to the ideals that he, and others in his position, had set forth. By 15 March, criticisms of how Cicero was comporting himself were passed onto him by Atticus, and Atticus added his own plea for Cicero to disguise the intensity of his grief.[49] More complaints were to follow, as well as a carefully composed consolatory letter from Sulpicius Rufus, residing then in Athens.[50] Among many other arguments, Sulpicius urges this: "Do not forget that you are Cicero, a man accustomed to giving instruction and advice to others. And do not imitate those bad doctors who, when it comes to other men's illnesses claim to possess medical knowledge, but then cannot cure themselves." Advice similar to what Cicero gave Titius follows. In his reply, Cicero acknowledges what Sulpicius said: "I think it is disgraceful that I did not bear my own misfortune as a man endowed with such wisdom as you thought that I should."[51] "But," he continues, in words similar to those of the *laudatio,* "sometimes I am overwhelmed, and can barely resist the grief...." His situation, he naturally feels, is different.

Cicero completed his *Consolation* and allowed it to be disseminated—although sadly it does not survive beyond a few quotations—but he continued to think about what had happened to him.[52] The problem of grief looms large in a major work of ethics that he wrote after the *Consolation,* set at the Tusculan villa, *The Tusculan Disputations.*[53] In it, according to the conventional interpretation, Cicero shares his views with an anonymous interlocutor on the nature of emotions and happiness. While the work owes a great debt to Stoic philosophy, and Stoic views of the emotions in particular, Cicero pays more attention to grief than Greek Stoic philosophers did in their analysis of emotion, and the practical problem of how to cope with grief, or (better) to cure it. Book 3 of the *Disputations* is given over to a review of various theories of human distress (one of the four major emotions, according to the Stoics, of which grief is an example). In this review, Cicero gives particular emphasis to the Stoic view: grief, like all the passions, may seem instinctive, but it in fact stems from a judgment that one had made about the value of what one has lost. Cicero also discusses, favorably, the Stoic claim that men feel that the gods are placated by grief, and so developed a view that it is a customary duty to grieve. "Out of this belief," he claims, "arise all of those dreadful different types of mourning: failure to wash, women's rending of their cheeks, beating of the chest, thighs, and head."[54]

One who gives comfort can take something from all of the different views on the origins of emotions surveyed by Cicero, "just as I in my *Consolation* pretty much threw everything into one effort at consolation; for my soul was in turmoil and every type of curing it was attempted."[55] He proceeds to outline what the ideal cure is, and while he admits that the Stoic views he favors can be difficult to swallow in a time of distress, he still maintains that they are the most powerful. Whatever evil there is in distress, Cicero insists, is not natural, but the result of a mistaken belief about the value of something. All alleviation of distress must go back "to the same foundational point, that all anguish is far removed from the wise man, because it has no meaning, because it is taken up in vain, because it does not stem from nature, but rather from a judgment, a belief, a sort of call to grieve, since we have decided that is what we ought to do."[56] While Cicero can still in this work admit to his earlier devastation by Tullia's loss, he now is suggesting a fuller philosophy to cope with such loss than the crisp formulations of consolatory letters.

If it was not fanciful in the least to view the wife of the *laudatio* as a proponent of philosophic thinking, it is not fanciful either to imagine that she had read Cicero's moving *Tusculan Disputations*—or had had a slave read it aloud to her (and, perhaps, her husband).[57] Very clearly, at any rate, the husband is challenging the sort of philosophic views one finds in Cicero's work by himself using the language of philosophy. When he says that "a natural sorrow jerks away my power of self-control," he is pointedly disavowing the Stoic view of emotions (2.63).[58] The value he has placed in his wife is not mistaken, not in the least: "Going back over my earlier troubles and fearing what the future may bring, I break down" (2.64–65). Here we almost seem to see them arguing one last time, taking the positions they always had. He is all emotion—emotionally untidy, but rugged, even beautiful—as he had been in the days of the proscriptions or when the wife made her proposal to divorce. She is calm, calculating, and prefers reasoned thought to reckless emotion. He shares his emotion at the end of the *laudatio* not just by talking about it, but through his language itself. The sentences become shorter and simpler. They veer back and forth in time, like the verses of a love poem. He is insistent: not to mourn her would be to deny that she was everything to him, just as, so many years before her, to divorce her would have been a complete betrayal.

† † †

Only one thing seems to provide any consolation to the husband, a thought that keeps occurring to him. As he puts it at one point, "Fortune...has not snatched everything away from me; she has allowed your memory to become established with my words of praise" (2.59–60). What the wife achieved will not be lost to the husband. He will draw strength from it. It will take precedence over all of his wife's opinions and instructions. It will allow her to remain alive. The enduring fame of the great man or woman was not a stock argument in the consolatory literature of Ciceronian Rome (it does appear in the works of Seneca, written a few generations later), but it is one at the heart of traditional Roman thinking.[59] After all, what was life but a ceaseless quest for glory?

Cicero himself wrote two books *On Glory* and set as his childhood goal what Peleus had said to Achilles in the *Iliad*: "Always to be best in battle and preeminent beyond all the others."[60] It is no accident that he should have quoted Homer to himself; Roman ideals were inspired, in part, by extensive childhood study of Homer. Romans could sympathize with the thought of their Trojan ancestor Hector, when he hoped to kill a Greek champion. If successful, Hector says, he will build a tomb by the shore so that a passing sailor might say, "This is the grave of a man who died long ago, one of the bravest whom bright Hector killed."[61] "My glory," Hector concludes, "shall never perish." In the face of mortality and a dim afterlife, this was a potent thought, more appealing to some than philosophy. Cicero himself, who quoted Hector's lines in his *On Glory*, also acknowledged the idea when he wrote of Cato the Elder: "I have discovered many excellent things in this man, but nothing is more admirable than how he bore the death of his son, a distinguished man of consular rank. You have the *laudatio*. When we read it, what philosopher don't we spurn?"[62] This captures something of the husband's attitude toward consolation in his speech.

But still the husband worries that even thinking of her praise will not be enough. Even as he contemplates her glory, "I seem now not so much capable of enduring these things" (2.65–66). The guilt at surviving her keeps coming back: "you deserved everything but it was not granted to me to give everything to you" (2.67–68). Cicero, surviving his daughter, felt those feelings of guilt too, and made what he considered a vow to build a shrine for her, as if she were a goddess. "Best and wisest of women," he said in the *Consolation*, "with the approval of the immortal gods themselves I shall hallow you, placed now in their company, in the thoughts of all mortals."[63] Where to build the shrine occupied Cicero's attention, and Atticus', for months to come.[64] Cicero's own estates were rejected. Something more public was needed, perhaps at Astura by the sea or on a piece of land along the Tiber River. Those gliding by, like Hector's imagined sailor, would be sure to see it—just as they did see the Mausoleum that Augustus built for himself and his family alongside the Tiber, after Cicero's death.[65] As the complex negotiations dragged on, and as Cicero did come to terms with his grief, the plan was finally dropped. The *Consolation* would do what the shrine was supposed to do; it would consecrate Tullia to immortality, just as ultimately it was Homer's poetry, and no funerary mound, that immortalized Hector.

The husband would find a way for his words, too, to immortalize his wife. Not only, then, does he challenge her view of emotions in the *laudatio*. He also, finally, took a different approach to mortality. But in doing so, he did not lose sight of how she tried to help him, even from beyond the grave.

6

Between the Torches

Although the husband does not mention it in the *laudatio*, he would have organized a funeral for his wife, first displaying her corpse in the house, then processing with it, and finally disposing of it by cremation. It is worth reconstructing the whole ceremony, to provide some essential context for the speech we have been examining throughout, which combines a traditional praise of the deceased with more intimate remarks addressed to the wife directly by the pyre. The funeral brings us closer to understanding the stone monument that the *laudatio* was turned into. Furthermore, funerals were an area of Roman life important to women, and to explore them helps to open up experiences the wife herself must have had—her own parents' funeral, for example—and of women's lives more generally. Funerals only made it into the mainstream historical record when they commemorated leading men or women, such as Julius Caesar. But within the lives of even the most ordinary Romans, they could be landmark events.

† † †

Important as funerals were, though, there are challenges in asserting what would have happened at any one in particular, and not just because customs varied over time and depended on the status and wishes of the deceased.[1] The textual sources, themselves of various dates, only provide particular details as opposed to full accounts, and so have to be synthesized—a risky procedure.[2] Fortunately, however, some more elaborate sculptural depictions also survive, which aim to make their viewers not just witnesses, but almost participants themselves in funerary rituals. In combination with the texts, they can give us something of the experience of at least some Roman funerals and the preliminaries to them, as well as Roman attitudes toward death more broadly.

Masterfully shown in one marble relief, probably originally the front of a sarcophagus found in Paris and dating to the AD 100s, are the first moments after death (Fig. 14).[3] As a person died, loved ones would gather round, to support the dying—and each other. A close relative might give a final kiss to capture the soul of the dying, and then close the dead person's eyes. Those around called out the name of the deceased— as if to make sure she or he really were dead—and began lamentation. It is this calling out and lamentation that we witness on the sarcophagus. A young girl lies dead, with her feet crossed, on a comfortably arranged bed. A man at the head of the bed—presumably her father—is seated, clutching his right knee with his hands as a gesture of grief. At the other end of the bed is a woman—presumably the girl's mother—also griev- ing; she rests her head on her hand. With the presumed father are two young men (the girl's brothers?), and with the mother, two girls (her sisters?); there are also two girls behind the couch (perhaps hired mourners), who seem to be the ones calling out the name of the deceased or perhaps are singing dirges. The artist has carefully distinguished the

FIGURE 14. Marble relief, representing a deathbed, found in Paris. Cluny Museum, Paris, France.

dead girl from the living women (whoever they are), by showing all of the women with disheveled hair. Striking too is the contrast between the girl's peaceful rest and the variety of gestures and poses of those standing or seated. It is a crowded scene, which the artist, through the open composition, invites us to enter. We take leave of the girl too.

Death, it can hardly be said enough, was prevalent in Rome, striking those of all ages, often unexpectedly—hence the useful concept of Fate.[4] Death was, one could almost say—in comparison with modern societies with lower mortality rates—more a part of life.[5] The dying and the newly dead were not isolated or hidden. Rather, custom prescribed that the living should gather around the dying, and the living should interact with the corpse in specific rituals. Relatives and friends were to take part in the process of dying, as a way to come to terms with this more common occurrence.

After the crying out of the deceased's name, the body might be placed on the ground, bathed, anointed, clothed, and garlanded, to prepare for a lying in state in the *atrium* of the house. Traditionally, women of the house might do these tasks themselves, but those of means increasingly hired professionals to help them.[6] So, too, women themselves also traditionally performed rituals of mourning around the corpse in the *atrium*, or they might hire mourners to sing dirges, beat their breasts, scratch their faces, wail, and scream, while visitors came to pay their respects.[7]

A unique representation of this lying in state is shown on a marble relief from a tomb on the outskirts of Rome, dating to around AD 100, belonging to a family of wealthy freedmen (Fig. 15).[8] Dominating the scene is a dead woman, laid out in the *atrium* of her house (its roof and columns can be made out in the background, along with funerary props: garlands hanging on the colonnade, incense-burners at the bottom, and on the sides, massive flaming torches and candles that light the scene). The deceased lies on two mattresses, with both placed on an elaborate couch that rests on a draped platform. These, like the rings she wears on her left hand, proclaim the woman's wealth. So, too, do the tablets at her feet, as they must be the will that she has left disposing of her property.

As in so much other Roman art, scale is not consistent: encircling this important woman are smaller figures, attending to her in death. A pipe player on the left provides music, and next to him is probably a hired female mourner, a *praefica*, leading the customary dirge that

FIGURE 15. Marble relief, representing a lying in state, from the Tomb of the Haterii. Vatican Museums, Rome, Italy.

lamented the dead. Behind the couch, an undertaker prepares to place a garland on the deceased's neck, while to his side there are two female mourners with hair down, raising their hands to beat their breasts. The procession below of men and women, also beating their breasts, may represent grieving relatives, and at the head of the couch are three additional female figures, seated, with disheveled hair, each clutching her knee, and each wearing a pointed cap: this is the cap worn by freed slaves, showing that these women have been manumitted by the will of the deceased. This scene lacks the pathos of the Paris relief, and its composition invites less direct participation on the viewer's part. This is not the death of a young girl, but of a more mature woman, able to leave a will; seemingly, we are closer to a good death. The crowdedness of the scene is a striking contrast to the isolation that the husband of the *laudatio* claims to feel, lacking as he does his wife to organize the sort of elaborate occasion that was expected.

After the lying in state, the body of the dead was carried in a procession to the grave or a separate place of cremation, with a stop in the

FIGURE 16. Marble relief, representing a funerary procession, from Amiternum. Museo Nazionale, L'Aquila, Italy.

Forum for those high-ranking individuals who were honored with a *laudatio* delivered from the Speaker's platform.[9] Across a relief from ancient Amiternum (near modern L'Aquila), identified as one part of a centurion's tomb, we see such a parade in progress (Fig. 16).[10] The deceased rests again on a couch with double mattresses, and beneath an elaborate canopy, adorned with representations of stars and the moon, which may suggest some notion of a celestial afterlife for him.

While the bier is visually impressive, in contrast to the other reliefs examined, it is less predominant: really the whole procession is the spectacle here. A master of ceremonies stands in front of the elaborate bier, directing its eight bearers. In front of them are the musicians—horn players, trumpeters, and flautists—as well as two women, one tearing at her hair, the other raising hands (perhaps in the role of *praefica*). Nine mourners come after the bier, including it seems the dead man's widow and children, as well as other relatives, friends, dependents. Also to be seen in the bottom left corner is an incense carrier. Interestingly, the deceased here is shown propped up: perhaps we are to imagine he was shown thus in effigy (a practice elsewhere attested), or it may simply be the artist's way of depicting who he was in life. He wears a tunic and toga and holds what appears to be a centurion's staff, while on top of the canopy can be made out a helmet. From the crying-out immediately after death, to the lying in state, to the funeral procession itself, there almost seems to be a sort of progression: after the fact of death is confronted, focus shifts, at least in part, onto who the deceased was in life.

There are no artistic representations of what followed the procession, the disposal of the corpse.[11] At the time of the couple in the *laudatio*, cremation was entirely typical and is safely assumed for the wife. The bier would be set on a pyre (sometimes, like the bier, a highly elaborated structure), the body anointed, the eyes opened, and final offerings made, of perfume, incense, and food. As at the moment of death, the deceased might again be kissed by a relative, who would light the pyre with a torch, and again there would be a calling out of the name of the dead person. After the cremation (a long process) was concluded, the pyre was doused with wine, the remains were gathered up into a container, and ultimately the container was interred in some sort of tomb. There were additional days of mourning, cleansing ceremonies at home, and a sacrifice and feast on the ninth day, possibly at the tomb: this banquet marked the complete separation between the living and the dead, with the dead receiving only certain simpler foods.

Formal opportunities for communion with the dead continued.[12] Graves and tombs might be decorated during the festivals of the violets and the roses in March and May, respectively. On the Parentalia, in February, as an occasion to venerate the ancestors, offerings were made to the dead collectively, and their tombs again decorated. The birthday of the deceased was also a time to specifically honor that person. While ideas about the afterlife varied, it was common to believe that the tomb was a resting place for the deceased, his or her eternal home—a place not to be disturbed.[13] *Sit tibi terra levis* ("may the earth be light for you") many epitaphs implore, a phrase so familiar it could be abbreviated *STTL* to save room on costly stone monuments.[14]

In the very last words of the *laudatio*, the husband offers a variation of this idea, when he says, "I pray that your *di manes* will grant you peace and protection" (2.69). The *manes* were, originally, the collective spirits of the dead, an undifferentiated whole, worshipped at the Parentalia; graves were considered to be consecrated to them.[15] The *di manes* (the "divine *manes*") then also came to mean one's family ancestors in particular, and this may be the sense in which the husband uses the term: he would be praying that his wife's deceased forebears will protect their daughter's tomb. Just around the time of the *laudatio*, though, the plural noun *di manes* came also to refer to an individual's own (divine) soul, and it is possible that the husband may (also) be suggesting that his wife's own spirit will help to determine the tranquility of her remains, in her final resting place.

What all this shows is that while there were subsequent occasions to commune with the dead, the cremation itself, or the interment, was a wrenching moment—a virtual repetition of the moment of death, but one at which you really did have to say your last goodbye. After that, it was the more nebulous world of the *di manes*. If no sculptural relief captures this final parting, it is evoked in a poignant lyric of Catullus, whose brother had died overseas and whose funeral Catullus, as he tells us, barely arrives to attend:

> Traveling through many lands and over many seas I have
> come, brother, for these wretched funeral rites, to give you the
> last dues of the dead and to speak, though in vain, to your
> silent ashes. Since Fortune snatched you from me—alas my
> poor brother, cruelly taken from me—things being as they are,
> accept these offerings which are made according to ancestral
> custom as a sad duty, offerings now dripping with your
> brother's tears, and forever, brother, greetings and farewell.[16]

Catullus dramatizes the moment of leave taking: while already his brother is gone, the poet undertakes an arduous journey not just to make the customary offerings, but also to address him a final time. Catullus needs to assure his brother—and, in truth, himself—how much his brother meant to him. Beneath the surface of the poem is the guilt that is more explicitly expressed in the *laudatio*. Nor is this the only similarity: the *laudatio* also is addressed in the second person, to the dead wife herself—something not true of all *laudationes*. And, just as Catullus turns the traditional, but fleeting, valedictory moment into a permanent commemoration of his brother, so did the husband find a way to make permanent his last farewell. The inscribed *laudatio*, in a sense, re-enacts the husband's separation from his wife, making us—as with the reliefs examined above—spectators of this sad scene.

† † †

Having traced the path from deathbed to pyre, we shall now look more at the tradition of the *laudatio* itself. Such a speech, celebrating the achievements of the deceased, was central to the funeral of a high-ranking Roman male.[17] Appropriately for these great patriots, the practice was distinctively Roman. It was the Athenian custom, for example, to give funeral speeches for all the men who had fallen in a particular campaign, *collectively* exalting them as well as the city, while also consoling their families.[18] The origins of the Roman ritual may have lain in a performance by the *praefica*, separate from the choral dirges she directed at the graveside, and focusing on the praises of the dead.[19] But certainly by the third century BC, the bier of a very distinguished man would be placed on or near the speaker's platform in the Forum, and the citizens were treated to a recitation of his praises by his son or another close relative. Making this even more of a family affair, around the bier sat actors who wore masks depicting the faces of the dead man's forebears (masks normally displayed in the family house). In fact, the *laudatio* itself customarily included ample praises of the family's ancestors.

By tradition, the rhetoric of the *laudatio* was not too obviously elaborate, in keeping both with the frequently young age of its speaker and, as Roman oratory became more sophisticated, the apparent simplicity of earlier times.[20] Only a few relatively short quotations of *laudationes* given in the Forum for men actually survive, and these come from the section praising the deceased himself, rather than the ancestors.[21] Probably toward the climax of the oration that Q. Caecilius Metellus gave for his father Lucius, a general in the First Punic War, came a list of "the ten greatest and finest things which wise men spend their lives pursuing," all of which the deceased achieved, better than anyone else at any point in Roman history.[22] What jumps out is the highly conscious sense that aristocratic life is dominated "by competition for prestige and recognition."[23] Exactly this same idea seems to occur in the papyrus scrap of a Greek translation of the *laudatio* given by Augustus for his son-in-law Agrippa in 12 BC, part of which reads: "You were raised to the supreme height of power with our support and through your own excellent qualities by the consent of all men."[24] Although this *laudatio* was spoken in the Forum, Augustus here does not address the citizens of Rome, as was customary, but the dead Agrippa himself—a point to which we shall return.

Where did women fit into all of this? By the late Republic, it is clear that they too received *laudationes*.[25] The majority of these were probably delivered graveside, as would be those for men not of Senatorial background—which is not to say that these speeches were uninfluenced by those given in the Forum.[26] But at least in part because the aristocratic funeral, and the *laudatio* with it, was not just about the dead, but the man's whole family, some women of Senatorial background were also honored in the Forum, with an address to the people.[27]

The first woman to receive such a public honor may have been Popilia, the mother of Q. Lutatius Catulus, the consul of 102 BC (so, at any rate, a character in one of Cicero's dialogues implies).[28] Other women received it in the first century BC, including Julius Caesar's young wife Cornelia, in 68 BC, and also that same year, Caesar's aunt Julia, the wife of the great general Marius.[29] Caesar himself gave both of these speeches, and a fragment of that for aunt Julia survives:

> My aunt Julia's maternal family is descended from kings, while
> her paternal family is joined with the immortal gods. For the
> Marcii Reges (this was her mother's family name) go back to
> Ancus Marcius; and the Julii, the family of which we are a
> branch, to Venus. Thus in this family is the deep respect owed
> kings, who have supreme power among men, and the
> sacredness of gods, in whose power even kings themselves lie.[30]

The focus on family is insistent, and probably this quotation came from that part of the *laudatio* concerned with the family. It may well be that the section on the family was the more important part of this speech; Caesar, still at an early point in his career, could use it to lend luster to himself. His precocious heir, the future Augustus, must have done the same, when at the age of twelve he made his public debut by orating for his grandmother, who was Caesar's sister. In the ensuing decades, Augustus gave *laudationes* for other relatives, such as Agrippa, and Augustus's sister Octavia, setting a good example for the speaker of our oration.[31]

And not just for him: aside from ours, the only other reasonably well-preserved *laudatio* also honors a woman. Inscribed on marble too (on a slab only half of which was ever recovered, though is presently missing), it has as its subject one Murdia, who was not of the highest nobility, but was well-off financially and lived around the same time as our wife, or perhaps slightly later.[32]

In its surviving portion, the speaker (Murdia's first son) devotes considerable attention to matters of inheritance. Murdia had married twice, with her first husband predeceasing her. He left his estate to their surviving son, but also gave Murdia a share. She then remarried and had several more sons and a daughter. In her will, she made all of her sons heirs, and gave her daughter a legacy equivalent to the sons' inheritances. Her surviving husband was also given a bequest. The speaker is obviously pleased, though, because she specifically "returned" to him the part of the first husband's estate that had gone to Murdia. But, he insists, she won praise from "her fellow citizens" too "because the distribution of the shares [of her inheritance] shows feelings of gratitude and loyalty to her husbands, impartiality toward her children, and justice in her strict adherence to what is right." The disposition of her estate disclosed virtues complementary to those she had before: "she was true to herself in maintaining through her obedience and honesty the marriages to worthy men her parents gave her." Loyalty to family trumps any other.

Murdia's son then goes on to say that *laudationes* for good women tend to be similar; the reason is that "the natural excellences upheld by their own carefulness do not require varied language." Still, "since it is difficult for a woman to acquire novel praise, because their lives are troubled by fewer vicissitudes, it is necessary that their shared qualities be recognized." A list follows of Murdia's virtues, her "modesty, honesty, sexual morality, obedience, wool-working, economical management, and loyalty." These, the encomiast believes, still earned her "the greater praise of all." Sadly, the text breaks off just as it seems the son is about to acknowledge some more distinctive virtues of his mother, her "bravery" and her "work, wisdom, dangers" (or "work and wisdom in times of danger").

Comparison of this text with the so-called *Laudatio Turiae* is illuminating. Both, not surprisingly, given the interests of wealthy Romans, discuss these women's estates, and in both, the women's independence in such matters is taken for granted; they had choices to make, and they both exercised them well, as far as their menfolk were concerned.[33] Murdia, it seems, like "Turia," could also cope with an unusual situation well. And like Murdia' son, the husband of the *Laudatio Turiae* still feels that despite his wife's extraordinary excellence, he must make some gesture toward the more traditional feminine virtues:

> Why should I mention the virtues of your private life: your
> sexual morality, your obedience, your considerateness, your
> reasonableness; your attentive weaving, your religious devotion
> free of superstition, your unassuming appearance and sober
> attire? Why should I talk about your love and devotion to
> family...? You have countless other things in common with all
> married women who keep up a good reputation. The qualities
> that I assert you have belong to you alone; very few other

women have lived in times similar enough so as to endure
such things and perform such deeds as Fortune has taken care
to make rare for women. (1.30–36)

The idea of "incomparability" that we saw in the male *laudatio* does apply to women too.

Perhaps even more revealing, though, are the differences between the two speeches, or at least in what survives of them. While both women are said to be singular, the wife of the *Laudatio Turiae* seems more singular. Murdia's son apologizes for including a catalogue of standard feminine virtues; the husband does not.[34] Of course his wife had all of those, and so much more too; even what she did in the face of childlessness was "nothing at all to marvel at, compared to the rest of your virtues" (2.30). The wife, in other words, is ever capable of surpassing her own good self, not just other good women. Also different is the husband's insistence that he is unable to express her excellence adequately: "It would be an endless task, if I tried to touch on all this.... But why say more? I will spare my remarks, which ought to be and can be short. I do not wish, in treating your very great exploits, to go through them unworthily" (2.9–10, 2.22–23). Such rhetorical devices, familiar from other Roman oratory, might have been common enough in *laudationes*, but they are especially effective in conjunction with the husband's several descriptions of his own feelings, including his repeated near loss of self-control.[35]

Much, then, as the husband tallies up the achievements of his wife, as any good *laudatio* would—for her it's not the number of won battles that counts, but how many times she saved her family—one still feels that there is an anguish in this text utterly lacking in the more smug *Laudatio Murdiae*. Part of this impression must be attributed to a final difference between the texts: as in the traditional *laudationes* for great men in the Roman Forum, Murdia is spoken of in the third person ("*She* made all of her sons equal heirs, and her daughter was given a portion"), whereas the husband addresses his wife directly throughout. Direct address may have been the tradition in graveside *laudationes*, perhaps even deriving from the laments that were also sung there.[36] But as Murdia was most likely herself to have had such a graveside speech, it seems that the husband had a choice here. Here we should recall that in speaking the *laudatio* for Agrippa, Augustus used the second person. He would have done so to add emotional impact to his speech.[37] Despite the need for Augustus and his family to show self-control at state funerals, there was value in bringing into the Forum something of the poignancy of the valedictory scene at the grave. With the rise of what was almost a royal family, mourning became a civic event.

† † †

The husband's *laudatio* has now been set within the context of the Roman funeral. Dwelling on all of the great virtues of his wife, in the sober tradition of *laudationes*, he also partakes in the grief that one might feel graveside, at the final parting. And, just like the funerary reliefs examined, his speech, once inscribed on his wife's tomb, transports us to the moment of farewell. His confessional tone might well be compared with what one finds in some of the poets of his day. We saw already how Catullus gave lasting expression to the feelings of the bereaved. Another poet, Propertius, did so as well.

Consummate love poet that he is, Propertius throughout his poetry begs to have his emotions indulged. In a poem to his friend Tullus, heading off in military service to the East, he cries out: "Let me, whom Fortune wished to lie ever prostrate, give up my dying breath to this everlasting worthlessness."[38] Repeatedly, he imagines his own demise and the presence of his beloved Cynthia at his funeral. Contemplating death by shipwreck, Propertius torments himself with an alternative:

> If there [in Rome] some fate had buried all of my sorrow, and a
> final gravestone rested on my love after it was laid under, then
> at my funeral she would have made an offering of her precious
> locks of hair and gently placed my remains in a soft bed of
> roses; over my ashes she would have cried out my name, praying
> that the earth should lie light on me.[39]

In another poem, he hopes that Cynthia will speak a sentence in his praise at his pyre: "Alas you proved true to me, true to me, alas!"[40] Propertius's poetry holds out, repeatedly, the thought that there is no moment of greater truth than the death of a loved one.

The poet's conception of love is not irrelevant to the speaker of the *laudatio*. While the husband, like Murdia's son too, mentions the traditional wifely virtue of "obedience," the rest of his remarks show that it was deep mutual regard that was the real basis of the marriage. So, too, for Propertius, it is not Cynthia's obedience that endears her to him, nor her beauty alone, but, on the deepest level, her reciprocation of his feelings for her. For her, Propertius will not leave Rome, not even for the chance "to experience Athens and its learning and to see the ancient wealth of Asia."[41] And just a couple of poems later, Cynthia abandons *her* plan to go overseas; "I am dear to her and because of me she holds Rome most dear and says that apart from me even a kingdom has no sweetness."[42]

Propertius and Cynthia's was not a married love, of course, nor in his kaleidoscope of shifting poetic images does it always look so special. But in his later books, the poet did start to explore the idea of a deep love within marriage, looking at it especially from a woman's point of view. The devotion of Galla to her husband Postumus, a soldier leaving to fight in Parthia, is celebrated in Book 3. Not a temptation will budge her, she will remain true, and "Aelia Galla surpasses the loyalty of Penelope!"[43] In Book 4, Propertius imagines a young Roman bride writing to her husband—both are called by Greek pseudonyms—after he has gone off to the wars. "Keep unsullied the pact of my marriage bed! On this condition alone would I wish for you to return."[44] And in his very last poem, Propertius had the matron Cornelia boast from beyond the grave that hers was a marriage broken only by death: "I lived a distinguished life between wedding and funeral torch."[45] Torches, part of the lying in state and funerary procession, were also a prop for the Roman marriage ceremony.[46] Cornelia was expressing, in a traditional way, her eternal faith to her husband.

"Rare are marriages as long as ours—marriages ended by death, not cut short by divorce" (1.27). Wifely obedience was one of the ancient marital ideals in Rome, but so too was the wife who stayed married only to one husband (like Cornelia), and so was the eternal marriage bond that was only broken by death.[47] This last idea is an important piece of background for Propertius's poetry. Though he is not married to Cynthia, they have the sort of bond (or so he hopes) that is eternal. "I shall be hers in life, hers in death," he says in one poem, and in another:

> By the bones of my mother and father I swear—if I am lying,
> may neither ghost spare me—that I shall stay true to you, my
> dear, until the final darkness [of death]; one love, one hour
> shall take us both away...my loyalty shall be in the end what it
> was in the beginning.[48]

Propertius almost seems to be suggesting throughout his poetry that the ideal of the eternity of the bond has dropped from marriage. In fact marriage is no longer a solemn pact between man and woman; but such a pact now might take place outside of marriage.[49]

This notion must have come to him in part through his predecessor Catullus, who in one short poem addresses his mistress (not wife), Lesbia, with great joy:

> My dear, you declare that this delightful love we have shall last forever between us. Great gods, see to it that she can promise sincerely and speak this honestly and with all her heart so that it may be allowed to us to keep this eternal bond of inviolate friendship for our whole lives.[50]

The fantasies of love poets may seem a long way from the husband and his *laudatio*, but for both, love and death were intertwined.[51] The lover looks forward all the way to death, the bereaved back on love. Even the stern collector of edifying *exempla* Valerius Maximus can recognize this nexus in the story he tells of the Senator Plautius.[52] Sailing back from Asia to Italy by command of the Senate, Plautius was met by his wife Orestilla in Tarentum, who fell sick and died; "when, while her funeral was underway, she was placed on the pyre, between the anointment and last kiss he drew his sword and fell on it." He was then placed, just as he was, next to his wife's body, both were cremated together, and their joint tomb, known as "The Tomb of the Two Lovers," was still visible in Valerius' day. "When love is very great and most honorable," Valerius concludes, "to be joined in death is far preferable to being separated in life." So he reveals for us again the emotionally pregnant moment before cremation at the pyre. His tale, with its more prosaic ending, does lack the immediacy of a poet like Catullus and of the husband in the *laudatio*. What unites the latter two is the way they directly share the emotions that love and death inspire.

Something else, we saw, also united them. In the moral legislation that he planned, Augustus was willing to undermine the traditional, if admittedly rather lofty, idea of the eternal marital bond, yoking marriage almost entirely to reproduction as he did. Love outside of marriage, no matter how strong, was to be limited for men, illegal for women. Much as they might have admired Augustus and in particular the peace that Rome was enjoying under him, the husband and Propertius alike felt inspired to challenge Augustus on this. Poet and praiser, each could say that while lacking children, he had a relationship based on faithfulness. The *laudatio* was an opportunity for the husband to praise his wife and tell her a final time what she meant to him; it also became, in published form, a chance to share his grief with others, reveal its origins, and in doing so defend a love that he shared with his wife.[53] The *laudatio* is a love poem in prose.

7

Missing Pieces, Other Pieces

From foiling the plot against her father's estate, to staging a protest in the Forum of Rome, to devising a plan to give her husband children, a good deal of the wife's life can be known. Some parts of the story, though, are missing, most obviously the three major gaps in the *laudatio*: (1) the beginning of the speech, concerned no doubt with the wife's parents, her early life, and her betrothal; (2) another portion from the first column, which would have illuminated the couple's early married life; and (3) the ten lines or so of the second column, describing events leading up to the triumviral proscriptions. While it seems unlikely that any of these would radically shift our picture of the wife, it is still a pity to be without them. Even a smaller fragment such as the one identified in 1950 would not only help to restore the text, but could settle chronological uncertainties and possibly reveal once and for all the wife's identity.[1]

Mommsen believed that even without these missing pieces, there were other evidences available, the literary accounts of Turia and her husband Quintus Lucretius Vespillo, the consul of 19 BC, and it is to these we now turn.[2] Should the identification still be entertained, or has it been absolutely ruled out of court, as some scholars maintain? Turia and Lucretius' story raises other questions that need answering now, as well: how did one-time enemies of Augustus such as Lucretius come to be reintegrated into Roman life, and how, years later, did they recall their experiences during the civil wars? If Turia is not the wife of the *laudatio*, what does it mean that we have *two* such detailed stories of heroic women from these years, one of them inscribed on stone at great cost?

FIGURE 17. Arch of Salvia Postuma. Pula, Croatia.

The story of Turia, the *laudatio,* and the public display of the *laudatio*: all point the way to a change in the profile of women in Rome, of lasting importance for their position in society.

Women were not to become the equals of men in public life, but they were, in the high Roman Empire, able to achieve public recognition, as devoted family members, and also as patrons, priestesses, benefactors, and builders. A marble arch, beautifully decorated with twisting grapevines and acanthus, stands to this day in Pula (ancient Pola), a pretty coastal town of Croatia, the gift of Salvia Postuma. At first glance, Pula and Rome, the majestic arch and the shattered *laudatio,* may seem worlds apart, but the stories of the two women are actually intertwined.

† † †

First, the question of identification. One name, of course, is preserved in the surviving *laudatio,* and several times at that: the wife's brother-in-law

Gaius Cluvius.[3] From the historian Cassius Dio, we know that, in 29 BC, one "Gaius Cluvius" was given consular status, despite never having served as consul.[4] A "Cluvius" (without *praenomen*) is also known from a letter written to him by Cicero, which shows him presiding over land distributions in Cisalpine Gaul in the mid-40s BC.[5] The latter Cluvius may also be the prefect of Julius Caesar, "C. Clovi(us)," who appears on some of Caesar's coinage (the variation in spelling is not significant).[6] Indeed, all three of these Cluvii could even be the same man, but there seems little positive reason to relate any (or all) of this testimony to the Cluvius of the *laudatio*, while against doing so is the latter's Pompeian sympathies. Moreover, "Cluvius" was not an uncommon name in these years.[7] Also popping up in Cicero's letters is one Marcus Cluvius, a rich financier from Pozzuoli (ancient Puteoli) who had an extensive portfolio of loans in Asia Minor, the collection of which Cicero helped by pulling strings; Cluvius, in turn, who died in 44 BC, left Cicero a part of his estate, while also bequeathing to Terentia 50,000 sesterces.[8] Obviously he cannot be the Cluvius of the *laudatio*, but, as we shall see, a background and profile like his might be exactly the right one for the wife's brother-in-law—and her husband.

We turn then from this unhelpful crowd of Cluvii to the wife and her husband themselves. As early as the start of the eighteenth century, Phillippe della Torre suggested that the heroine of the fragments, then known, of the *laudatio* was the Turia whose story was told by Valerius Maximus, a writer of the imperial period.[9] In his vast handbook of exemplary deeds and sayings, he included her in a chapter on the loyalty of wives toward their husbands:

> Quintus Lucretius, after being proscribed by the triumvirs, was hidden by his wife Turia between the ceiling and the roof of their bedroom. With only one slave girl in on the plan, Turia kept her husband safe from imminent death, at great risk to herself. It was because of her singular loyalty that while others of the proscribed were only barely making their escapes in strange and hostile lands, undergoing the greatest torments of body and mind, Lucretius kept his life in his bedroom and in his wife's embrace.[10]

The later writer Appian, who in his *Civil Wars* recounts the fate of several dozen of the proscribed, adds additional details:

> Lucretius had been wandering about with two loyal slaves but was driven by a lack of food to go back to his wife in Rome,

carried on a litter by the slaves, just as a sick man would be. One of those carrying him broke a leg and Lucretius continued on by leaning on the other man. When he was at the gates where his own father, proscribed by Sulla, had been apprehended, he saw a detachment of soldiers running out and, struck by the coincidence, he hid himself with his slave in a tomb. When some grave-robbers came to explore the tombs, the slave gave himself up to the robbers to strip until Lucretius could escape to the gates. There Lucretius waited for the slave and, after sharing his own clothing with him, he went to his wife and was hidden by her in the middle of a double roof, until some of his friends saved him from the proscribers. Afterwards, in the time of peace, he served as consul.[11]

Later still, Cassius Dio says nothing of Turia, but he does explain how in 19 BC, when Augustus was abroad and unrest broke out in Rome, one of the envoys to him, Quintus Lucretius, was made consul by Augustus, "even though he had been placed on the list of the proscribed."[12] This must be the same Lucretius as Appian's, and Valerius', and—from various records—we can give his full name as Quintus Lucretius Vespillo.

One thing clearly stands out about this man: political ambition. Because his father was proscribed by Sulla, he too was barred from the membership in the Senate until 49 BC, when Caesar lifted Sulla's ban on the sons of the proscribed.[13] Evidently, the younger Lucretius jumped at the chance to enter public life. What is more, despite his proscription by the triumvirs and all the danger he found himself in at that time, he agreed to go on a delegation to Augustus in the unsettled year 19 BC, and further agreed to return to a disturbed Rome to serve as consul.

Now of all the stories of the proscribed in Appian (and elsewhere), that of Turia and Lucretius most closely matches the circumstances of the couple in the *laudatio*. This was one of the main reasons Mommsen accepted della Torre's identification. Moreover, it was most unlikely, Mommsen believed, that two different couples could have had such similar experiences—even though the number of the proscribed reached into the hundreds, if not thousands, and Appian makes clear that there were many tales of the proscribed he chose not to include in his history. To these general points, Mommsen added a more specific argument: Caesar, in his *Civil War*, mentions that a Lucretius Vespillo was in charge of a Pompeian fleet off the coast of Illyria, adjacent to Macedonia—

exactly where the husband of the *laudatio* was when his wife struggled to avenge her parents' murder.[14] This could independently confirm della Torre's identification.

Doubts, however, were cast on Mommsen's view with the publication of the Via Portuense fragment of 1898, which initially was interpreted as referring to events of the triumviral period. Since, in this fragment, the husband is clearly away from Rome, it seemed that he could not be Lucretius Vespillo, safe "in his bedroom and in his wife's embrace." While this objection no longer remains salient (the Portuense fragment refers rather to 49–48 BC), others have since been made.[15] There are discrepancies between the *laudatio* and the literary accounts of Lucretius and Turia, most notably in who helps the wife in question (her sister and brother-in-law, or a slave) and in how the pardon was obtained (by the wife herself, or the husband's friends). Without too much difficulty, these can be reconciled: the wife of the *laudatio* could have received help from a variety of individuals, but her husband naturally puts the spotlight on her, and her family.[16]

Far more worrisome—if he is Lucretius Vespillo—is the failure of the husband anywhere in what survives of his speech to mention the consulship of 19 BC, or indeed any public service at all. As one scholar has put it, "If a consular, a man with a long political career behind him, had composed the inscription, it is very strange, I would say even un-Roman, that there is no hint of political ambitions and acquired *dignitas*. These things would have been an essential and precious part of the life of such a model Roman wife as the deceased."[17] So no hint of Vespillo's political ambition—and, it has also been claimed—the speaker of the *laudatio* betrays a "modest education" and "deficient rhetorical training," so rough are his remarks in places; add to that an "absence of family pride" and he is "an utterly improbable ex-consul."[18]

While a heartfelt funeral speech is not the place to look for rhetorical pirouettes, it is true that the *laudatio* does not exude the values typical of a Senator of an established Senatorial family like Lucretius, who clawed his way into power as soon as he could. In its outlook, it is far more similar to the admiring account of the equestrian Titus Pomponius Atticus, written in the 30s BC by Atticus' friend, Cornelius Nepos (also of similar background).[19] Despite some whitewashing, Nepos manages to capture the essence of his subject by showing him as obsessed with protecting his own estate. This was why Atticus went abroad during the civil war between Marius and Sulla, and why he returned only when the situation had stabilized.[20] This was why he made only essential repairs on his inherited house in Rome, foregoing costly redecoration.[21] So self-sufficient was Atticus, as we saw earlier, that he kept monthly expenditures down to 3000 sesterces, despite inheriting two million sesterces from his father and a further ten million from a rich uncle he had cultivated (known to have been a rapacious money lender).[22]

Along with financial discipline went concerted efforts to stay out of the troubled waters of public life. Atticus shunned all political offices, "though they were available to him either through the favor he incurred or his standing"; to enter the Senate, Nepos claims, would have involved Atticus in lawlessness and (costly) bribery.[23] Atticus even refused to travel with provincial governors as prefect—a post held by equestrians to provide support for the governor, especially with financial, legal, or logistical matters.[24] As a prefectship could offer much emolument for its occupant, Atticus would have incurred a large debt of gratitude for accepting one. Moreover, especially in a time of civil war, with its constant need for requisitions, a prefect might make enemies. Thus, by the choices Atticus made, Nepos concludes, "he protected not only his standing in society but also his ease."[25]

Nevertheless, Atticus did find ways to show generosity to friends and associates, not least at moments of danger to them. When the civil war between Caesar and Pompey broke out, "from his own private holdings he gave everything that his friends setting out for Pompey had needed; at the same time he managed not to offend Pompey, although Pompey was close to him."[26] Later in the 40s BC, he gave help to Brutus, and to Brutus' mother, and during the proscriptions to all of his friends who needed it.[27] All such help, Nepos insists, was rendered without calculation (though Nepos himself makes it clear that it helped Atticus to navigate the dangers of civil war).[28] It was complemented by unwavering devotion to family; when Atticus' mother died at the age of ninety, he boasted in his *laudatio* for her that they not quarreled once.[29] It was not nature alone that guided Atticus on this path of duty, "although we all obey her"; it was also his learning, "for he had so fully grasped the teachings of the major philosophers that he relied on them for managing his life, not for show."[30]

The parallels with the *laudatio* are numerous. Like Atticus, the wife showed devotion to her family and was generous with others. Like him, she had absorbed "the teachings of the major philosophers." For her and her husband, management of their estate was of the greatest importance, seemingly transcending any political honors. They too valued tranquility. Of these parallels, it is the emphasis on financial affairs that seems most salient; so prominent a theme is this in the extant portions of the *laudatio* that it is tempting to believe that the couple not only is of equestrian background, but never really transcended an equestrian outlook, and is therefore unlikely to be Turia and Lucretius, the consul of 19 BC.[31] Of course, it can be replied, Lucretius himself was not entirely a typical Senator: as the son of the proscribed, he had no hope of entering political life until 49 BC, and so may not have devoted himself as a young man to such Senatorial pursuits as oratory, but rather to management of his estate. But, as we saw, given the opportunity, his ambition very quickly flowered. The seeds must have been there all along.

Furthermore, if we posit an equestrian background and outlook for the wife and her husband, rather than having to explain some odd gaps, details of their life together come into sharper focus. Not only does their evident pride in how successfully they have managed their estate make sense, it would also become clear why the husband (and almost certainly Cluvius too) went off in 49 BC. Over his long years governing vast overseas territories, Pompey had put to work numerous equestrians and other wealthy men, as prefects and in other positions.[32] It is Nepos himself, so attuned to equestrian experience, who tells us that when the war broke out with Caesar, there were many men who owed much to Pompey, "having acquired through him either offices or wealth; some of these men followed Pompey on campaign most unwillingly, while others remained at Rome, causing the greatest offense to him."[33] The husband seems a good candidate for one of these unwilling warriors, more personally obligated to Pompey than ideologically motivated. And if this is correct, his proscription in 43 BC would more clearly yet be a consequence of his wealth, conspicuous to all at least since the time he had picked up Milo's house at the auctions following that man's condemnation. Again, it is Nepos who makes especially clear how equestrians were proscribed solely for their estates.[34]

To be sure, it is important not to imagine too sharp a divide between equestrians and Senators.[35] Each helped the other, and they could be personally close. Atticus' life is only the most spectacular of many examples; think of Vedius Pollio, who in his will left his stunning seaside villa to Augustus, or the military officer Marius of Urbinum, who accumulated a vast fortune that he assured Augustus he would leave to him, but did not.[36] Likewise, wives of Senators and equestrian women easily comingled.[37] If the wife of the *laudatio* was not married to a Senator, that in and of itself would be no bar for her to speak with Senatorial women, or ultimately even Caesar, Lepidus, and Augustus himself. The clout of equestrians was on the rise in the civil wars, foreshadowing the great role they would play in the Roman Empire as imperial agents and administrators, often more powerful than Senators themselves.[38]

† † †

If, as seems very likely but not absolutely certain, the couple of the *laudatio* is not Turia and Lucretius, the story of Turia and Lucretius remains useful for illustrating how onetime enemies of Augustus came to reconcile with him. Given Augustus' final victory, it was imperative that they make amends, if they were to get on; but at the same time, they would want to lose as little face as possible. They were not, they would insist, nor had they ever been, public enemies, despite their proscription.[39] As in other postwar periods where reconciliation was at a premium, what proved most useful, for both sides, was to decontextualize memories: in all the tales of the proscriptions that came to be preserved, the blame was squarely put on Antony, or Lepidus; or the focus was on the loyal, or disloyal, spouse, slave, or friend.[40] The latter is clearly seen in Valerius Maximus' framing of Turia's story: "Through her singular loyalty she brought it about that…Lucretius kept his life in his bedroom and in his wife's embrace." Of Augustus' responsibility, not a word. A second tactic was to embed in memories of the proscriptions a contrast with the peace that followed.[41] Appian does this effectively by bringing up the earlier proscription of Lucretius' father—a reminder of the first major civil war in Rome—and then concluding his account with the remark that "… in the time of peace, Lucretius served as consul." The horrors of civil war underscore the felicity of Augustan Rome.

Both of these tactics are utilized in the *laudatio*. The husband decontextualizes the proscriptions by focusing on how he was saved during them by his wife; no mention of those who died, no acknowledgment of what caused all of their suffering in the first place. The finger *is* pointed, of course, at Lepidus, sitting implacably at his tribunal. The ugly scene there becomes, in the hindsight of the husband, the means by which Lepidus was shown up at the time, and by which he came to trouble in the longer run. Augustus, who precipitated civil war for his own advancement in 44 BC and repeatedly afterward, becomes only a force for civic reintegration, restoring the husband to citizenship, and then restoring the *res publica*. "The period of peace and prosperity" makes, thank goodness, for a happy ending to their hardships (2.25–26).

Nepos, in his earlier *Atticus*, also illustrates these same tendencies. We read of Antony, "moved by such hatred for Cicero that he was hostile not only to Cicero but to all of his friends and wished to proscribe them."[42] Augustus' double-cross? Tactfully omitted. Then we read of Atticus, helping "as many people as possible by whatever means he could," including the equestrian Lucius Saufeius, a devotee of philosophy who had moved to Athens but retained valuable estates in Italy. It was thanks to Atticus that "Saufeius was informed by the same messenger that he had both lost and recovered his property."[43] In addition to serving up such edifying tales, Nepos frequently hints at the contrast between the dark days and the better times to follow: danger "would happen at night," Saufeius' property was sold "according to the practice by which things were then done," and "such was the mutability of fortune at that time, that sometimes one side, sometimes the other was on either the highest peak of prosperity or in the gravest peril."[44]

The biography of Atticus and the *laudatio* are the earliest extant accounts of the proscriptions, and are invaluable for giving a sense of how they came to be remembered in a literature drawn on by Valerius Maximus, Appian, and others. But while these memories were partial, it also needs to be recognized that they were abundant. There was a need to remember, somehow, the civil wars and the proscriptions especially. This sprang not just from the suffering endured at the time, nor from the difficulty of voicing protest or even mourning the dead, but also from a desire to commemorate those who had taken risks to help the proscribed. Otherwise, stories such as that of Turia would never have been preserved at all.[45]

Prominent in memories of the civil war years was the strength that women had shown. Like the woman of the *laudatio*, like Turia stashing her husband in the attic, there were others who took risks during the proscriptions: Tanusia, who hid her husband too (in a chest, at least for a time) and then presented him at the theater to Augustus with a plea for clemency; Sulpicia, who dressed as a slave so that she could run away to her husband in exile; and the wife of Acilius, who used her jewelry to buy her husband safe passage to Sicily.[46] Velleius Paterculus, lacking room for detailed stories in his history, still comments that "wives showed the highest loyalty to the proscribed."[47]

Tales were told of bravery at other times too. Marcus Brutus' stepson Bibulus released memoirs of the assassin and also celebrated Brutus' wife (and Bibulus' mother) Porcia. She was the only woman, according to the later sources that drew on Bibulus' work, to know in advance of the plot to kill Caesar.[48] When Brutus refused to explain his evident anxiety to her, she gashed her thigh with a knife used for clipping nails and then showed the wound to Brutus as a badge of her bodily strength, reminding him that she was no ordinary woman, not "like a concubine…but a partner in your joys, and a partner in your sorrows."[49] Brutus relented and even felt strengthened by his wife's own boldness.

Cato's daughter was every bit the patriot as any man was, as another of Bibulus' stories attested. When, months after the Ides of March, Brutus was preparing to depart from Italy, Porcia happened to see a painting of Hector's farewell to Andromache; composed until then, she broke down.[50] Brutus, though, insisted that he would not address his wife with the words Hector used in the *Iliad,* "Work the loom and distaff and give orders to your handmaidens." Though Porcia's body, he explained to a friend, may have been incapable of manly heroism, "still in her spirit she shows the greatest bravery on behalf of her country, just as we do." Not even Cicero could have dismissed her as a *mulier timida.*

Augustus' sister Octavia was another woman remembered for strength in defense of family and country—and without having to resort to Porcia's penknife.[51] Her marriage to Antony in 40 BC was contracted to improve relations between the triumvirs, and (according to later accounts) in the ensuing years, she actively maintained the role of peacemaker, following in the footsteps of Antony's mother, Julia.[52] In 37 BC, when the men were once again quarreling with another, of her own volition, Octavia went to her brother and smoothed the way for a meeting with Antony by answering some of Augustus' complaints and winning over his friends.[53] Augustus had to make peace, she said, for if there were war, "it is uncertain which of you is fated to conquer, which to be conquered, but either way my situation will be wretched."[54] This fine sentiment is attributed to her by Plutarch; whether she said it exactly this way or not, it illustrates why women in these years were well suited to be mediators. With split loyalties, they could bring mutually suspicious parties together. But as noncombatants, they could then seize the moral high ground: women had done nothing to start civil war, yet were very much its victims. This was the same point the matrons had made during the tax protest in 42 BC.[55]

Relations between Antony and Augustus were patched up in 37 BC, sparing Italy as it had been in the fall of 40 BC, but Octavia's subsequent diplomatic efforts foundered. After her husband's failed expedition to

Parthia in 36 BC, she came East with soldiers, supplies, and money. Antony accepted the presents without seeing her, and Augustus harped on Antony's apparent callousness, blaming it on intoxication for Cleopatra.[56] As Plutarch tells it, Augustus insisted that Octavia initiate divorce, but she refused and begged her brother to let the whole matter drop, since she did not want to unleash war on Rome.[57] She stayed in Antony's house, cared for his children (from Fulvia, as well as her own), and continued receiving Antony's friends and helped them in their business with Augustus.[58] Even when, in 32 BC, Antony finally divorced her, she took all of his children with her, to continue caring for them.[59] She was in visible distress, though, because it now seemed inevitable that "it would appear that she also was one of the war's causes." If the tears were not real, it would have been wise to feign them: Octavia needed to distinguish herself from her predecessor Fulvia, on whom the earlier Perusine war had been blamed.[60]

Just like Fulvia, Octavia undeniably figured into her brother's brilliant campaign to turn public opinion to his side. This campaign, and the later legends that grew up around Antony and his love for Cleopatra, have doubtlessly colored the way her life came to be told; context was sometimes lost here too. But the stories would have had no resonance unless their audience, at least to some degree, already valued Octavia, and women like her. Indeed, her role as peacemaker, which clearly for a time she did play, harkened back to some of the most distinguished deeds of the women of Rome's legendary past—the Sabine women, for example, who, abducted soon after Rome's foundation, stepped forward into the battle lines when the Sabine men marched on Rome and ended the hostilities.[61]

Through her own actions, and through her brother's machinations, Octavia had a public profile in the 30s BC unlike that of any Senatorial woman even a decade before—a profile confirmed by the extraordinary honors that she, and Livia, received in 35 BC.[62] They, like other women from these years, even those from the losing side such as Porcia, were seen as embodying core Roman values thought to have fallen by the wayside in the civil wars, above all loyalty to family and loyalty to country. These two loyalties, women could insist with unique conviction, in fact were inextricably intertwined. With victory secured, and Antony and Cleopatra safely buried in Alexandria, Augustus himself may have wished to emphasize women's role as family members, sitting at home and weaving.[63] But as Bibulus' memoirs, as the literary tales of the proscriptions, as the lavishly inscribed marble *laudatio* show, there long remained a yearning to remember what women had done to keep the *res publica* going. Had the wife not saved her husband, he points out in his eulogy (2.1–2), there would have been no chance for Augustus himself to restore him.

When Octavia died in 11 or 10 BC—a couple of years before the wife of the *laudatio*—her funeral was most elaborate.[64] Mourning was public, meaning a suspension of ordinary business, and Senators dressed in black. Her body lay in state in the Temple of the Divine Julius, from where Augustus gave one eulogy for her, while her son-in-law Drusus delivered another from the Speaker's platform at the other end of the Forum. Both of these, we can be sure, dwelled on all that she had done for her family and for her country; the story of how she helped to save one couple during the proscriptions by appealing to her brother, at a theatrical show, may have been recalled.[65] Whatever was said, Octavia's state funeral itself is a sign of the new recognition women were receiving in Augustan Rome. This recognition has often been associated primarily with the rise of monarchy in Rome and women's production of possible heirs, but as Octavia's own story well shows, it goes back to the prominence of women in the civil wars, especially after 44 BC.[66]

† † †

But even looking back to the aftermath of the Ides of March is not enough to explain fully women's enhanced profile. Well before Augustus' establishment of monarchy, in the heyday of Servilia and Terentia, it was commonly believed that women—and the family more generally—really could come through for one another.[67] One sees that not only in literary texts such as Cicero's letters, but also in the late Republican funerary monuments that even ordinary inhabitants of the city of Rome put up for themselves. The one-time slave and butcher, Lucius Aurelius Hermia, celebrated his companion, Aurelia Philematium, "a woman who was not promiscuous, my one and only wife, loving sharer of my soul, faithful to a faithful husband" who "lived with equal affection" (Fig. 18).[68] Philematium herself proclaims that her husband "prospered before the eyes of all thanks to my unremitting devotion." These are doubtless Hermia's words, since Philematium predeceased him, but they pay a handsome tribute to all he owed her. Without her, Hermia is suggesting, he feels he would not have succeeded, at least not so well. The strength of their union is emblematized in the poignant relief that shows Philematium clasping her husband's hand and raising it to her face—an anticipation of a later iconographic tradition whereby joined hands symbolized marriage.[69]

FIGURE 18. Stone funerary monument for Aurelia Philematium and her husband Aurelius Hermia. British Museum, London, United Kingdom.

FIGURE 19. Funerary monument for Sextus Maelius Stabilio, Vesinia Iucunda, and Sextus Maelius Faustus. North Carolina Museum of Art, Raleigh, USA, purchased with funds from the State of North Carolina, 79.1.2.

The idea of family solidarity is captured well in another relief, of the Augustan age, again depicting freed slaves (Fig. 19). Made of marble, and designed to decorate the street façade of a tomb, it shows on the left Vesinia Iucunda and Sextus Maelius, a wife and husband, as their tightly clasped hands suggest.[70] The younger man on the right is perhaps their son, but since he too is identified as a freedman, he could have been born to them only while they were still in slavery. Dozens of similar reliefs survive, from the late Republican and imperial periods, cumulatively demonstrating how important it could be for one-time slaves to commemorate the families that they could only legally form after manumission.[71] Fellow slaves helped each other get through the horrors of slavery, and—the reliefs suggest—once freed, these former slaves wanted nothing so much as citizenship and the ability to recognize, properly, their loved ones. Maelius and Vesinia are the image of perfect Romans: he in his toga, she with the veil that connotes modesty, both celebrating a marriage that was to be remembered even in death.

Roman society consisted of far more than freed slaves, but they were a large and dynamic group within it, and their aspirations point to more widely held ideals. A remarkable study of epitaphs commemorating spouses from varying levels of society shows that already by the late Republic marriage was commonly thought to entail mutual obligation.[72] Indeed, while the old ideal of "obedience" still appears (as it does in the *laudatio*), "obedient" is rarely used as an epithet for wives; most common in the city of Rome are "well-deserving" and "very dear"—exactly the epithets most common for men.[73] Marriage was, at least in the ideal, a nearly equal partnership; the good qualities of spouses were largely reciprocal, and derived from their affection for one another.[74]

This should not blind us, of course, to the often-significant difference in age between man and woman at the time of marriage. With women typically marrying in their teenage years, even sometimes their early teenage years, it seems likely that the marital relationship initially might have been rather paternalistic.[75] It is suggestive that Aurelia Philematium is made to say on her funerary monument that her husband, who had been a slave with her, was "truly far beyond a father to me" and that he met Aurelia when she was just seven years old.

Part of why civil war, and memories of civil war, mattered, we can conclude, was that civil war reminded Romans of just how important marriage, with its emphasis on mutual obligation—on the cardinal Roman virtue, *fides*—could be. The *laudatio*, like Turia's story, shows how couples were tested in their loyalty to one another, how they passed the test, and how they emerged with a strengthened bond. The funeral speech, along with reliefs like that of Vesinia and Maelius, does not just reflect Augustus' own promotion of the family, but can also be seen as evidence of sentiments that Augustus himself needed to respond to, to succeed fully. Of enormous value to him here was his sister Octavia and, even more, his wife Livia, to whom he was obviously devoted, as his biographer Suetonius saw.[76] Livia, whose life almost uniquely embodied the transition from republican to monarchical government, was of particular importance in enhancing the heightened profile of women in Augustan Rome, and for reasons going beyond Augustus' evident devotion to her.[77] She helps to forge the link between the wife of the *laudatio* and Salvia Postuma, the arch builder from Pula.

† † †

It was especially in the years immediately following Octavia's death that Livia gained greater recognition, and in ways that reached out to other Roman women.[78] After her son Tiberius celebrated a victory over the Dalmatians in Rome in 9 BC, she along with Tiberius' wife and Augustus' daughter Julia hosted a public banquet for the women of the city.[79] Two years later, she hosted another dinner for women, after Tiberius' celebration of a full Illyrian triumph; at the same time, mother and son also codedicated a new building named after her, the Portico of Livia, built on property left to Augustus by Vedius Pollio.[80] The conversion of that unsavory man's ostentatious house and gardens into a public park was shrewd politics. The people could come and stroll in the shade, marveling at the single grapevine that wove through the trellises overhead as well as the great works of art on display.[81] Within the portico itself was a shrine dedicated by Livia to Concord, a good reminder at once of women's role as a force for domestic and civic harmony.[82] Livia could be admired too in the form of new statues voted to her by the Senate after the death of her other son Drusus in 9 BC, at which time she was also voted honorary status as a mother of three children, the new category created by the Augustan marital legislation.[83] (She of course only had two, but the exemption is not surprising in a culture so familiar with legal dodges; the Vestal Virgins were also made mothers of three, as were even some celibate divinities so that they could benefit from inheritances![84])

It is obvious that all of these honors for Livia were tied to milestones in the lives of her men—one son's victories, the other's death. This fit in with Augustus' attempts to promote a "virtuous domesticity," a domesticity that might have been traditional, except that it was so publicly advertised.[85] But what also must be appreciated is the ever-growing emphasis on Livia's financial independence.[86] Though already freed from guardianship in 35 BC, she had this privilege reaffirmed when she became an honorary mother of three children.[87] Later still, she, along with other high-ranking women, was voted a dispensation from the *lex Voconia*, allowing her to be named as an heir in Augustus' will.[88] When the imperial freedman Polybius read out this will, after Augustus' death in AD 14, it emerged that Livia was to inherit one third of the estate, worth tens of millions of sesterces.[89] It was perhaps some of this money that Livia used to reward a Senator with one million sesterces when he reported that he had seen Augustus' soul ascend into the heavens from his funeral pyre; this was important testimony for Livia, because she would be the first priestess in the cult of her dead husband.[90] Livia helped girls who lacked dowries; she gave financial assistance to fire victims; she even reportedly came to fires in progress to urge the firefighters on.[91] With her own money, she built or refurbished religious shrines, and made a dedication to the great sanctuary of Jupiter on the Capitol.[92] She was a patron to individuals and communities, and was publicly recognized as such.[93]

Many in Roman society, from Senators on downward, were eager to honor Livia—more eager, in fact, than was her own son Tiberius.[94] Although the Senate voted Livia an arch that commemorated her benefactions, Tiberius ensured that it was never built.[95] For him, such honors were too untraditional, and indeed many were unprecedented. Not in her wildest dreams would Servilia have imagined such a role for herself, even if she and others of her generation broke new ground in acting as independently as they did. Like the Augustan principate itself, Livia was made into who she was not simply by herself and Augustus, but by a broader band of society—in recognition for what she did, and also as a way to recognize women more widely. As a wife and mother, Livia gained distinction, but she was distinguished for more than that—for her patronage, her piety, her civic munificence. Also not forgotten was her heroism in the civil wars: at a critical moment she had come through for her first husband and son, and in doing so, like other women, including the wife of the *laudatio*, she helped to uphold some key Roman values under threat.

Livia's own sense of herself had to have grown out of her experience in the civil wars. As for the wife of the *laudatio*, despite all the hardships, those experiences were empowering to Livia. They made her, as they did Octavia, into a nearly legendary figure—they were the Sabine woman for a new generation. Such legend was a reflex of larger trends, yet at the same time, it was potent enough to inspire others. Roman women felt more able to celebrate their own roles as wives, mothers, sisters, and daughters, and as civic agents too, by emulating Octavia and Livia's prominent example, and then that of other imperial women.[96] In the long run, this was to be especially true outside of Rome, since within that city the imperial family, men as well as women, came to monopolize

FIGURE 20. Sketch of the Arch of Salvia Postuma. Reconstruction drawing by Margaret L. Woodhull adapted from G. Traversari, *L'arco dei Sergi*, Padua, 1971.

all forms of public glory.[97] Even the most powerful Senators and their wives were well advised to keep a low profile there; not to do so could bring disaster. But outside Rome, in Italy and in the provinces, in citizen colonies and other leading cities, women became the Livias of their home-towns. They served as priestesses, gave to their communities, wielded patronage, and were honored publicly.[98]

Let one rather early example stand for many. It was already in the life-time of Livia that Salvia Postuma, living in the Roman colony at Pula, decided to honor herself and her family members by adorning her city, just by one of its main gates, with a new arch, constructed in marble and decorated in the latest Augustan style (Fig. 17).[99] On its attic rested statues of three men important to Salvia, identified by large inscriptions. One was her husband, another her brother-in-law, both of whom had served as magistrates in Pula; the third, an officer in the Roman army, who must have been her son. Because he himself never held office in Pula, it seems likely that he died relatively young, and Salvia's arch served to glorify him by other means. A statue was later added of Salvia herself, as an inscrip-tion shows—suggesting that she herself had become a prominent member of the community, of course in part by adorning Pula with so fine a marble monument. She did not shrink from taking credit for her building; the most prominent inscription on the arch is its dedication: SALVIA POSTUMA, THE WIFE OF SERGIUS, BUILT THIS WITH HER OWN MONEY (*SALVIA POSTUMA SERGI DE SUA PECUNIA*).

This arch, with its dedicatory inscription, encapsulates a remarkable history. Over the centuries of the Roman Republic, women had increas-ingly won control over their own property; in the age of Augustus it was acknowledged that they could be free of guardianship altogether. This was in the context of the marriage legislation, and the recognition of Roman women as mothers. But other contributions that women made were being acknowledged now too. While the old ideals associated with modesty were never to be shattered completely, women could make forays into the civic sphere, and there they emblazoned their accomplishments, including contributions to the public good. Behind Salvia Postuma's arch lie the highly visible examples of Octavia and Livia, and with that pair, a whole generation of women, including the wife of the *laudatio*.

8

The Monument Itself

A visitor to the Rome of Augustus—to *maxima Roma*, as contemporary poets dubbed it—would have found a city full of new monuments.[1] There were the sumptuous porticoes, like Livia's, with their shaded walks and peerless art collections. There were the theaters and baths, including Agrippa's particularly lavish complex, of which the heated rooms confirmed its builder's engineering prowess. In 2 BC, an entire new Forum was dedicated by Augustus, its two sides comprising statue galleries honoring the great men of Rome's past, the men "who had made the empire of the Roman people very large from something very small"—it was, as a modern scholar has dubbed it, "the first hall of fame."[2] Perhaps most visually striking of all was the massive mausoleum Augustus had built on the banks of the Tiber River.[3] Upon its base of gleaming white marble sat a great mound of earth with evergreen trees planted thickly right up to the top—and on the mound, towering over the trees and visible from afar, a bronze statue of Augustus.

After his death in AD 14, Augustus' remains were interred in the tomb, joining those of relatives who had predeceased him, including the beloved Octavia. A visitor who came to pay his respects to the late emperor and drew close to the Mausoleum could have observed two new bronze pillars, on which was recorded Augustus' own account of his life, the so-called *Res Gestae* (*Achievements*).[4] And that was not the only text. Already years earlier, for his stepson Drusus who died in 9 BC, Augustus had inscribed on the Mausoleum commemorative verses that he had composed himself—separate from a prose biography of Drusus that he also wrote.[5] And joining Drusus' epitaph, around fifteen years later, were Senate decrees honoring Augustus' two grandsons, Gaius and Lucius, both of whom had died as young men.[6] These are lost, but a marble inscription set up by the town council of Pisa survives in that city, and its contents give a sense of what was in the decree for Gaius in particular—high language about Gaius waging war beyond the Empire's furthest boundaries, the bellicose peoples he had subdued and the wounds he suffered, the cruelty of Fate in snatching him from the Roman people.[7]

What in fact happened was that the installation of a Roman client on the Armenian throne went unexpectedly awry, and Gaius was lured to a parley at which he was wounded.[8] He died from complications of the wound some months later, not before letting Augustus know that he wished to retire to private life. If the Pisan decree fails to reveal any of that, it is valuable all the same for showing that the colonists of this northern Italian town had taken note of a key development in the monumental culture of Augustan Rome: the elaborate display of texts. Republican Rome certainly had its share of monuments—statues, victory columns, whole roads of tombs leading out of the city. What was new, under Augustus, was a more generous incorporation of text into monuments, or monumental complexes, almost as a design element itself.[9]

FIGURE 21. Fragment of marble pillar commemorating the Centennial Games, 17 BC. Museo Nazionale Romano, Rome, Italy.

The trend was facilitated by the increased importation of northern Italian marble, the hardness of which allowed for a much crisper style of lettering than travertine and tuff did, more legible even than writing on bronze.[10] Working with the precious marble, stonecutters put greater care into their carving of letters, using thick and thin strokes to create what would become a font that is still used today, "Roman." Its beauty and clarity can be admired even on the battered remains of a column set up to commemorate the Centennial Festival of 17 BC at which Rome celebrated the dawning of a new age (Fig. 21; cf. Fig. 23).[11] (From the column itself, which displays an elaborate dossier of documents pertaining to the Festival, we learn that the Senate ordered its construction, along with another in bronze; both would help turn an ephemeral event into a lasting inspiration.)[12] Looking closely at the column, one can notice two other features that contribute to readability: between most words, mid-height, comes small, triangular punctuation; and the text as a whole is divided into paragraphs, at the start of which there is an outward indentation of several letters.[13]

All the marble and its lettering were new, and what was also new under Augustus was a more self-conscious sense that monuments, in heightening the memory of the ephemeral or the dead, were leaving a standard for the future to conform to. Monuments were, like laws, one of the ways Augustus could "hand down exemplary practices for future generations to imitate," to borrow a phrase from the *Achievements* that he wrote for his Mausoleum.[14] His Forum, with its statue galleries, clearly was didactic. As Augustus himself stated in an edict, his aim in building it was that "both he himself, as long as he lived, and the leaders of following generations would be required by citizens to conform to these men as a model."[15] The *Achievements* itself also was no doubt put up in part to inspire imitation, as had been the decrees for Gaius and Lucius. When another prince, Germanicus, died a few years after Augustus, the Senate decreed that it would be useful to display a copy of Tiberius' eulogy for him for the edification of future generations of the young.[16] The custom was by now well established.

† † †

As we now look more closely at the marble slabs on which the *laudatio* is preserved, and try to imagine their original context, we can first ask what place women had in the new monumental culture of Augustan Rome. They were, it seems, excluded from the galleries of Augustus' great Forum.[17] But Octavia, treated to an elaborate state funeral, could be buried in her brother's tomb, and her extant epitaph from there survives.[18] It is quite simple (as were those of the men interred in the Mausoleum), but it is not impossible that some more elaborate inscribed text commemorating her once existed. Certainly by the time she died, Romans were familiar with the idea of giving a woman an elaborate funerary inscription, as a moving elegy by Propertius, the final poem in his last collection, published in or slightly after 16 BC, shows.[19] It takes the form of an address by the recently deceased matron Cornelia to her husband Paullus, a prominent aristocrat in Augustan Rome, but the address is envisioned as engraved. "I was wedded to this couch, Paullus," Cornelia says, "and destined to leave it so that I shall be recorded on this tombstone as married to one man alone."[20]

The poem is worth lingering over, for it is also a prime document of how high-ranking Roman women were being recognized in Augustan Rome as making contributions to society, contributions worthy of men.[21] Cornelia can list off her distinctions in a manner more reminiscent of male epitaphs. Right at the start, she mentions three of these: her marriage to Paullus; her children, "such excellent vouchers for my reputation"; and the "triumphal chariot of my ancestors," whose glory she has perpetuated.[22] These, and other achievements still—above all, her upstanding morality—are elaborated in what follows. Propertius casts Cornelia as an example for other women: "no woman shall be any guiltier of disgraceful behavior by sitting next to me," she boasts, not even the most virtuous women of Rome's past.[23] She is an "example to be followed" within her own house.[24] At moments, Cornelia is even made to describe her achievements, and women's achievements, as *equivalent* to those of men. Through her own life, she upheld the censor's law; and her daughter was "born to be the embodiment of her father's censorship" (Paullus held the office of censor in 22 BC).[25] We seem, in Propertius' final poem, a world away from his earlier books of poetry, with their celebration of Cynthia and the life of love out of marriage; it is likely no coincidence that the Julian laws had intervened.[26]

"The final reward for a woman's triumph is this," Cornelia concludes, "when in candid conversations she is praised for completion of her marital union."[27] "Triumph" is not a casual choice. As proud as any of her male ancestors, Cornelia basks in the public recognition that she has received, even recognition by Augustus, who was her stepfather (Cornelia's mother Scribonia had briefly been married to Augustus, giving him is only child, Julia). "I am praised by a mother's tears," she says, "and the laments of the city of Rome, and my remains are vindicated by Caesar's groans. He grieves that I who lived in a way worthy of being his daughter's sister died, and we have seen a god's tears stream."[28] All this came only at her funeral, but already she had "earned the noble matron's robe of honor" for her three children.[29] And now, after her funeral, Propertius' poem itself serves to provide a lasting tribute to her.

To turn to real epigraphy now, while it cannot be precisely dated, the *laudatio* for Murdia is with some confidence assigned to the age of Augustus—it certainly is not earlier—and it provides an excellent example of an elaborate monumentalizing of a woman's life.[30] The contents of the speech have already been examined, but here we must recognize how the decision of Murdia's son to display his speech (surely on her tomb) was designed to confirm, and spread further, the praise that he claims Murdia won from "her fellow citizens." The son had his *laudatio* inscribed on a large marble slab, later split in two pieces, only one of which has so far been discovered (although it is, at the time of writing this, missing). A transcription reveals a layout similar to that of the pillar commemorating the Centennial Festival. The heading is given in larger lettering, while the speech itself is subdivided into paragraphs, each of which was indented outward, with mid-height interpuncts between words.

In celebrating his wife by reproducing his *laudatio* in marble, the husband, then, was very up to date. Like Murdia's son, he took inspiration from what he saw around him—from the praise women were winning (as in Propertius' elegy for Cornelia, or Octavia's *laudatio*), and from the monuments of Augustan Rome themselves. He incorporated a large amount of text, his own speech—the equivalent, in a sense, of an official document like a Senate decree. He had it inscribed in marble. And again its lettering was like that of the Centennial Festival pillar: beautifully executed, with interpuncts between words, spaces left at the ends of paragraphs, and outward indentations at their start. Legibility was enhanced (as on other monuments) by painting the letters red.[31]

Frustratingly, we can say little more about the tomb itself.[32] It was unlikely to have been as elaborate as that of Caecilia Metella on the Appian Way, modeled on that of Augustus and a landmark through the centuries (Fig. 22).[33] (But Metella's tomb shows us another example of a lavish commemoration of a woman from these years.[34]) Quite possibly

FIGURE 22.   Mausoleum of Caecilia Metella. Rome, Italy.

it did include a statue of the deceased. If so, in fine Augustan fashion, statue and inscription would work together, turning passers-by into viewers and readers at once. Those who knew the deceased would recall their memories of her; those who did not, impressed by the elaborate text on display, might stop to learn something of who she was. The inscription did not simply preserve her memory; it publicized it.

It is doubtful that even Cicero, meditating on the shrine for Tullia, would have thought to inscribe so much text on it, for the revolution in monumental design really only followed his death.[35] Perhaps tellingly, he never even built the shrine itself. The real modernity of the inscribed *laudatio* is shown by comparing it with the most elaborate epitaph to survive for any Roman woman before the wife's lifetime, a short set of verses for one, Claudia, who perhaps died in or after giving birth to twins, one of whom also perhaps died.[36] Inscribed on travertine about a century before the *laudatio*, the lines were copied in Rome in the Renaissance, after which the stone itself disappeared:

FIGURE 23. Epitaph of Caecilia Metella from her mausoleum, Rome, Italy. Epigrapher A. E. Gordon calls this inscription "one of the most beautiful in Latin": Gordon (1983), p. 99.

> Stranger, I have only a little to say; stop and read it through.
> This is the unbeautiful grave of a beautiful woman. Her parents gave her the name Claudia. She loved her husband with her heart. She gave birth to two sons, one of whom she leaves behind on the earth, the other she has buried beneath. Her speech was pleasant and her bearing proper. She looked after the house and spun the wool. I have spoken; pass along.

> hospes, quod deico paullum est, asta ac pellege.
> heic est sepulcrum hau pulcrum pulcrai feminae.
> nomen parentes nominarunt Claudiam.
> suom mareitum corde deilexit souo.
> gnatos duos creauit; horunc alterum
> in terra linquit, alium sub terra locat.
> sermone lepido, tum autem incessu commodo.
> domum seruauit, lanam fecit. dixi. Abei.

Here the focus is unremittingly domestic. There is no sense, as in the Cornelia poem or our *laudatio*, that Claudia's achievements can be compared to those of men and merit widespread public recognition. Claudia is virtuous, but not exceptional or exemplary.

† † †

While clearly the husband took advantage of recent innovations in official monumental design, at the same time his celebration of his wife was also a highly personal one. As we have seen, his *laudatio* itself employed a confessional mode, more akin to that of contemporary poets than the writers of Senatorial decrees. Furthermore, it is inscribed in a way that makes it look like a script the husband might actually have read aloud. While in many respects, the layout of the inscribed text evokes that of official monuments; it stands out for the occasional use of "extra-wide intervals between words…employed to designate pauses in the pronunciation of the text."[37] These intervals, in other words, come at points when the speaker would wish to pause. Here are just a few examples from two separate points in the speech (with the intervals marked "#"):

1. War came to an end throughout the world, the republic was restored, and we were granted a period of prosperity and peace. # We did, it is true, desire children, whom for some time circumstances refused us. If Fortune had allowed herself to proceed with her customary regard for us, what would either of us have lacked? # But proceeding otherwise, she began to put an end to our hopes.
2. What desire or need to have children could have been so great for me, that I could have broken faith, and traded certainty for uncertainty? # But why say more?

The stonecutter, it has been suggested, can only have known to put the pauses where he did because they were in the text handed over to him.[38] Since even *laudationes* in the Forum are said to have been read from scripts, it is an attractive suggestion that the text the husband gave for inscription was the one he had read at his wife's graveside, having written it in advance.[39] Our sense that the monument is in some way recreating the funeral, and the moment of leave-taking in particular, is thus increased.

There is, however, a still more specific way in which the husband aimed to make the monument distinctive. We should remember that tombs, typically, did not stand in isolation, but lined the roads that led to and from Rome. And they were on those roadsides because they were meant to be seen (Caecilia Metella's being an extreme example). Tombs jostled for the traveler's attention, and so in a sense, could even be in competition with one another—just as honor-bound Romans were in real life. From Augustan Rome itself, there is relatively little with which to compare the wife's monument; however, from the town of Corfinium, part of an elaborate funerary inscription for a woman survives, and this gives a sense of what the husband might have been responding to.[40] This lady's name also is missing, but quite a bit else survives: she was married for thirty-nine years to a "single husband" and left "three surviving children from him." Of the two sons, both equestrian, one rose high in local politics, the other in the army, each with the support of no less than Augustus himself. And their sister—"most irreproachable" of course—was well on her way to emulating her mother's example, having given birth to two children.

The epitaph reeks of pride in fulfilling Augustus' marriage legislation. One need not criticize the lady of Corfinium, or her commemorators, for this, but we can imagine what the husband might have thought, when he encountered epitaphs like this, as he quite likely did, on the roads outside of Rome. In passing his moral legislation, Augustus had not entirely banished the old ideals of the marriage bond that lasted until death and the wife who married one man (as the Corfinium epitaph itself shows). But he had asserted, powerfully, that what mattered most about marriage was the procreation of children.[41] Marriage was to be a matter of what was good for the state; it was less a solemn bond between two individuals.

Augustus' position had been shared by those censors of the mythic good old days. In haranguing the Senate on the importance of passing his new legislation, the emperor in fact read aloud a speech from one of them, Metellus Macedonicus, which argued that men should be compelled to marry "for the sake of producing children."[42] Nothing of this speech survives, but the words of a slightly later censor—in fact, Macedonicus' nephew—speaking on the same subject, are recorded, and give a hint of the tone of such rhetoric:

> If we could exist without a wife, citizens, we would all free
> ourselves of that annoyance. But since Nature has required
> that with them we cannot live very comfortably, but without
> them we cannot live at all, we must give thought to our
> ongoing survival rather than transitory pleasure.[43]

Undeniably there is misogyny here—women are to be valued only for their role in procreation—and Augustus, for all that he may have respected in his own wife, Livia, and in his cherished marriage to her, on some level shared this outlook, at least as a lawmaker.[44]

But if the censors of old insisted that men should marry, Augustus was now compelling women to marry. And not necessarily just once: by the Julian law of 18 BC, widows who failed to remarry within a year, and divorcées within six months, were to be penalized.[45] The clear implication is that some of these women wished to remain detached, perhaps (on the part of widows anyway) out of loyalty to their first husbands, but also surely because unmarried life brought with it certain freedoms. Some of these freedoms, though, Augustus also tried ruthlessly to curtail, through his criminalization of extramarital sex on the part of women.

Augustus did not flinch at regulating all aspects of women's lives, as a chilling story, told by the Tiberian writer Valerius Maximus, shows.[46] A woman named Septicia, he tells us, decided to marry "Publicius, a very old man, when she could no longer bear children." Her aim, Valerius claims, was to disinherit her sons from her first marriage, which she in fact did, and upon her death they appealed to Augustus. He agreed to intervene, stating that both Septicia's marriage and will should be deemed invalid; Publicius could not even retain the dowry given to him, for "the marriage had not been contracted for the sake of producing children." To this tale, Valerius adds his own nasty commentary, in the form of an apostrophe to Septicia: "You reject those to whom you gave birth, now sterile you marry, you spitefully upset the order of succession and show no shame in making over your whole estate to the man beneath whose body, already laid out for burial, you spread your wasted old self." To be sure, Septicia did defy convention by disinheriting her sons, and a father who disinherited his children would have come in for criticism too (as other stories of Valerius show). But Septicia is faulted most heavily here for daring to marry after her child-bearing years—as if she could have had no other grounds for doing so, as if she should be defined entirely by her fertility.

It is not an anachronistic judgment to register the hostility toward women latent in Augustus' legislation or explicit in the moralizing of Valerius Maximus or the censor's speech. We know that Augustus' laws were disliked, by women as well as men, and women, including almost certainly his own daughter Julia, defied them.[47] But we also have the testimony of the *laudatio*—and not purely by accident. In his speech, the husband challenged, implicitly, the Augustan legislation and the attitudes that lay behind it, and his decision to inscribe it puts him on record, as it were: he was publicly acknowledging, even celebrating, his refusal of his wife's offer to divorce him despite her childlessness.[48] He had so many other reasons to value her. She deserved a lavish tomb every bit as much as the lady of Corfinium. Next to that fertile woman, she could stand in pride, for all eternity.

† † †

When it comes to relations between the sexes, the age of Augustus should be remembered, then, not just for the Augustan laws on marriage and adultery, important as those were. Already in the late Republic, we saw recognized the idea that marriage could be an affectionate and mutually supportive partnership; even Claudia, in the old epitaph, was praised for loving her husband "with her heart."[49] Despite the Augustan legislation, this view persisted, and if anything became more widely held, or at least more widely expressed, even now among the top orders of Roman society.[50] Propertius' elegy for Cornelia in fact is a fine example: as she ends her speech, Cornelia becomes more intimate, imagining her husband so bereft that he sobs for her, dreams of her, speaks to an image of her—a small painting most likely—during a sleepless night (cf. Fig. 5).[51] This willingness to discuss the domestic more openly, in part, grew out of the traumas of the civil wars, and the emergence of Octavia and Livia as new exemplars.[52] And it found fertile ground in the different political landscape of imperial Rome: as the old noble families died off, and with them their dynastic style of politics—politics Servilia-style—the new members of the ruling class (of course with exceptions) fostered a different moral climate, fully in evidence in the letters the Senator Pliny the Younger published around the year AD 100.[53] The views, in other words, that the husband gave concrete embodiment to in his *laudatio* were to be echoed, even amplified, in the years to come.

As already Propertius could celebrate the love of married couples in his later elegies, so too would imperial poets (while the poetry of extra-marital love did come to an end). Statius' consolation to the imperial freedman Abascantus for the loss of his wife Priscilla describes the grief Abascantus feels, even a year after her death. "Enduring harmony," the poet proclaims, "linked you in an unbroken chain; you were joined with united hearts."[54] Priscilla was married before, but Abascantus should be assured that it was he she cherished, "with all her heart and soul."[55] It was as if she were a virgin bride. In another poem, Statius addresses his own wife—who also had been previously married—and praises her in similar language; it is you, he says, "whom Venus, in a benevolent disposition, linked to me in the flower of my years and keeps for my old age."[56] A few years later, Pliny the Younger relies on poetic tropes to express his feelings for his wife. A series of letters reveals that she had left for Campania to convalesce, Pliny greatly missed her, and she wrote back expressing her own sadness.[57] Away from him, she read his books, while he (so he writes) kept poring over her letters. In her absence he pictures her—he cannot sleep, he retraces his steps to her suite, but leaves like a shut-out lover. Pliny's wife, Statius' wife, Priscilla: all are presented very much as companions, who take an active interest in supporting their husbands' careers. None is celebrated for giving her husband a child.

Another letter of Pliny, concerning the loss of his friend Macrinus' wife of thirty-nine years, "a wife who would have set an example even long ago," makes for an especially apt comparison with our *laudatio*.[58] Macrinus has suffered a "severe blow"; while all of the pleasure he and his wife took in one another may be a consolation, it also intensifies the loss. The paradox would have been familiar to the husband of the *laudatio*, as would Pliny's emphasis on the couple's reciprocal regard: "What respect that woman showed her husband, while earning the highest respect herself!" Other prose writers supply further examples of the strong mutual bonds Pliny describes. Pliny's friend Tacitus wrote in the biography of his father-in-law, Agricola, that Agricola's marriage gave him support; Agricola and his wife "lived in remarkable harmony, each putting one another ahead of themselves because of their mutual affection."[59] Another friend of Pliny, Suetonius, tells of the distress the future emperor Tiberius felt when he was compelled by Augustus to divorce his wife; chancing to see her, he could not stop following her in tears.[60]

Even Valerius Maximus, for all his talk of women's tendency to mental weakness—how good it was when they would not even touch wine or when they were divorced by their husbands if caught walking with their heads uncovered or talking in public with the wrong people— even Valerius devotes a chapter of his handbook to the theme of "marital love."[61] Here is to be found the story of Plautius' suicide on the pyre of his wife who followed him to Tarentum, and others like it. For the sententious Valerius, though, what really counts is not so much mutual affection as mutual faithfulness. Tiberius' younger brother Drusus, he assures us, "kept his lovemaking within the confines of his fondness for his wife," while Antonia, for her part, "balanced the love her husband felt with her own remarkable faithfulness."[62] After his death, though "in the bloom of youth and beauty," she never slept with another man.

If married love was celebrated more publicly by leading Romans of the high empire than in the Republic, the historian might ask, what impact did this have on people's actual behavior? It would be hard to answer from the edifying anecdotes that our sources tend to relate. But there is at least one more concrete indicator of a change in customs stemming from husbands' increased appreciation of their wives as partners. In the republican era, a governor's wife did not accompany him when he was assigned a provincial command.[63] This started to change in the civil wars, with first Sulla's wife, Caecilia Metella, accompanying him to Athens, and then Pompey's wife, Cornelia, fleeing with him in 49 BC.[64] Fulvia and Octavia both left Italy to see Antony, Livia traveled abroad with Augustus, and other women of the imperial household accompanied their husbands on overseas assignments.[65] By this time, it is clear, the wives of governors not infrequently were accompanying their husbands, sparing couples the potentially painful separations from days before. Readers of the New Testament will think of the wife of Pontius Pilate, the prefect of Judea for ten long years. Latin literature abounds with examples. Seneca's aunt Helvia spent years in Egypt when her husband was governor there; Tacitus' wife was present with him during his prolonged service abroad under Domitian; Pliny's wife, Calpurnia, accompanied him to Bithynia, although she had to leave him when her grandfather died and her aunt needed consoling (the two had raised Calpurnia when her father died).[66]

It is Tacitus who records a debate that took place in the Senate in AD 21 concerning governors' wives.[67] On this occasion, Severus Caecina, an old-fashioned and hard-bitten Senator who had seen forty years of service abroad, proposed that "no magistrate to whom a province had been assigned should be accompanied by his wife."[68] Certainly his wife had never accompanied him, despite their harmonious marriage, and when women traveled overseas (Caecina maintained), the result was lax discipline and compromised government. In his counterargument, Valerius Messalinus did not actually take a more favorable view of women, pointing out that if let alone in Rome they could get into trouble. But he does mention too what for many Senators surely was a key point: if Caecina's ban went into effect, husbands would be deprived of partnership in their prosperity and adversity. Tiberius' son Drusus ended the whole discussion when he pointed out how Livia had accompanied Augustus, and how much he wished always to travel with his own "dearest wife."[69] Once again, Livia's example set the agenda for others.

So in the face of Caecina's proposal, the Senate recognized the ready-received support men derived from their wives, who were far more to them than just the mothers of their children. But as with the marital legislation of Augustus, here too with new recognition came more regulation. Wives could be tried alongside their husbands for provincial maladministration and were liable to financial penalty and exile—even if their husband had already died.[70] In one of his letters, Pliny dwells at length on the fate of one such widow, Casta, the wife of Classicus, governor of one of the Spanish provinces.[71] Women's liability in cases such as this was a perverse recognition of just how much of a partnership marriage could be thought to be.

What seems clear in all this is that the husband's speech would have struck a chord with many Roman men in his generation and beyond. They were not the first to love their wives, to value them as partners. But at least

FIGURE 24. Base of the column of Antoninus Pius, depicting the apotheosis of the emperor (who died in AD 161) and his wife Faustina. Vatican Museums, Rome, Italy. Though Faustina predeceased her husband by twenty years they are united in death, "a standard theme in the funerary art of freedmen," now seen in this imperial commission: Kleiner (1992), pp. 285–288.

some of them, even of very high rank, were willing to be more vocal about that partnership, in works of literature and in public debate. Cicero betrayed his reliance on Terentia in private letters that he wrote to her at a time of crisis, only published after his death. Pliny's self-published, and therefore more self-conscious, letters hold up a model of marriage as companionship; it was a part of the good life as Pliny saw it. For the modern historian, the husband's lavish inscription is a portent, a very full expression of an attitude that was to become more prominent during the long imperial peace.

† † †

Let us, though, in conclusion turn from what the speech shows about attitudes toward gender in Rome, to what it has revealed about an actual Roman woman. Most striking is how, during the years of civil war, the wife gained and used power. With her sister's help, she avenged her parents' murder; on her own, she staved off the run of her family's estate and protected her and her husband's inheritance. In his absence, she defended his house from physical attack, smuggled money and supplies to him, and helped to secure his pardon. After he was proscribed, she took charge of the situation, finding a hiding place for him, securing another pardon, and staging a public protest when Lepidus, in charge of Rome, refused to recognize the pardon. The wife had legal knowledge and political ability, not to mention real bravery. For a time, like other high-ranking women in Rome, she was visibly a part of the political process.

Close reading of the *laudatio* showed other dimensions of her life. She had a clear talent for managing property, recognized by her husband. Religion was of some importance to her. Philosophy provided her with a framework for coping with life's misfortunes. In the face of her own death, and the grief that she knew would engulf her husband, she tried to help him in advance by sharing with him some of the fruits of her knowledge.

Of fundamental importance to her was taking care of her family. Not only did she avenge her parents' murder, stand by her sister in the inheritance dispute, and come to her husband's rescue more than once, she also took in female relatives and made sure they had dowries sufficient for their status. She looked after her mother-in-law. Having failed to produce heirs for her husband, she even offered to divorce him, find him a fertile wife, and help raise the new children—without insisting on taking back all of her property, as she legally could. The *laudatio* shows the pressure on women to produce children, heightened in the moral (and then legal) climate of Augustan Rome.

Civil war was a defining experience for her, testing her in ways that she otherwise might not have been. Her achievements were most conspicuous then, and along with the achievements of other women, including Augustus' wife Livia, led to lasting changes in how women might comport themselves in public. Outside the city of Rome, women in the imperial age regularly made benefactions to their communities from their own resources, and in other ways were involved in civic life, serving as public priestesses for example. Women helped their husbands when they were governing overseas. But important as civil war was for the wife and her generation, we must recognize that the lengths she went to in caring for her family transcended civil war; her offer to divorce and her deathbed assistance to her husband both happened only afterward. Women cared for their families at all times.

The wife's own perspective on her life does not survive, but in fact it is hard to get much of a sense of most men's perspectives on their own lives either, even though they did write much more, and it is their writing that mostly survives. All the same, the wife is no simple icon—an emblem of domesticity or family life or the like.[72] In her husband's words, her personality emerges, her indomitability and her practicality above all. He helps us to see an all-too-human vulnerability too; her proposal to divorce him rested on a sense of her own failings that he did not share, at least not ultimately.

In ancient Rome, women were constrained in ways that men were not. There certainly was misogyny. There was also, for high-ranking women, the important ideal of *pudicitia*, entrenched by custom, even if it was related also to men's concerns about the legitimacy of their children. While women gained more public recognition under Augustus, the price paid was complete legal oversight of their sexual lives—another constraint. As for men too, with peace and prosperity came a sacrifice of personal freedom. Women like the wife showed great ingenuity in circumventing at least some of these constraints when they needed to, and they sometimes did so with the help of men. For women, although their roles in life were circumscribed more narrowly than men's, were also dearly loved.

APPENDIX 1

A Brief Note on Chronology

This brief note serves to explain the chronology that I have adopted in my reconstruction of the wife's story in chapters 1–6 of the text and to discuss some alternate views.

1. Most securely dated are the events of lines 2.0–24: the mention of "Caesar Augustus" (12) and "his colleague Marcus Lepidus" (13) makes it clear that we are in the triumviral period, while the absence of Augustus from Rome dates the episode at the tribunal of Lepidus to later 42 or very early 41 BC. Very late 42 BC should be the right date since it was at this time that Octavian was dispensing pardons to the proscribed.[1]

2. The contents of the Portuense fragment (lines 2.1a–11a), first published by Vaglieri in 1898 and so unknown to Mommsen, were initially referred to the time of the proscriptions. But here, the wife is seen supporting her husband (or fiancé) in his absence from Rome (note especially 2.5a, *apsentiam meam*). The "civil war" referred to (*belli civilis*, 2.10a), during which Milo's men attacked the husband's house, must be earlier than 43 BC. The attack should have taken place in 49 or (more probably) 48 BC, when Milo was still alive, aiming to take control of Rome, and bands of men were rallying to his side. The husband must have bought at least one property of Milo's when it was auctioned in 52 BC.[2]

3. The absence of the husband (2.5a) should be related to the narrative given in 1.1–26. There, too, the husband is shown as absent, repeatedly (1.4, 1.8, 1.12, 1.17). In his absence, the wife avenged her parents' murder and upheld her father's will. A crucial supplement to the text comes at 1.3 ([*ante nuptiar*]*um diem*, "before the day of the

wedding"), without which the legal situation described in lines 13–26 makes no sense. Thus we can posit that the wife and husband were betrothed by 49 BC, but did not marry until after his return to Rome in late 48 or (more likely) 47 BC, when others pardoned by Caesar were allowed back.[3] The likeliest date for their marriage seems to occur in 47 BC, as well.

Kierdorf, and subsequently Flach, have proposed that the events of 1.1–26 did not take place during the civil war between Pompey and Caesar, but earlier.[4] The husband's Macedonian sojourn, they suggest, must have been on other grounds—for example, posting as quaestor. (Cluvius, similarly, would have been in Africa on government service or on business.) Following this chronology, the date of the marriage can be placed a few years prior to 49 BC, and the wife's death placed no later than 9 BC.

This alternate chronology does have the virtue of giving a more chronological structure to the *laudatio* as a whole: life before marriage and marriage would be the subjects of Column 1, and then the vicissitudes of the couple's marriage of Column 2. I do not favor it, however, on the grounds that it is uneconomical to create within the speech two major absences for the husband, especially when the absence of 1.1–26 seems to have been prolonged—exactly what one would expect if he were away during the civil war.[5] Furthermore, the wife's defense of her husband's house in 49–48 BC (2.9a–11a) is most economically linked to the co-residence with his mother attested at 1.11, furnishing the wife an opportunity to take care of her mother-in-law (1.32–33).[6] As for the structure of the *laudatio* as a whole, the husband has organized it not only by pure chronology, but also so as to present his wife's most special virtues and achievements—and the ones most relevant to him—later (in the text of Column 2).

4. The wife and husband had a marriage that lasted until its forty-first year (1.28). It has been pointed out that the Roman numeral XXXXI (= 41) comes at a point in the text where there was a break in the stone, and it is possible that the number of years in marriage could have been only XXXI (= 31).[7] But thirty-one years is much less exceptional a span of marriage than forty-one (cf. Plin. *Ep.*8.5). The transcribed text should not be altered, and we can place the wife's death no earlier than 8 BC, and more likely in 7 or 6 BC.

Thus, my proposed chronology is as follows:

52 BC: husband purchases house of Milo

49 BC: husband and Cluvius leave Rome and Italy; his wife-to-be handles inheritance dispute

47 BC: wife and husband marry after his restoration by Caesar

late 43 BC: husband proscribed

late 42 BC: wife's confrontation with Lepidus; restoration of husband by edict of Augustus

7 or 6 BC: death of wife

APPENDIX 2

Reading Text and Translation

General Note: For scholarly study of the text of the *laudatio*, the edition of Flach (1991) is now the fullest and best resource, containing not only Flach's own text, but a full selection of other conjectures as well as detailed information on the various fragments, their measurements, letter counts per line, and other useful details. Flach's text has been reprinted in the updated entry for the *laudatio* in the *Corpus Inscriptionum Latinarum* (6.41062).

The following reading text indicates which letters are fully or almost fully preserved and shows in square brackets what I believe to be a plausible reconstruction. I based the text on that in Wistrand (1976), but studied others available, above all that of Flach. I have deviated from Wistrand's restorations in the following lines (1.4, 1.7, 1.10, 1.13, 1.31, 1.42, 1.48, 1.52; 2.8a, 2.10a, 2.11a, 2.16, 2.22, 2.29, 2.41, 2.58, 2.59, 2.60); in almost all of these lines I follow the restorations proposed by Flach, very often his own, doing so usually on grounds of likely line length. Scholars will consult Flach's edition or the entry in *CIL* for the details. Also note that I have not rendered *apices* (marks resembling acute accents generally cut over long vowels).

The translation printed here attempts to render into English the printed text, including all restorations. I modeled the translation on that in Wistrand's edition, and owe some specific renderings to it. I also consulted the translations of Flach (1991) and Durry (1950) into German and French respectively, and those of Braund (1985), pages 267–271 and Cooley (2003), pages 384–388. I owe some of my renderings to these translations as well.

Here is a good point to acknowledge not only my great indebtedness, but also gratitude to all of those who have worked on the text and translations of it.

COLUMN 1

Some lines missing.

(1) ...[mo]rum probit[ate]... (2) rum...permansisti prob[a]...

(3) Orbata es re[pente ante nuptiar]um diem utroque pa[rente in rustica soli-] (4) tudine una o[ccisis. Per te maxu]me, cum ego in Macedo[niam provinciam issem,] (5) vir sororis tua[e Cluvius in A]fricam provinciam, [non remansit inulta] (6) mors parentum.

(7) Tanta cum industria m[unere es p]ietatis perfuncta ef[flagitando et] (8) vindicando ut, si praes[to fu]issemus, non ampliu[s praestitissemus. At] (9) haec habes communia cum sanctissima femina, [sorore tua.]

(10) Quae dum agitabas, ex patria domo propter custodia[m non cedisti; sumpto] (11) de nocentibus supplicio, evest[i]gio te in domum ma[tris meae contulisti, ubi] (12) adventum meum expectast[i.]

(13) Temptatae deinde estis ut testamen[tum,] quo nos eramus heredes, rupt[um diceretur] (14) coemptione facta cum uxore: ita necessario te cum universis pat[ris bonis in] (15) tutelam eorum qui rem agitabant reccidisse: sororem omni[no illius hereditatis] (16) fore expertem, quod emancupata esset Cluvio. Qua mente ista acc[eperis, qua iis prae-] (17) sentia animi restiteris, etsi afui, compertum habeo.

(18) Veritate caussam communem [t]utata es: testamentum ruptum non esse ut [uterque potius] (19) hereditatem teneremus quam omnia bona sola possideres; certa qui[dem sententia] (20) te ita patris acta defensuram ut, si non optinuisses, partituram cum s[orore te adfir-] (21) mares; nec sub condicionem tutelae legitumae venturam, quoius per [legem in te ius non] (22) esset, neque enim familia[e] gens ulla probari poterat, quae te id facere [iure

COLUMN 1

(1) ...through your virtuous character...you remained a virtuous woman...

(3) You were orphaned suddenly before the day of our wedding when both of your parents were killed together in the solitude of the countryside. It was mainly through your efforts that the death of your parents did not go unavenged: I had gone to Macedonia, and the husband of your sister, Cluvius, to Africa.

(7) You insistently demanded punishment and you got it, so strenuously performing your familial duty that even if we had been present, we could not have done anything more. But this accomplishment you have in common with that most irreproachable woman, your sister.

(10) While you were occupied with this, you did not leave your father's house because you were guarding it. But after you did obtain punishment of the guilty, you immediately went to the house of my mother, where you awaited my homecoming.

(13) Then there was an attempt to make both you and your sister recognize that the will, in which we were heirs, was broken, because of the *coemptio* your father made with his wife. In consequence (it was said), you along with your father's entire estate automatically would revert to the guardianship of those who were pursuing this matter; your sister would be cut out of the inheritance altogether, because she had come under the *manus* of Cluvius. With what resolution you dealt with all this, with what presence of mind you resisted, I know full well, even though I was then away.

(18) You defended our shared position by stating the facts: the will had not been broken, with the result that each of us should hold onto our inheritance rather than having you alone take possession of the whole estate. It was your firm intention to uphold the acts of your father, so much so that even if you did not win your case, you insisted that you would share the inheritance with your sister; nor would you enter into the situation of agnatic guardianship, of

cogeret;] (23) nam esti patris testamentum ruptum esset, tamen
iis qui intenderen[t non esse id] (24) ius, quia gentis eiusdem non
essent.

(25) Cesserunt constantiae tuae neque amplius rem sollicitarunt; quo
facto [offici in patrem,] (26) pietatis in sororem, fide[i] in nos pa-
trocinium succeptum sola peregisti.

(27) Rara sunt tam diuturna matrimonia, finita morte, non divertio
in[terrupta; nam contigit] (28) nobis ut ad annum XXXXI
sine offensa perduceretur. Utinam vetust[a consortio habu-] (29)
isset mutationem vice m[e]a, qua iustius erat cedere fato
maiorem.

(30) Domestica bona pudici[t]iae, opsequi, comitatis, facilitatis, lani-
ficii stud[i, religionis] (31) sine superstitione, o[r]natus non con-
spiciendi, cultus modici cur [memorem? Cur dicam de cari-] (32)
tate, familiae pietati, [c]um aeque matrem meam ac tuos parentes
col[ueris eandemque quietem] (33) illi quam tuis curaveris, cetera
innumerabilia habueris commun[ia cum omnibus] (34) matronis
dignam f[a]mam colentibus? Propria sunt tua quae vindico ac
[perpaucae in tempora] (35) similia inciderunt, ut talia paterent-
tur et praestarent, quae rara ut essent [mulierum] (36) fortuna
cavit.

(37) Omne tuom patrimonium acceptum ab parentibus communi
diligentia cons[ervavimus;] (38) neque enim erat adquirendi tibi
cura, quod totum mihi tradisti. Officia [ita par-] (39) titi sumus
ut ego tu[t]elam tuae fortunae gererem, tu meae custodiam
sust[ineres. Multa] (40) de hac parte omittam ne tua propria
mecum communicem. Satis sit [hoc] mi[hi tuis] (41) de sensibus
[indi]casse.

which there was no claim against you in law, since for your family no clan could be regarded as having the right to compel you to do this; even if the will of your father had been broken, those who were bringing action had no such right, since they were not members of the same clan.

(25) They gave way to your steadfastness and did not pursue the matter further. In having achieved this, you completed the defense that you had undertaken, all on your own, of respect for your father, devotion to your sister, and loyalty to us.

(27) Rare are marriages as long as ours—marriages ended by death, not cut short by divorce. It was granted to us that ours lasted into its forty-first year without any wrongdoing. I wish that our long-enduring union had been altered by something happening to me, not you; it would have been more just for the elder partner to yield to fate.

(30) Why should I mention the virtues of your private life: your sexual morality, your obedience, your considerateness, your reasonableness; your attentive weaving, your religious devotion free of superstition, your unassuming appearance and sober attire? Why should I talk about your love and devotion to family? You took care of my mother as well as you did your own parents and saw to her security as you did for own people, and you have countless other things in common with all married women who keep up a good reputation. The qualities that I assert you have belong to you alone; very few other women have lived in times similar enough so as to endure such things and perform such deeds as Fortune has taken care to make rare for women.

(37) Through careful management together we kept intact all of your fortune, as it was handed down from your parents; there was no effort on your part to acquire what you handed over in its entirety to me. We shared the duties in such a way that I stood as protector of your fortune, while you kept a watch over mine. On this point there are many things I will leave out so as not to associate with myself what is uniquely your own. Let it suffice for me to have said this about your feelings.

(42) [Liberali]tatem tuam c[u]m plurumis necessariis tum praecipue pietati praesti[tisti.] (43) [Licet cum laude item qu]is alias nominaverit,
unam dumtaxat simillimam [tui]...(44)...[h]abuisti sororem tuam;
nam propinquas vestras [dignas eiusmodi] (45)...[of]ficiis domibus
vestris apud nos educavistis. Eaedem u[t condicio-] (46) [nem
dignam famili]ae vestrae consequi possent, dotes parastis, quas
quide[m a vobis] (47) [constitutas comm]uni consilio ego et C. Cluvius excepimus et probantes [liberalitatem,] (48) [ne vestro patrimo-]
nio vos multaretis, nostram rem familiarem sub[didimus vestrae]
(49) [nostraque praedia] in dotes dedimus. Quod non ventitandi
nostri c[aussa rettuli,] (50) [sed ut illa consi]lia vestra concepta pia
liberalitate honori no[s duxisse consta-] (51) [ret exequi de nos]tris.

(52) [Complura alia benefici]a tua praetermittenda [mihi sunt...]

Some lines missing.

(1a) ...(V)XORIS

(2a) [Amplissima subsi]dia fugae meae praestitisti,—ornamentis (3a) [me
instruxisti], cum omne aurum margaritaque corpori (4a) [tuo detracta
trad]isti mihi—et subinde familia, nummis, fructibus (5a) [callide de-
ceptis a]dversariorum custodibus apsentiam meam locupletasti.

(6a) [Pro vita rogabas apse]ntis,—quod ut conarere virtus tua te horta-
batur; (7a) [verbis tuis victa me m]unibat clementia eorum, contra
quos ea parabas; (8a) [nihilo minus tamen v]ox tua est firmitate
animi emissa.

(9a) [Interea agmen ex repe]rtis hominibus a Milone, quoius domus
emptione (10a) [potitus eram cum ille esset] exul, belli civilis oc-
casionibus inrupturum (11a) [et direpturum fortiter reiecist]i [atque
defe]ndisti domum nostram.

About twelve lines missing.

(0) [...]m extare[...] (1) me patriae redditum a se, [na]m nisi parasses
quod servar[et] cavens saluti meae (2) inaniter opes suas

(42) You extended your generosity to very many friends, and especially to the family you are devoted to. Although someone might mention with praise other women on the same grounds, your only equal has been your sister. It was you and she who brought up with us in our houses your kinswomen who deserved such help. So that these same women could achieve a match worthy of your family, you provided them dowries. Gaius Cluvius and I mutually consented to take upon ourselves the amounts you settled on; we approved of your generosity, and so that you would not deprive yourselves of your own property, we substituted our own wealth for yours, and turned over to the dowries some lands of ours. I do not speak of this to brag about ourselves, but to make clear that we considered it an honor to fulfill with our resources those plans of yours, made with devotion and generosity.

(52) I must skip over quite a number of your other kindnesses...

(1a) ... OF MY WIFE.

(2a) You gave me plentiful support for my escape. You provided me with your jewelry, when you tore off your body all your gold and the pearls and handed them over to me. Then you enriched me, while I was away from Rome, with slaves, money, and supplies, cleverly deceiving the enemy guards.

(6a) You begged for my life while I was away, something your courage kept urging you to try. The clemency of those against whom you produced your words was won over and shielded me. Yet what you said was spoken with strength.

(9a) Meanwhile, a gang of the men gathered by Milo, whose house I had acquired through purchase when he was in exile, was going to take advantage of the opportunities offered by civil war, force their way in, and loot everything. Bravely you drove them back and defended our house.

(o) ... exist ... that I was restored to my country by him; for if you had not, in looking out for my survival, produced something for him to pollice[ret]ur.—Ita non minus pietati tu[a]e quam Caesari (3) me debeo.

(4) Quid ego nunc interiora [no]stra et recondita consilia s[e]rmo- nesque arcanos (5) eruam? ut repentinis nu[n]tiis ad praesentia et inminentia pericula evoca- (6) tus tuis consiliis cons[er]vatus sim—ut neque audac[i]us experiri casus (7) temere passa sis et mod[es]tiora cogitanti fida receptacula pararis (8) sociosque consilioru[m t]uorum ad me servandum delegeris sororem (9) tuam et virum eius C. Cl[uvi]um, coniuncto omnium periculo: infinita sint, (10) si attingere coner.—Sat [es]t mihi tibique salu- tariter m[e latuisse.]

(11) Acerbissumum tamen in vi[ta] mihi accidisse tua vice fatebo[r, reddito me iam] (12) cive patriae beneficio et i[ud]icio apsentis Caesaris Augusti, [quom per te] (13) de restitutione mea M. L[epi]dus conlega praesens interp[ellaretur et ad eius] (14) pedes prostrata humi [n]on modo non adlevata, sed tra[cta et servilem in] (15) modum rapsata, livori[bus c]orporis repleta, firmissimo [animo eum admone-] (16) res edicti Caesaris cum g[r]atula- tione restitutionis me[ae atque vocibus eti-] (17) am contumelio- sis et cr[ud]elibus exceptis volneribus pa[lam ea praeferres,] (18) ut auctor meorum peric[ul]orum notesceret.—Quoi no[cuit mox ea res.]

(19) Quid hac virtute efficaciu[s], praebere Caesari clementia[e locum et cum cu-] (20) stodia spiritus mei not[a]re inportunam crudeli- tatem [Lepidi egregia tua] (21) patientia

(22) Sed quid plura?—Parcamu[s] orationi, quae debet et potest e[sse brevis, ne maxu-] (23) ma opera tractando pa[r]um digne peraga- mus, quom pr[o magnitudine erga me] (24) meritorum tuorum oc[ulis] omnium praeferam titulum [vitae servatae.]

save, his pledge of support would have been to no avail. Thus no less to your devotion than to Caesar do I owe my existence.

(4)   Why should I now divulge our private and hidden plans and our secret conversations? How I was saved by your plans when I was provoked by unexpected news to court immediate and present danger; how you did not allow me to tempt fate in a rash away; how you made me think more calmly and prepared a secure hiding place for me; how you made your sister and her husband, Gaius Cluvius, partners in your plans to save me, at a risk shared between all of you: it would be an endless task, if I tried to touch on all this. It is enough for you and me that I was safely in hiding.

(11) Nevertheless I have to say that the most distressing thing to happen to me in life was what happened to you. Thanks to the favorable decision of Caesar Augustus, then away from Rome, I was re-stored as a citizen of our country. You then confronted his col-league Marcus Lepidus, who was in charge in Rome, about my reinstatement. Prostrate on the ground before his feet, not only were you lifted up, you were also dragged and carried off like a slave. Your body was covered with bruises, but most strenuously you kept reminding him about Caesar's edict with its rejoicing over my restoration, and although you had to endure Lepidus' insulting words and cruel wounds, you kept on putting forward your case in the open so that the person responsible for my trials would be publicly disgraced. It was not long before his behavior brought him to harm.

(19) What could have more effective than this courage of yours, to offer Caesar an opportunity for clemency and, while preserving my life, to brand the ruthless cruelty of Lepidus through your own excep-tional willingness to endure hardship?

(22) But why say more? I will spare my remarks, which ought to be and can be short. I do not wish, in treating your very great exploits, to go through them unworthily. In recognition of the greatness of all the good deeds you did on my behalf, I shall display to the eyes of all an inscription that tells how you saved my life.

(25) Pacato orbe terrarum, res[titut]a re publica quieta deinde n[obis et felicia] (26) tempora contigerunt.—Fue[ru]nt optati liberi, quos aliqua[mdiu sors nobis invi-] (27) derat.—Si fortuna procede[re e]sset passa sollemnis inservie[ns, quid utrique no-] (28) strum defuit?—Procedens a[li]as spem finiebat.—Quid agitav[eris prop- ter hoc quae-] (29) que ingredi conata sis, f[ors] sit an in quibusdam feminis [conspicua et memorabi-] (30) lia, in te quidem minime a[dmi]randa—conlata virtutibu[s tuis reliquis praetereo.]

(31) Diffidens fecunditati tuae [et do]lens orbitate mea, ne tenen[do in matrimonio] (32) te spem habendi liberos [dep]onerem atque eius caussa ess[em infelix, de divertio] (33) elocuta es—vocuamque [do-] mum alterius fecunditati t[e tradituram non alia] (34) mente, nisi ut nota con[co]rdia nostra tu ipsa mihi di[gnam et aptam con-] (35) di- cionem quaereres p[ara]resque ac futuros liberos t[e communes pro-] (36) que tuis habituram adf[ir]mares,—neque patrimoni nos[tri, quod adhuc] (37) fuerat commune, separa[ti]onem facturam,—sed in eodem [arbitrio meo id] (38) et, si vellem, tuo ministerio [fu]turum:— nihil seiunctum, ni[hil separatum te] (39) habituram, sororis soc[rusve] officia pietatemque mihi d[einceps praestituram.]

(40) Fatear necessest adeo me exa[rsi]sse ut excesserim mente, adeo [ex- horuisse cona-] (41) tus tuos ut vix redderer [mi]hi. Agitari divertia inter nos [ante quam nobis] (42) [f]ato dicta lex esset,—pos[se te a]liquid concipere mente, qua[re vivo me desineres] (43) esse mihi uxor, cum paene [e]xule me vita fidissuma perman[sisses!]

(44) Quae tanta mihi fuerit cu[pid]itas aut necessitas habendi li[beros, ut propterea] (45) fidem exuerem, mutare[m c]erta dubiis?—Sed quid plura? [Coniunx permansisti] (46) aput me; neque enim ced[er]e tibi sine dedecore meo et co[mmuni infelici-] (47) tate poteram.

(25) War came to an end throughout the world, the republic was re-stored, and we were granted a period of prosperity and peace. We did, it is true, desire children, whom for some time circumstances refused us. If Fortune had allowed herself to proceed with her cus-tomary regard for us, what would either of us have lacked? But proceeding otherwise, she began to put an end to our hopes. What you planned because of this and what you attempted! Perhaps in some other women this would be remarkable and worth com-memorating, but in you it is nothing at all to marvel at, compared to the rest of your virtues, and I pass over it.

(31) You were despairing of your fertility and pained over my child-lessness. So that I would not, by keeping you in marriage, have to put aside any hope of having children and become unhappy on that account, you mentioned the word "divorce." You would, you said, turn our house over to another woman's fertility, but your plan was that in keeping with our well-known marital har-mony, you would find and arrange a suitable match worthy of me; you insisted that you would regard the children born as shared, and as though your own; nor would you require a sepa-ration of our property, which up until then we had shared, but it would still remain in my control and, if I wished, under your management; you would hold nothing apart, nothing separate, and you would henceforward fulfill the duties and devotion of a sister or mother-in-law.

(40) I must say that I became so enraged that I lost my mind; I was so horrified at your designs that it was very hard to regain my composure. To plan for a divorce between us before Fate gave its decree to us—for you to be able in any way to conceive the thought that you would cease to be my wife, while I was still alive, when you had remained utterly faithful to me, at the time I was exiled and practically dead!

(44) What desire or need to have children could have been so great for me, that I could have broken faith, and traded certainty for uncer-tainty? But why say more? You remained with me my wife; I could never have assented to your proposal without bringing great shame upon me and unhappiness on both of us.

(48) Tibi vero quid memorabi[lius] quam inserviendo mihi o[peram dedisse te] (49) ut quom ex te liberos ha[b]ere non possem,—per te tamen [haberem et diffi-] (50) dentia partus tui alteriu[s c]oniugio parares fecunditat[em?]

(51) Utinam patiente utriusqu[e a]etate procedere coniugium [potuisset, donec e-] (52) lato me maiore, quod iu[sti]us erat, suprema mihi praest[ares; ego vero super-] (53) stite te excederem, orbitat[i f]ilia mihi supstituta.

(54) Praecucurristi fato. Delegast[i] mihi luctum desiderio tui nec libe[ros foturos mise-](55) rum reliquisiti. Flectam ego quoque sensus meos ad iudicia tu[a et monita tua sequar.]

(56) Omnia tua cogitata praescri[p]ta cedant laudibus tuis, ut sint mi[hi solacio ne nimis] (57) desiderem quod immort[ali]tati ad memoriam consecrat[um est sempiternam.]

(58) Fructus vitae tuae non derunt [m]ihi. Occurrente fama tua firma[bo animum atque](59) doctus actis tuis resistam fo[rt]unae, quae mihi non omnia erip[uit, sed cum meis laudi-] (60) bus crescere tui memoriam [pas]sa est. Sed quod tranquilli status e[rat mihi tecum totum] (61) amisi, quam speculatricem e[t p]ropugnatricem meorum pericul[orum cogitans calami-] (62) tate frangor nec permane[re] in promisso possum.

(63) Naturalis dolor extorquet const[ant]iae vires: maerore mersor et quibu[s angor luctu metuque] (64) in necutro mihi consto: repeten[s p]ristinos casus meos futurosque eve[ntus timens animo con-] (65) cido. Mihi tantis talibusque pr[aesi]diis orbatus, intuens famam tuam n[on iam tam par pa-] (66) tiendo haec quam ad desider[ium] luctumque reservatus videor.

(48) But what is more worthy of commemoration on your part than this? Looking after me, you devoted yourself, when I could not have children from you, to have them nevertheless through your efforts. Your goal, since you despaired of own ability to bear children, was by marriage with another woman to furnish me her fertility.

(51) I wish that each of our lifespans had allowed our marriage to continue until I, the older spouse, had been carried off—which would have been more just—leaving you to perform last rites for me; I would have left you as my survivor, a substitute daughter for me in my childlessness.

(54) Fate decreed that you should precede me. You consigned me to grief through longing for you, and you left no children to comfort me in my misery. But I for my part will steer my feelings to your views and follow your directions.

(56) Let all of your opinions and precepts yield to your praises, which may be a comfort for me so that I do not long too much for what has been consecrated to immortality for eternal commemoration.

(58) The fruits of your life will remain available to me. With the thought of your glory presenting itself, I shall strengthen my resolve; instructed by your deeds, I shall stand up to Fortune, who has not snatched everything away from me. She has allowed your memory to become established with my words of praise. But all of that tranquility that I had I have lost along with you. When I think of how you foresaw and warded off all of the dangers that befell me, I am shattered in misfortune and I cannot abide by my promise.

(63) A natural sorrow jerks away my power of self-control. I am overwhelmed by sadness and cannot stand firm either against the grief or the fear that anguish me. Going back over my earlier troubles and fearing what the future may bring, I break down. Deprived of such great defenses as I have just described, contemplating your glory, I seem now not so much capable of enduring these things. Rather I seem kept alive for longing and grief.

(67) Ultumum huis orationis erit omn[ia] meruisse te neque omnia contigisse mi[hi ut praestarem] (68) tibi. Legem habui mandata tu[a]; quod extra mihi liberum fuerit pr[aestabo.]

(69) Te di manes tui ut quietam pat[ia]ntur atque ita tueantur opto.

(67) The conclusion of this speech will be that you deserved everything but it was not granted to me to give everything to you. I have treated your final wishes as law; whatever further it is free for me to do, I shall.

(69) I pray that your *di manes* grant you peace and protection.

Notes

Prologue

1. Cf. Durry (1950), p. 69. In my discussion of the discovery and reconstitution of the *laudatio*, I have drawn especially on Durry (1950), pp. xlv–liii, as well as Gordon (1950) and Horsfall (1983).

2. Mommsen (1863).

3. Bodel (2001) is a helpful introduction to the importance of inscriptions for ancient history. Keppie (1991) introduces the inscriptions themselves.

4. de Rossi (1856).

5. See the full discussion below, pp. 117–124.

6. Mommsen (1863), pp. 477–478.

7. Vaglieri (1898); and again, see the full discussion below, pp. 117–124.

8. Mommsen (1863), pp. 467–475.

9. Durry (1950), pp. lvx–lxxvi provides a useful summary of reactions to Mommsen's views.

10. Vaglieri (1898) and Gordon (1950).

11. For what follows, see especially Horsfall (1983), pp. 85–86.

12. My figure for the height of the inscription slightly differs from Horsfall's (by about three inches), since I follow the reconstruction of Vaglieri (1898) for the dimensions of the gaming board.

13. Gordon (1950), p. 226.

14. For example, in an important paper Lindsay (2009) discusses legal and prosopographical matters.

15. Hemelrijk (2004) is a fine example of this approach. On the history of Roman women, two general works, Pomeroy (1975) and Fantham, et al. (1995), have not been surpassed. James and Dillon (2012) is a good starting point for exploring subsequent research, while D'Ambra (2007) generously showcases visual evidence.

16. A brief book by Storoni Mazzolani (1982) is the fullest discursive reconstruction of the wife's story prior to this study.

17. Cutolo (1983–1984) is an extensive exploration of the *laudatio* as a piece of litera-ture, an approach used later in this book when assessing the significance of the speech for understanding attitudes to women in Rome.

Chapter 1

1. Translations of the *laudatio* are taken from Appendix 2. Translations of other texts are my own, usually based on those in the Loeb Classical Library. Particularly extensive debts are acknowledged below.

2. As Mommsen (1863), p. 468 suggested.

3. See further below, pp. 34–37.

4. Mommsen (1863), p. 466, repeated, e.g., by Durry (1950), p. 30.

5. The major ancient accounts of the outbreak of civil war in 49 BC are Caes. *B Civ.* 1.1–1.33; Plut. *Caes.* 1.29–1.39; *Pomp.* 1.59–1.63; App. *B Civ.* 2.32–2.41; Dio 41.1–41.14. Two now-conventional reconstructions are offered by Rice Holmes (1923), vol. 3, pp. 1–50 and Rawson (1994a); a bold reassessment of Pompey's strategy is offered in Welch (2012).

6. See Welch (2012), pp. 43–91.

7. Suet. *Aug.* 32.1.

8. Suet. *Aug.* 3.1.

9. Brunt (1971), p. 552. Throughout this chapter, I owe a great debt to Brunt's discus-sion of "Violence in the Italian Countryside" (pp. 551–557) and also MacMullen (1974), pp. 1–27.

10. Caes. *B Civ.* 1.24.2, 3.4.4.

11. Caelius and Milo: Caes. *B Civ.* 3.20–3.22; Vell. Pat. 2.68.1–3; Dio 42.22–42.25.

12. Asc. 31 C.

13. Cic. *Att.* 8.13.2 (= 163 SB). My translations of Cicero's letters throughout this book are indebted to those of Shackleton Bailey.

14. Dyson (1992), pp. 69–74 is a useful supplement to Cicero's speech that I have drawn from here; for a lively translation of *For Cluentius*, see Grant (1975), pp. 111–253.

15. Murder of aunt Cluentia: Cic. *Cluent.* 30.

16. Cic. *Cluent.* 36–39 (quotation from 36).

17. See esp. Cic. *Cluent.* 19–30, 40–41, 45–48.

18. For what follows, and much more in this vein, see Castor (2006).

19. See further Brunt (1971), pp. 551–557 and, with a somewhat different perspective, Dyson (1992), pp. 56–88.

20. Cic. *Cluent.* 161.

21. Cic. *Mil.* 74.

22. Cic. *Tull.* 8–12.

23. Lintott (1968), pp. 107–131; Brunt (1971), pp. 553–557.

24. On this point and what follows, see Buckland (1908), pp. 91–97; Bradley (1994), pp. 112–114.

25. See further Gaughan (2010).

26. Lintott (1968), pp. 22–34.

27. Cic. *Mil.* 8–11 (quotations from 9, 10).

28. In the following discussion of these rights, I have relied on three superb works of scholarship: Gardner (1986), esp. pp. 5–29; Gardner (1993), pp. 85–109; and Evans Grubbs (2002), esp. pp. 16–80.

29. In addition to the works mentioned above, see also below, p. 173, n. 38.

30. On this important point see Gardner (1993), pp. 101–107; Evans Grubbs (2002), pp. 46–60.

31. A woman from Arretium, name unknown (Cic. *Caec.* 97) and Titinia (Cic. *Brut.* 217).

32. *Dig.* 48.2.11 *pr.*

33. At this time Augustus was calling himself "Gaius Julius Caesar" (after his father), while modern historians often refer to him as "Octavian" (from *Octavianus*, a named that could be added to "Gaius Julius Caesar" indicating that the birth father was Octavius). The young Caesar gained the new name "Augustus" only in 27 BC, but to avoid confusion, I often call him "Augustus" even when describing events before 27 BC.

34. *RG* 2.

35. In addition to the mention of *pietas* at 1.7, note 1.32.

36. Watson (1967), pp. 25, 121–122.

37. Lindsay (2009), p. 191.

38. Again, see Watson (1967), pp. 117–122; and also Watson (1971), pp. 180–181. Crook (1986), focused specifically on women in Roman succession, is also a most helpful resource, as is Gardner (1986), pp. 163–203.

39. My interpretation of the lines is similar to that of Gardner (1998), pp. 33–34.

40. Catull. 68.119–68.124.

41. Pointed out by Frier (1985), p. 37, in a marvelous discussion of "the problem of litigiousness" (pp. 27–41).

42. See, again, Dyson (1992), pp. 68–69. Berry (2000), pp. 3–58 is an excellent introduction to and translation of the speech.

43. Some scholarship, e.g., Dyck (2003), has argued for the guilt of Cicero's client; if this view is correct, the whole affair would be an even more spectacular example of a family feud centering over land.

44. Frier (1985), p. 17.

45. Helpful discussions include Crook (1986), pp. 65–67; Dixon (1985); and Gardner (1986), pp. 170–177.

46. Crook (1986), p. 65.

47. Two articles of Daube are essential reading: Daube (1964) and Daube (1986).

48. Father's failure to register: Cic. 2. *Verr.* 1.104. Inserted clause: Cic. *Fin.* 2.55. Deathbed request: Cic. *Fin.* 2.58.

49. Suet. *Iul.* 83.1 with Treggiari (1991), p. 366.

50. Already Mommsen (1863), p. 471 suggested that the wife's husband was to be her guardian.

51. Aug. *RG* 15.1 with Plut. *Ant.* 16.1–16.2, *Brut.* 22.3; App. *B Civ.* 3.21–3.23.

52. Nep. *Att.* 9.4. Cf. Cicero's efforts to protect the property of Milo's wife, Fausta, after her husband's condemnation and forced exile in 52 BC: Cic. *Att.* 5.8.2–5.8.3 (= SB 101).

Chapter 2

1. Langlands (2006) is a landmark study of *pudicitia* from which (esp. pp. 37–77) I have drawn.

2. Treggiari (1991), pp. 299–317 in a rich discussion brings out the problems with attributing the double standard solely to the matter of legitimacy.

3. Lendon (2011), esp. pp. 385–386.

4. Cic. *Fam.* 7.23.4 (= 209 SB).

5. Suet. *Aug.* 64.2. On Baiae: Griffin (1985), pp. 90–91.

6. Prop. 1.11.29. My translations of Propertius are based on those of Goold (1990), while I follow the text of Heyworth (2007).

7. Warde Fowler (1905), by redating the events of Vaglieri's fragment, achieved a major advance in our understanding of the wife's experience in the civil war.

8. For events in Rome and Italy though 47 BC, Dio 41.1–18, 36–40; and 42.17–33, 49–55 are the major narrative sources, while the contemporary account of Caesar (*B Civ.* 1.1–33; 3.1–2, 20–22) and the Ciceronian corpus (discussed more below) are of great value. Rice Holmes (1923), esp. vol 3, pp. 1–50, 220–235, 276–292 and Rawson (1994a) are two modern overviews, but I especially recommend two more focused articles, Welch (1995) and Ramsey (2004), which inform my account in this chapter.

9. See Dio 41.7–8 and 42.27 in addition to the Ciceronian evidence in the following notes.

10. Cic. *Fam.* 14.8.1 (= 144 SB), 14.14.1 (= 145 SB). In the first letter, Cicero advises Terentia to have the house "barricaded and guarded." Cf. letters to Atticus at this time (e.g., *Att.* 7.13.1 [= 136 SB]).

11. Cic. *Att.* 11.9.3 (= 220 SB). After Pharsalus, Caesar was granted authority to treat Pompeians as he wished (Dio 42.20.1).

12. See esp. letters Cicero wrote to Atticus in mid-47 BC, e.g., Cic. *Att.* 11.15 (= 226 SB) and *Att.* 11.25 (= 231 SB).

13. Ramsey (2004) discusses the liquidation of Pompey's estates in particular. For evidence of confiscation more generally, see, e.g., Cic. *Fam.* 4.7.5 (= 230 SB); 4.13.2 (= 225 SB); 9.10.3 (= 217 SB). Servilia: Suet. *Iul.* 50.2; Macrob. *Sat.* 2.2.5; cf. Cic. *Att.* 14.21.3 (= 375 SB).

14. Frederiksen (1966), also an essential article for understanding Italy in the early 40s BC.

15. Dio 42.49.4, cited by Frederiksen (1966), p. 132. Cicero (*Att.* 14.4.2 = 358 SB) would echo the sentiment.

16. Harris (2006).

17. See esp. Caes. *B Civ.* 3.1.1–3 and Dio 41.37–38, with Frederiksen (1966), p. 133.

18. For Caelius' activities in 48 BC, see Caelius' own letter to Cicero, *Fam.* 8.17 (= 156 SB); Caes. *B Civ.* 3.20–22; Vell. Pat. 2.68.1–3; Dio 42.22–25; Welch (1995).

19. The major sources are Ascon. 30–56 C and Cic. *Mil.*, both translated and equipped with a helpful introduction by Berry (2000), pp. 162–223.

20. Caes. *B Civ.* 3.21–22; Dio 41.36.2, 42.24–25; Vell. Pat. 2.68.2–3.

21. See esp. Plut. *Ant.* 8–10 and Dio 42.21, 42.27–28 with Welch (1995).

22. Antony's mission: Welch (1995), pp. 184, 190.

23. Dio 42.29–33.

24. Treggiari (2007) is a masterful reconstruction, to which I owe much, and which any interested in Terentia must read in full. Here I limit myself to making points useful to my own larger discussion. Dixon (1986) and Claassen (1996) are earlier useful studies of Terentia.

25. All biographies of Cicero discuss this period of his life, e.g., Shackleton Bailey (1971), pp. 61–72; Treggiari (2007), pp. 56–70 gives the story of Terentia and her daughter Tullia.

26. Flower (2006), pp. 102–103.

27. Cic. *Fam.* 14.4.3 (= 6 SB).

28. See further Dixon (1986), pp. 95–97.

29. Cic. *Fam.* 14.2.2 (= 7 SB), 14.3.2 (= 9 SB) with Treggiari (2007), p. 60 as well as Lintott (1968), pp. 16–21 on mourning.

30. Cic. *Red. Pop.* 8.

31. Cic. *Red. Sen.* 17. Cf. Cic. *Sest.* 54 and various letters, e.g., *Fam.* 14.4.4 (= 6 SB); 14.3.3 (= 9 SB).

32. Cic. *Fam.* 14.1.5 (= 8 SB); cf. *Fam.* 14.2.2 (= 7 SB).

33. Cic. *Fam.* 14.1.5 (= 8 SB), 14.2.3 (= 7 SB).

34. Cic. *Fam.* 14.1.5 (= 8 SB).

35. Cic. *Fam.* 14.3.1 (= 9 SB).

36. Cic. *Fam.* 14.2.2 (= 7 SB). See also Cic. *Dom.* 59; *Sest.* 54, 145; *Cael.* 50.

37. Cic. *Fam.* 14.2.3 (= 7 SB), 14.1.1 (= 8 SB)

38. Cic. *Fam.* 14.1.5 (= 8 SB).

39. Cic. *Fam.* 14.3.5 (= 9 SB).

40. Cic. *Fam.* 14.3.5 (= 9 SB).

41. On this period of Terentia's life, see esp. Treggiari (2007), pp. 100–130.

42. Treggiari (2007), pp. 83–99 gives a full discussion of the search for a new husband (and see pp. 75–77 for the marriage to Furius Crassipes).

43. For Caelius' recommendation of Dolabella, see esp. Cic. *Fam.* 8.6.2 (= 88 SB); cf. *Fam.* 3.10.5 (= 73 SB).

44. Note especially Cicero's disavowal to Appius Claudius, the man Dolabella was prosecuting: Cic. *Fam.* 3.10.5 (= 73 SB). As Atticus was close to Claudius, letters to him must be read cautiously; Welch (1996), p. 465, n. 83 notes the divergence between what Cicero felt and what he wrote to Atticus at this time. I thank Kathryn Welch for additional advice in correspondence on this matter.

45. Cic. *Fam.* 7.32.3 (= 113 SB).

46. Cic. *Fam.* 14.18.1 (= 144 SB).

47. Cic. *Fam.* 14.18.2 (= 144 SB); cf. *Fam.* 14.14 (= 145 SB); *Att.* 7.14.3 (= 138 SB).

48. Tullia: Cic. *Att.* 10.8.1 (= 199 SB). Caelius: *Fam.* 8.16 (= 153 SB).

49. See, e.g., Cic. *Fam.* 14.6 (= 158 SB); *Att.* 11.11.2 (= 222 SB). Dixon (1986), pp. 102–111 should be read now with Treggiari (2007).

50. Financial worry is a leitmotif of Book 11 of Cicero's letters to Atticus, written from January 48 BC to later 47 BC; this book, when read continuously, reveals how after Cicero's departure from Italy, civil war took a toll on his personal and family life, and is a most useful *comparandum* for the *laudatio*. For financial worries, see, e.g., Cic. *Att.* 11.2.1 (= 212 SB), 11.11.2 (= 223 SB), 11.25.3 (= 231 SB).

51. Cic. *Att.* 11.24.2 (= 234 SB); cf. *Att.* 11.25.3 (= 231 SB).

52. In addition to Treggiari (2007), pp. 122–123, see Gardner (1998), pp. 220–221.

53. See, e.g., Cic. *Fam.* 14.13 (= 169 SB); *Att.* 11.2.2 (= 212 SB), 11.23.3 (= 232 SB).

54. Cic. *Fam.* 14.13 (= 169 SB).

55. Cic. *Att.* 11.7.2 (= 218 SB) and see further below, pp. 38–39.

56. In addition to Treggiari (2007), pp. 128–130, 155–161, see Claassen (1996).

57. Cic. *Att.* 11.24.3 (= 234 SB).

58. Cic. *Att.* 11.14.3 (= 225 SB), 11.15.2 (= 226 SB).

59. Plut. *Cic.* 41.2–3.

60. Cic. *Fam.* 14.20 (= 173 SB). Treggiari (2007), p. 196, n. 36 explains: "It was common sense to warn a host in advance, since it took time to stoke up the bath furnace."

61. Cf. Treggiari (2007), p. 129: "Cicero had lost his old feelings for his wife."

62. Griffin (1985), p. 12. Plin. *NH* 9.106–123 gives an interesting account.

63. Pearl sellers and Livia's pearl setter: Treggiari (1975), p. 55. Caesar: Suet. *Iul.* 43. Augustus: Aug. *RG* 21.2; Dio 51.22.2–3; Suet. *Aug.* 30.2.

64. Juristic texts: Oliver (2000). War effort: e.g., Liv. 5.50.7; 26.36. Caelius' loan: Cic. *Cael.* 30, 51–55.

65. Cf. the safe of Cluentius' mother Sassia: Cic. *Cluent.* 179–181.

66. Gardens: Cic. *Cael.* 36, with Griffin (1985), p. 89 for swimming and sex. Dresses: Quint. *Inst.* 8.6.52, with Griffin (1985), p. 10 for "see-through Coan dresses."

67. Cf. Warde Fowler (1905), p. 264. Others, e.g., Wistrand (1976), p. 41 refer this episode to after the battle of Pharsalus in 48 BC. Another possibility is that she was supplying him in early 48 BC, perhaps for instance during the entrapment of the Pompeians at Dyrrachium (cf. the details in letters Cicero wrote to Atticus from in and around Pompey's camp in early 48 BC, *Att.* 11.1–4 [= 211–215 SB]).

68. Caes. *B Civ.* 1.31; 2.23–44; App. *B Civ.* 2.44–46; Dio 41.41–42, 42.56.2.

69. Asc. 54 C; Cic. *Fam.* 8.3.2 (= 79 SB), *Att.* 4.3.3 (= 75 SB), 5.8.2–3 (= 101 SB); *Mil.* 64.

70. Lindsay (2009), p. 194, arguing that the house of the *laudatio* is that on the Palatine.

71. Just as Cato's wife, Marcia, was entrusted with the care of Cato's household and children when he left Rome in 49 BC (Plut. *Cat. Min.* 52.5).

72. Asc. 33 C; cf. Dio 40.49.3–4 (the house nearly burned).

73. Cic. *Att.* 4.3.3 (= 75 SB).

74. Patterson (1992), pp. 200–204.

75. Cic. *Att.* 11.2.3 (= 212 SB) seems to refer to a threat on Cicero's townhouse, reported to him by the architect Vettius Chrysippus. The house of Sextus Pompey's mother, Mucia, was threatened with destruction in 39 BC (App. *B Civ.* 5.69).

76. See esp. Cic. *Att.* 11.7.2–4 (= 218 SB), a letter discussed further below (cf. also Cic. *Att.* 11.14.1 [= 225 SB] etc.).

77. Flach (1991) reconstructs the lines to contain a reference to the wife's recovery of the husband's confiscated property; against this view, see Kruschwitz (1999).

78. Cic. *Fam.* 5.6.1 (= 4 SB). For the larger pattern here, see, e.g., Dixon (1983).

79. Plut. *Ant.* 2.1–2.

80. Cic. *Fam.* 14.16 (= 163 SB), well discussed by Treggiari (2007), p. 121. Of Volumnia, Traina (2001) offers a portrait.

81. On the genre and its social context see, in addition to Traina (2001), Wiseman (1985), pp. 26–38.

82. Cic. *Att.* 10.10.5 (= 201 SB).

83. Cic. *Phil.* 2.57–58; cf. *Phil.* 2.62, and also Plut. *Ant.* 9.4.

84. Cic. *Fam.* 14.16 (= 163 SB).

85. Cic. *Att.* 11.7.2 (= 218 SB), with Treggiari (2007), p. 121.

86. Evans Grubbs (2002), pp. 91–102 usefully sets out legal evidence. Other key discussions I have relied on are Gardner (1986), pp. 67–80, 97–116, Crook (1990), Treggiari (1991), pp. 323–396, and Saller (1994), pp. 204–224.

87. Crook (1990), p. 164.

88. See below, pp. 84–85.

89. See above, p. 23 and Cf. Treggiari (1991), p. 377.

90. On dodges, see above, p. 23.

91. See above, pp. 23–24.

92. Pearce (1974); Treggiari (1991), p. 374–379.

93. Plut. *Ant.* 1.2–3.

94. Told in a letter written by Cicero's brother, *Fam.* 16.26.2 (= 351 SB), discussed by Treggiari (2007), p. 33.

95. Treggiari (2007), p. 33.

96. On the household as an economic unit, Saller (2007) is a useful overview. Two articles by Treggiari, Treggiari (1973) and Treggiari (1975), give a vivid sense of the staffs of urban houses.

97. Nep. *Att.* 13.

98. See the account given by Plutarch (*Crass.* 2).

99. A telling detail is Cicero's assumption that his brother's wife, Pomponia, had her husband's seal in his absence from Rome—with which she could send letters in his name (Cic. *Att.* 11.9.2 [= 220 SB]).

100. Livia had a "*lanipendus* to weigh out wool for each day's work to the slaves" notes Treggiari (1973), p. 245. See also Treggiari (1991), pp. 243–244.

101. As Caesennia, a woman of Tarquinii, did in the 80s BC: see Cic. *Caec.* 11.

Chapter 3

1. For events from 47 through 44 BC, major ancient sources include App. *B Civ.* 2.95–154; Dio 43–44; various lives of Plutarch (esp. *Caes., Cat. Min., Ant.*) as well as

works of Cicero and the continuators of Caesar's *Civil War*. Rice Holmes (1923), vol. 3, pp. 236–352 and Rawson (1994a) are two modern narratives; Welch (2012), pp. 93–119 usefully foregrounds Caesar's political problems.

2. Lintott (2009) gives a basic account of the Ides of March; Toher (2006) is an important study of the earliest extant account given by Nicolaus of Damascus.

3. Rice Holmes (1928), vol. 1, pp. 1–71, Syme (1939), pp. 97–186, and Rawson (1994b) give good overviews of major events. In Osgood (2006), pp. 12–61, I discuss the sources, especially Cicero's writings, and cite other studies. Ramsey (2001) and Welch (2012), pp. 121–162 are important reconsiderations of the politics of the period.

4. See above, p. 173, n. 33.

5. Servilius Ahala: e.g., Liv. 4.13–14; Dion. Hal. *Ant. Rom.* 12.4; Plut. *Brut.* 1.5. Servilia's descent: Plut. *Brut.* 1.5, *Caes.* 62.1. The most important account of Servilia is to be found in Münzer (1999), pp. 308–344, and I am indebted to it, as well as to Syme (1939) *passim* and Bauman (1992), pp. 73–76. In an important article, Geiger (1973) challenges some of Münzer's conclusions. Skinner (2011) treats Servilia's close contemporary Clodia Metelli, whose biography is instructive for Servilia's world. Brennan (2012) also includes Servilia in a useful sketch of perceptions of women's power in the late Republic.

6. App. *B Civ.* 1.44; Liv. *Per.* 73.

7. Plut. *Cat. Min.* 11.1–3. He left only a young daughter (Plut. *Cat. Min.* 11.4).

8. Caesar betrothed his daughter to a Servilius Caepio, but broke off the engagement in 59 BC: Suet. *Iul.* 21; Plut. *Caes.* 14.7; etc. Münzer (1999), pp. 310–311 thought this Servilius Caepio was Servilia son's Brutus, who through adoption gained the name Servilius Caepio (see p. 49 below); against this view, see Geiger (1973), p. 153.

9. Even over her younger half-brother, Cato—her mother's son through a remarriage—Servilia was said to have maintained "a maternal power" (Asc. 19 C). For Servilia in 44 BC, see below, p. 50.

10. One of her contemporaries who researched the histories of Rome's great families, Messalla Rufus, claimed that the Servilii had an old bronze coin that seemed to grow bigger and smaller in sympathy with the family fortunes (Plin. *NH* 34.137).

11. Caesar and the Julii: Badian (2009).

12. Death of M. Junius Brutus (*tr. pl.* 78 BC): esp. Plut. *Pomp.* 16.2–5, *Brut.* 4.1–2; Liv. *Per.* 90; Val. Max. 6.2.8. Hatred of young Brutus: Plut. *Pomp.* 64.3, *Brut.* 4.3.

13. Marriage to Junius Silanus: Plut. *Cat. Min.* 21.2. Three daughters' husbands: (1) Aemilius Lepidus (see, e.g., Cic. *Att.* 14.8.1 [= 362 SB], Vell. Pat. 2.88.1); (2) Servilius Isauricus (*AE* 1934.84); (3) Cassius the tyrannicide (e.g., Cic. *Att.* 14.20.2 [= 374 SB, recording a miscarriage of "Tertulla"]; Plut. *Brut.* 7.1; Tac. *Ann.* 3.76.1).

14. Cic. *Brut.* 331; cf. *Or.* 153 (Servilius Ahala as Brutus' ancestor). Adoption: see above, p. 178, n. 8.

15. *RRC* 433.

16. Shackleton Bailey (1976), pp. 129–131. See, e.g., Cic. *Phil.* 10.25–26; *SEG* 17.75.

17. Plut. *Brut.* 4.1–5, *Pomp.* 63.3; Dio 44.13.1.

18. Plut. *Brut.* 5.1.

19. Plut. *Brut.* 5.2–4, *Cat. Min.* 24.1–2; Suet. *Iul.* 50.2.

20. Cic. *Att.* 2.24.3 (= 44 SB).

21. Cic. *Att.* 2.24.3 (= 44 SB).

22. Vell. Pat. 2.52.5; Plut. *Brut.* 6.1–2, *Caes.* 46.4; Dio 41.63.6; App. *B Civ.* 2.111.

23. Cic. *Or.* 35, *Att.* 12.21.1 (= 260 SB).

24. Marriage to Claudia: Cic. *Fam.* 3.4.2 (= 67 SB); *Brut.* 267, 324. Divorce: Cic. *Att.* 13.9.2 (= 317 SB), 13.10.3 (= 318 SB). Marriage to Porcia: Plut. *Brut.* 13.3, *Cat. Min.* 73.4; Dio 44.13.1.

25. Cic. *Att.* 13.22.4 (= 329 SB), on which Shackleton Bailey comments *ad loc.*: "Apparently Brutus' mother Servilia and his new wife Porcia were on bad terms."

26. Junia Tertia's marriage to Cassius: Plut. *Brut.* 7.1.

27. Friendship: Cic. *Att.* 15.11.2 (= 389 SB); Nep. *Att.* 11.4. Atticus' biography is reconstructed by Shackleton Bailey (1965–1970) vol. 1, pp. 3–59 (mentioning on p. 5 Atticus' "interest and flair for backstairs politics") and Welch (1996).

28. Cic. *Att.* 5.4.2 (= 97 SB).

29. Welch (1996), mentioning on p. 452 Atticus' "financial empire."

30. Cic. *Att.* 15.9.1 (= 387 SB), 15.10 (= 388 SB); App. *B Civ.* 3.6, 4.57.

31. Cic. *Att.* 15.11 (= 389 SB).

32. Cic. *Att.* 15.11.2 (= 389 SB).

33. It is not clear she ever did so: the commission, in fact, provided a good pretext for Brutus and Cassius to raise ships for war: see Cic. *Att.* 16.4.4 (= 411 SB) etc. with Welch (2012), p. 134. That she could make the promise, though, is telling.

34. Brutus' departure: Cic. *Att.* 16.7 (= 415 SB), *Phil.* 1.8–10, 10.9, 10.23–24 etc. Cassius' departure: Cic. *Fam.* 12.14.6 (= 405 SB), *Phil.* 11.27–28, etc.

35. Cic. *Att.* 15.3.4 (= 416 SB); *Fam.* 12.7 (= 367 SB); *Ad Brut.* 2.3.3 (= 2 SB), 2.4.5 (= 4 SB), 1.13.1 (= 20 SB), 1.15.13 (= 23 SB), 1.18 (= 24 SB).

36. Cicero's proposal survives in *Phil.* 11. See also Cic. *Fam.* 12.7 (= 367 SB), *Ad Brut.* 2.4.2 (= 4 SB).

37. Cic. *Fam.* 12.7.1 (= 367 SB; source for next sentences too).

38. Cic. *Fam.* 12.10.1 (= 425 SB); Vell. Pat. 2.64.4; App. *B Civ.* 3.96. It was perhaps around this time that another of Servilia's sons-in-law, Servilius Isauricus, also abandoned Cicero and the Senate by betrothing his daughter to Octavian (Suet. *Aug.* 62.1).

39. See esp. Cic. *Ad Brut.* 1.3 (= 20 SB), 1.12.1–2 (= 21 SB), 1.15.13 (= 23 SB).

40. Nep. *Att.* 9.2, 9.4.

41. Cic. *Ad Brut.* 1.18.1 (= 24 SB).

42. Cic. *Ad Brut.* 1.18.6 (= 24 SB).

43. Nep. *Att.* 11.4. According to Plutarch (*Brut.* 53.4), Antony sent the ashes of Brutus to Servilia.

44. Compare the tradition about her daughter-in-law Porcia, discussed below, pp. 125–126.

45. Overviews of the triumviral period can be found in Rice Holmes (1928), Syme (1939), Pelling (1996) and Osgood (2006). Two recent interesting discussions, focusing on constitutional and political aspects, are Lange (2009) and Welch (2012).

46. My discussion of the proscriptions here draws on my earlier account, Osgood (2006), pp. 62–82, where fuller details can be found. The study of Hinard (1985) remains

important, and see also now Powell (2008), pp. 55–64 and Powell (2009). Milnor (2005), pp. 186–238 discusses the memory of the proscriptions, on which see further below, pp. 124–125.

47. The edict is given by App. *B Civ.* 4.8–11.

48. Lindsay (2009), p. 194.

49. App. *B Civ.* 4.5.

50. Nep. *Att.* 12.4.

51. Val. Max. 7.3.9.

52. See, e.g., Vell. Pat. 2.72.5, 2.77.2; App. *B Civ.* 4.36, 5.143; Dio 47.12.

53. Val. Max. 6.7.3 (see also App. *B Civ.* 4.39).

54. App. *B Civ.* 4.22, 4.36, 4.41, 4.44.

55. App. *B Civ.* 4.44.

56. Osgood (2006), pp. 79–81.

57. Val. Max. 6.7.2 (note also 6.7.3).

58. Val. Max. 9.11.7 (see also App. *B Civ.* 4.24).

59. App. *B Civ.* 4.23.

60. Cf. Nep. *Att.* 9.4; Plut. *Ant.* 21.3.

61. Dio 47.14.1–2. But later Octavian was forced to relent: Dio 48.8.5.

62. App. *B Civ.* 5.12 and especially Dio 48.3 describe this period. My reconstruction here is greatly indebted to Gowing (1992), who follows Mommsen (1863), pp. 476–477 on dating.

63. Dio 48.3.6.

64. Gowing (1992), p. 287, noting that Suet. *Aug.* 27.2 provides evidence of curtailment of the proscriptions around this time.

65. Gowing (1992), pp. 287–288.

66. See above, p. 38.

67. Gowing (1992), pp. 291–294.

68. See esp. Vell. Pat. 2.67.3; App. *B Civ.* 4.12; Plut. *Ant.* 19.2; Dio 47.6.3. Julia's brother had recently helped her by advocating more lenient treatment by the Senate of Antony in February of 43 BC: Cic. *Phil.* 8.1–2 (to be read with App. *B Civ.* 3.51).

69. App. *B Civ.* 4.37 (source of quotation); cf. Plut. *Ant.* 20.3; Dio 47.8.5.

70. The story of Tanusia and her presentation to Octavian at the theater of her proscribed husband whom she had hid illustrates the same strategy: see Dio 47.7.4–5 with Sumi (2004), pp. 203–204. Cluett (1998) also discusses women's appearances in public in the triumviral years.

71. Father: see, e.g., Liv. *Per.* 80. Husband: see esp. Plut. *Ant.* 2.1–2.

72. Julia in 40 BC: App. *B Civ.* 5.52, 5.63; Dio 48.15.2; cf. Plut. *Ant.* 32.1.

73. Dio 47.14, 47.16–17; App. *B Civ.* 4.32–34. For what follows, I draw on Osgood (2006), pp. 82–84; in addition to the works cited there, see also Cluett (1998); Milnor (2005), pp. 222–226; Sumi (2004); and Welch (2010), pp. 312–314.

74. App. *B Civ.* 4.32.

75. On her speech, in addition to App. *B Civ.* 4.32–33, see Val. Max. 8.3.3; Quint. *Inst.* 1.1.6. Daughter of Hortensius: Val. Max. 8.3.3; Quint. *Inst.* 1.1.6. Sister of proscript Hortensius: Vell. Pat. 2.71.2; Suet. *Aug.* 72.1. Sister-in-law of Servilia: deduced from *ILS* 9460.

76. See above, p. 31.

77. Liv. 34.1–8.3; Val. Max. 9.1.3. Hemelrijk (1987) gives a full and illuminating comparison of events in 195 and 42 BC.

78. Daube (2003), pp. 570–571.

79. Daube (2003), p. 571.

80. Daube (2003), pp. 571–572.

81. Daube (2003), pp. 584, 587–590.

82. Copy of speech: Quint. *Inst.* 1.1.6. Appian: *B Civ.* 4.32–33. Hopwood (forthcoming) makes a robust case for the view that Appian's speech preserves echoes of the original and Hopwood also suggests that Hortensia's speech inspired Livy as he wrote up his account of the debate over the *lex Oppia*.

83. Liv. 34.7.8–9.

84. Colley (1992), pp. 237–281 (quotation from p. 263).

85. Colley (1992), pp. 250, 262, 280–281. Blurring of roles in triumviral Rome: Hemelrijk (2004) and Osgood (2006), pp. 82, 84–86, 160, as well as Severy (2003), pp. 34–44 and Milnor (2005), pp. 186–239 for the association made, in later times, of blurred gender roles and civil war. See also below, pp. 125–127, 132.

86. Asc. 32 C. There are a number of studies of Fulvia, but Welch (1995) is especially illuminating. In my account, here I draw on my own earlier remarks, Osgood (2006), p. 160.

87. Asc. 40 C.

88. Welch (1995).

89. Brundisium: Cic. *Phil.* 3.4, 5.22, 13.18; Dio 45.13.2, 45.35.3.

90. App. *B Civ.* 3.51; see also Cic. *Phil.* 12.1–2 for Fulvia at this time.

91. Threats in summer of 43 BC: Nep. *Att.* 9.2–6. Appearance before the army in 41 BC: App. *B Civ.* 5.14 (cf. 5.19); cf. Dio 48.5.2, 48.6.1–3.

92. App. *B Civ.* 5.19–21; cf. also Plut. *Ant.* 30.1.

93. Cf. Welch (1995), p. 193. In a more recent discussion, Welch (2012), pp. 218–230 assigns a greater role to Mark Antony in this plan.

94. Dio 48.4–7, 48.11–13.1. Livy seems to have given a similar version (*Per.* 125–126). This tradition goes back to claims made by Octavian and his supporters in 41 BC, as is shown by the abusive inscriptions found on sling-bullets they fired against Lucius and his army: see Hallett (1977).

95. Dio 48.5.2–3; Suet. *Aug.* 62.1.

96. Fulvia's exhortations to Antonian generals: App. *B Civ.* 5.33.

97. Flight of Fulvia: App. *B Civ.* 5.50, 5.52; Dio 48.15.1. Julia's trip to Sicily: see above, p. 57.

98. Plut. *Ant.* 30.3; App. *B Civ.* 5.55, 5.59, 5.62; Dio 48.28.3.

99. See above, p. 57.

100. Plut. *Ant.* 30.3; App. *B Civ.* 5.59; Dio 48.28.3. Hemelrijk (2004), pp. 191–193 gives a perceptive discussion.

101. Vell. Pat. 2.74.3.

102. Plut. *Ant.* 10.3.

Chapter 4

1. Treggiari (1991), p. 8, citing, e.g., Plaut. *Capt.* 889; Suet. *Iul.* 52.3; Daube (1977), pp. 18–34 = Daube (2003), pp. 959–966.

2. Cf. Daube (1977), pp. 18–34 = Daube (2003), pp. 959–966.

3. Plin. *NH* 7.139–140.

4. Val. Max. 7.1.1 (but cf. 7.5.4).

5. Cornelia: Plin. *NH* 7.57; Sen., *Ad Helviam* 16.6. Claudia Fortunata: *AE* 1934.67.

6. Plin. *NH* 7.60.

7. Treggiari (1991), pp. 83–124 discusses the search for a marital power (including fertility, pp. 101–102).

8. Sor. *Gyn.* 1.34 (trans. Temkin [1956]). Gourevitch (1984) and Flemming (2000) discuss women in Roman medicine.

9. Sor. *Gyn.* 1.34–35.

10. E.g., Horsfall (1983), p. 93. Cf. the more nuanced statement of Treggiari (1991), p. 427: "If a couple failed to have children, it was usual to assume sterility in the wife."

11. E.g., the divorces of Sp. Carvilius Ruga (Val. Max. 2.1.4; Gell. *NA* 4.3.1–2; 17.21.44; etc.) and of Nero (Suet. *Ner.* 35.2). Cf. Juv. 2.137–138.

12. E.g., Aristot. *Gen. an.* 746.b12–747.a24; Caelius Aurelianus, *Gynaecia* 2.64–65. Brown (1987), pp. 336–340 gives an overview; see also Gourevitch (1984), pp. 144–148.

13. Lucr. 4.1233–1277.

14. Plin. *NH* 7.57.

15. See, e.g., Bongaarts and Potter (1983), pp. 41–43.

16. For fertility within the Roman demographic regime, see discussions by Parkin (1992), pp. 111–133 and Scheidel (2001), pp. 34–46, and for some of the implications Evans Grubbs (1995), pp. 107–108. Cf. Stone (1977), pp. 42–82, a vivid account of the demography of early modern England. Frier (1994) is a key study of fertility in Roman marriage, and see also Hin (2011).

17. Suet. *Aug.* 63.1.

18. Cic. *Att.* 10.18.1 (= 210 SB), with Treggiari (2007), p. 111. Hanson (1987) shows that "seven months' children" were often deemed to have a chance of surviving (seven being a "lucky" number), while children born dead were "eight months' children." The convention, she suggests, may have provided some comfort in the face of high infant mortality.

19. Cic. *Fam.* 6.18.5 (= 218 SB); Asc. 5 C with Treggiari (2007), p. 135.

20. Plin. *Ep.* 8.10–11, 10.2. Evans Grubbs (2006), pp. 316–320 gives a sketch of Pliny's family life.

21. Plin. *Ep.* 8.10.2.

22. See Brown (1987), pp. 336–337, 345–346.

23. Plin. *Ep.* 10.94.2.

24. Mart. 2.91.5, 11.53.5.

25. Lucr. 4.1236–1238.

26. Hopkins (1983), pp. 99–100, n. 85, 102, 242; Saller (1994), pp. 42, 64.

27. Shaw (1987) discusses the age of Roman women at marriage. On the age of the wife of the *laudatio*, Cf. Horsfall (1983), p. 93 and below, p. 92.

28. Forty and end of fecundity: Sor. *Gyn.* 1.34; Plin. *NH* 7.61. This likely corresponds to historical reality: Bongaarts and Potter (1983), pp. 41–43; Frier (1994), p. 321.

29. Richlin (1997), an important study of Pliny's references to women's health that informs this whole paragraph. Flemming (2000), pp. 129–184 also includes discussion of Pliny among other authors.

30. Foods, etc.: e.g., Plin. *NH* 22.83, 28.97, 28.253, 30.131. Ointments and suppositories: e.g., *NH* 28.52, 28.253. Waters of Sinuessa: *NH* 31.8.

31. Substances: e.g., Plin. *NH* 28.247, 28.250, 28.253. Amulets: *NH* 28.246, 36.151. On amulets, see also Bonner (1950), pp. 79–94 and Hanson (1995).

32. E.g., Plin. *NH* 32.24 (coral), 33.84, 37.50.

33. Schulz (2006), esp. pp. 95–120.

34. Ov. *Fast.* 2.423–452; Plut. *Rom.* 21.3–5; North (2008).

35. Natio: Cic. *ND* 3.47. Juno Lucina: Ov. *Fast.* 2.435–152, 3.244–258, with Schulz (2006), pp. 50–52, 55–57 and Dolansky (2011).

36. Dion. Hal. *Ant. Rom.* 2.25.7; Val. Max. 2.1.4; Plut. *Quaest. Rom.* 14; Gell. *NA* 4.3.1–2, 17.21.44. Full discussion in Watson (1965). On divorce in Rome, Treggiari (1991), pp. 435–482 is the essential starting place.

37. Plut. *Sull.* 6.11.

38. See below, pp. 113–114.

39. For events of 40 BC, see above, pp. 61–63; on the triumviral period, p. 179, n. 45.

40. Vell. Pat. 2.77.3; Suet. *Tib.* 4.3; Tac. *Ann.* 5.1.1.

41. Barrett (2002) is the essential study to date, and Bartman (1999) the visual complement. A path-breaking article by Purcell (1986) also remains essential, as are also articles by Flory, including Flory (1984), Flory (1988), Flory (1989), Flory (1993), and Flory (1995), and also Welch (2010).

42. Death of Livia's father, Livius Claudianus: Vell. Pat. 2.71.3 (cf. 2.94.1); Dio 48.44.1.

43. See esp. Suet. *Tib.* 4 for his life.

44. Vell. Pat. 2.75.1, 2.76.1; Suet. *Tib.* 4.2; Tac. *Ann.* 5.1.1, 6.51.1; Dio 48.15.3.

45. Vell. Pat. 2.75.2–3; Suet. *Tib.* 6.1–3; Dio 48.15.3–4.

46. Suet. *Tib.* 4.3, 6.2; Dio 48.15.3–4.

47. Vell. Pat.2.75.3; Suet. *Tib.* 4.3; Tac. *Ann.* 5.1.2; Dio 48.34.3.

48. Suet. *Aug.* 62.2; Dio 48.34.3.

49. Vell. Pat. 2.79.2; Suet. *Tib.* 4.3; Tac. *Ann.* 5.1.2; Dio 48.44.3.

50. Pontiffs: Tac. *Ann.* 1.10.5; Dio 48.44.2. On the chronology, see Barrett (2002), pp. 313–314.

51. For what follows I rely on Welch (2010), p. 318, relating Vell. Pat. 2.79.2–3 with Plin. *NH* 15.136–137.

52. In addition to Plin. *NH* 15.136–137, see Suet *Galb.* 1; Dio 48.52.3–4; Flory (1989); Flory (1995).

53. See sources in the previous note. On "The Poultry," see Klynne (2004), with earlier literature cited there.

54. See Flory (1989), esp. pp. 348–349, with earlier literature cited there.

55. For the legendary piety of Rome's *matronae*, see, e.g., Liv. 3.7.7–8; 5.25.8–9; 21.62.8; 27.37.8–10; further discussion below, pp. 131–134. Terentia apparently lived up to the ideal: Cic. *Fam.* 14.4.1 (= 6 SB); 14.7.1 (= 155 SB).

56. Welch (2010), esp. pp. 320–321, 325.

57. Dio 49.15.1; Cf. Ehrenberg and Jones (1955), p. 51.

58. Suet. *Aug.* 69–70; Flory (1988).

59. Dio 49.18.6.

60. Dio 49.38.1; Flory (1993). Osgood (2006), p. 334 gives further references.

61. Roller (2010) is an excellent study, through which all of the evidence and other discussions can be located. Below I cite only major sources, of which Plutarch's *Antony* is the most important. Kleiner (2005) proposes that Cleopatra and her encounters with the Romans made a deep and lasting impact on Roman culture, especially the arts.

62. Plut. *Ant.* 25–29; App. *B Civ.* 5.1, 5.8–11; Dio 48.24.2–3; 48.27.2.

63. Meeting of 37: Plut. *Ant.* 36; cf. Jos. *BJ* 1.362, *AJ* 15.96.

64. Cleopatra's arrival: Plut. *Ant.* 51; cf. Dio 49.31.4.

65. Plut. *Ant.* 53–54.1; App. *B Civ.* 5.138; Dio 49.33.3–4.

66. Plut. *Ant.* 54.3–6; Dio 49.41.1–4; Welch (2006).

67. Plut. *Ant.* 53.1; 54.1–2; 58.4; Dio 50.3.5, 50.26.1–2.

68. Antony's divorce: Liv. *Per.* 132; Plut. *Ant.* 57.2–3; Dio 50.3.2. Full details in Osgood (2006), pp. 298–349.

69. Osgood (2006), pp. 352–364, 368.

70. Osgood (2006), pp. 370–375, 387–388.

71. Octavian later boasted that he had 700 Senators served under his standards at the time of Actium (*RG* 25.3), apparently out of approximately 1000 (Dio 52.42.1).

72. See, e.g., Suet. *Aug.* 16.4; App. *B Civ.* 5.126; Dio 49.12.4; 54.15.4–8.

73. Crook (1996) is a superb account of Roman political history from 29 BC through 14 AD; for wider perspectives on this period, see Zanker (1988), Galinsky (1996), Wallace-Hadrill (2008), Levick (2010), and Galinsky (2012). On the triumphs of 29 BC: Osgood (2006), pp. 384–385.

74. Effigy of Cleopatra: Prop. 3.11.53–54; Plut. *Ant.* 86.3; Dio 51.21.8.

75. Handouts: Aug. *RG* 15.1, 15.3; Dio 51.21.3. Games: Dio 51.22.4–9.

76. Suet. *Aug.* 41.1; Dio 51.21.5.

77. Fuller details at Osgood (2006), p. 397. On the decoration of Augustan interiors, Galinsky (1996), pp. 179–197 and Clarke (2005) give good overviews, and see also Leach (1982).

78. Portico of Pompey: Prop. 2.32.11–16; 4.8.75; Ov. *Ars. am.* 1.67; 3.387. Portico of the Danaids: Prop. 2.31–32; Ov. *Ars. am.* 1.73–75; 3.389–390; *Am.* 2.2.3–4; *Tr.* 3.1.60–62. Public display of art: Plin. *NH* 35.26; Suet. *Aug.* 57.1.

79. Griffin (1985), pp. 1–31 is a brilliant evocation. On the postwar mood, see also Syme (1986), pp. 1–49 and Fantham (2006), pp. 32–44.

80. Hor. *Carm.* 1.37.1–2, 4–8.

81. Introductions to Propertius can be found in Hubbard (1974), Lyne (1980), and Keith (2008).

82. Prop. 1.1.1–2.

83. Prop. 1.11.13–14.

84. Prop. 1.6.29–30.

85. See, e.g., Griffin (1985), pp. 15–29; Wyke (1987); Treggiari (1991), pp. 299–307; Williams (1996), p. 132.

86. Apul. *Apol.* 10; cf. Ov. *Tr.* 2.2.427–440.

87. Volumnia: Cic. *Fam.* 9.26 (= 197 SB); Anderson, et al. (1979), pp. 152–155.

88. Griffin (1985), pp. 27–28; Wiseman (1985), pp. 44–49.

89. Shaw (1987) discusses the young age of marriage for Senatorial women in Rome.

90. Williams (1996), pp. 131–133, citing the same letter I do in the next paragraph. Richlin (1981) and Treggiari (1991), pp. 307–309, 461–465, 507–508 give fuller discussions of the evidence and its problems.

91. Cic. *Att.* 6.1.25 (= 115 SB); Syme (1961).

92. Williams (1996), p. 132.

93. Sen. *Clem.* 1.18.2, *De Ira* 3.40.2–5; Plin. *NH* 9.77; Tac. *Ann.* 1.10.5, 12.60.4; Dio 54.23.1–6.

94. E.g., Prop. 1.8, 2.16, 2.24B, 3.7; cf. 1.14

95. In addition to the works cited above, see Rich and Williams (1999).

96. Temple restoration: Aug. *RG* 20.4. Temple of Apollo: Aug. *RG* 19.1; Dio 53.1.3; Ehrenberg and Jones (1955), p. 53. On the temple Zanker (1988), pp. 85–89 and Galinsky (1996), pp. 213–224 are good discussions.

97. Vell. Pat. 2.81.3; Dio 49.15.5; Suet. *Aug.* 29.3.

98. See sources in previous note with the important discussion of Wiseman (2009). On Apollo: Zanker (1988), pp. 48–53, 85–89.

99. Aug. *RG.* 24.2; Suet. *Aug.* 52; cf. Dio 53.22.3.

100. Aug. *RG* 34.2; Ehrenberg and Jones (1955), no. 22; Zanker (1988), p. 96: "*pietas*....became the focal point of the new emperor's cultural and political program."

101. Williams (1962); Severy (2003), pp. 33–61, esp. 47. Dio 54.16.6 hints at Augustus's connection between civil war and immorality around this time.

102. Hor. *Carm.* 3.24.25–26, 28–29.

103. Hor. *Carm.* 3.6.25–32.

104. Hor. *Carm.* 3.14.5, 7, 14–16. The poem is well discussed by Treggiari (2005), pp. 130–131.

105. Suet. *Tib.* 9.1; Dio 53.26.1.

106. This aspect of the *laudatio* has been briefly noted in previous scholarship, e.g., Evans Grubbs (2006), pp. 315–316; Lindsay (2009), pp. 195–196.

107. For the traditional view of planned moral legislation in 28 BC: Williams (1962), pp. 28–29. Badian (1985) was the major attempt at refutation, but his arguments have been answered by Spagnuolo Vigorita (2010), pp. 1–9.

108. Prop. 2.7 (quotation from 13–14).

109. Dio 54.16.6 gives a hint of the opposition to moral reform around this time.

110. The scholarly literature on these laws is immense. Some discussions from which I have drawn, in addition to that of Spagnuolo Vigorita (2010), are Brunt (1971), pp. 558–566;

Treggiari (1991), pp. 60–80; and McGinn (1998), pp. 70–84. Evans Grubbs (2002), pp. 83–87 is a helpful summary.

111. Gai. *Inst.* 2.111, 2.144, 2.286; Dio 56.10.1. An alternative view holds that by the initial Julian law, there was no penalty for the married but childless (cf. Dio 54.16.2). But having children certainly was rewarded (see, e.g., Gell. *NA* 2.15.3–8; *Fragmenta Vaticana* 197; cf. Dio 53.13.2).

112. Ulp. *Reg.* 14–16.1.

113. Upper-class focus: Wallace-Hadrill (1981).

114. Treggiari (1991), pp. 277–298; McGinn (1998), pp. 140–147.

115. Full discussion in Spagnuolo Vigorita (2010), pp. 19–27.

116. For what follows, I draw on Lindsay (2009), pp. 195–197.

117. Suet. *Aug.* 34.2; Dio 54.16.7.

118. Suet. *Aug.* 34.2.

119. Tac. *Ann.* 15.19; cf. Suet. *Tib.* 35.2.

120. Gai. *Inst.* 2.286a.

121. Noy (1988), discussing the *s.c. Gaetulicianum*, preserved on papyrus.

122. Lindsay (2009), pp. 196–197 for this and what follows.

123. Prop. 2.7.19–20.

124. Noted, e.g., by Daube (1977), p. 32 = Daube (2003), p. 965.

Chapter 5

1. My account of Roman attitudes toward death throughout this chapter owes a great debt to Hope (2009), a book that I highly recommend, especially for its integration of many types of evidence. Other useful volumes I have consulted are Toynbee (1971), Hopkins (1983), Champlin (1991), Carroll (2006), Edwards (2007), Hope (2007), and Hope and Huskinson (2011).

2. *CIL* 6.4379, quoted by Hope (2009), p. 24.

3. Hope (2009), pp. 37–39, 41, 44.

4. Hope (2009), pp. 27–33. This is the context for understanding the Roman will, a document of immense cultural significance: Champlin (1991).

5. See above, p. 85.

6. Good discussion in Noy (2011), pp. 4–7, citing epigraphic and literary evidence (e.g., *AE* 1991.805; Cic. *Fin.* 2.58).

7. See above.

8. Prop. 4.7.73–76. Other *mandata* in Propertius: 1.21; 2.1.71–78, 2.13.17–42; 4.11.63–96.

9. Cosmeticians: Treggiari (1975), p. 52.

10. Hope (2009), pp. 18–22, 132.

11. Hope (2009), pp. 132–137; Manning (1981), pp. 12–20. Some examples from the Ciceronian corpus are *Fam.* 4.5 (= 248 SB), 5.14 (= 251 SB), 5.16 (= 187 SB); *Ad Brut.* 1.9 (= 18 SB). In his Epicurean poem *De rerum natura*, Lucretius enriches Epicurus's view that "death is nothing to us" (because the soul is material and so mortal) with elements

of this more popular consolatory tradition, which itself owed something to Epicureanism: see *DRN* 3.830–1094, with the valuable commentary of Kenney (1971).

12. Cic. *Fam.* 5.16.2 (= 187 SB). Wilcox (2005a) gives a discussion.

13. Cic. *Fam.* 5.16.6 (= 187 SB).

14. Hemelrijk (1999) is a full and rewarding study.

15. Hemelrijk (1999), pp. 146–184; Stevenson (2005).

16. Cic. *Att.* 13.21a.1–2 (= 327 SB); Hemelrijk (1999), p. 55; Skinner (2011), pp. 14–17.

17. Quint. *Inst.* 6.3.112.

18. Hemelrijk (1999), p. 51.

19. Sen. *Ad Marciam* 2.3–3.2; 4–6.

20. Sen. *Ad Helviam* 17.3.

21. Wistrand (1976), p. 67, 75. Wistrand's commentary on the philosophic language in the final section of the *laudatio* is most illuminating.

22. Prop. 4.11.2, 4.

23. Stat. *Silv.* 5.1.177–80, 181.

24. Courtney (1995), pp. 168–169, 378–379 gives text, translation, and commentary of the relevant inscribed texts (*CIL* 6.12652).

25. Toynbee (1971), pp. 33–34; Hope (2009), pp. 50–54; Noy (2011).

26. Treggiari (1998), pp. 14–23 discusses grief and guilt in Rome, using the example of Cicero; see also Treggiari (1991), pp. 495–498 and further below, pp. 95–99.

27. Lattimore (1962), pp. 187–190, 204

28. I assume the wife's age on the basis of the typical age of a Roman woman at the time of her first marriage (Shaw [1987]) as well as her maturity in handling threats at this time. See also Horsfall (1983), p. 93 and Lindsay (2009), p. 190.

29. Men's age at marriage: Saller (1987). Women's age: Shaw (1987).

30. In addition to Saller (1987), see Treggiari (1991), pp. 400–403 and Saller (1994), esp. pp. 12–69.

31. Women's role in Roman death rituals is discussed briefly within the surveys of Hope (2009), pp. 71–85, 125–132 and Graham (2011); and more specifically by Richlin (2001); Corbeill (2004), pp. 67–106; Mustakallio (2005); and Šterbenc Erker (2011). See also below, pp. 101–107.

32. See above, p. 61.

33. Val. Max. 7.1.1.

34. Hemelrijk (2004), pp. 188–190; Hope (2009), pp. 126–127.

35. Cic. *Q. Fr.* 3.6.3 (= 26 SB).

36. Sen. *Contr.* 4 praef. 4–5.

37. See, e.g., Suet. *Aug.* 65.2; Sen. *Consolatio ad Marciam* 15.2–3; Tac. *Ann.* 3.3–6, 4.8.

38. *Consolatio ad Liviam* 349–350.

39. Tac. *Ann.* 3.6.2.

40. Eck, et al. (1996), lines 123–132, 145–151. Lott (2012), pp. 125–158 gives the Latin text and an English translation.

41. Shackleton Bailey (1971), pp. 201–215; Treggiari (1998), pp. 14–23; Treggiari (2007), pp. 135–138.

42. Cicero and Tusculum: Cic. *Att.* 12.46 (= 287 SB); Plut. *Cic.* 40.3.

43. Cic. *Att.* 12.14 (= 251 SB, quotation from 12.14.3); Cic. *Att.* 12.40.2 (= 281 SB).

44. Atticus as Epicurean: e.g., Cic. *Fin.* 1.16; *Att.* 14.20.5 (= 374 SB), 15.4.2 (= 381 SB). Library: e.g., *Att.* 4.8.2 (= 79 SB); Nep. *Att.* 13.3.

45. Arrival in Astura: Cic. *Att.* 12.13 (= 250 SB). View of sea: Cic. *Att.* 12.9 (= 246 SB); *Att.* 12.19.1 (= 257 SB).

46. Cic. *Att.* 12.15 (= 252 SB).

47. Cic. *Att.* 12.14.3 (= 251 SB); cf. *Att.* 12.18.1 (= 254 SB), 12.20.2 (= 258 SB), 12.28.2 (= 267 SB); *Tusc.* 3.76.

48. Cic. *Att.* 12.4.3 (= 251 SB).

49. Cic. *Att.* 12.20.1 (= 258 SB).

50. Further complaints: e.g., Cic. *Att.* 12.21.5 (= 260 SB); 12.38a.1 (= 279 SB). Letter of Sulpicius: *Fam.* 4.5 (= 248 SB, quotation from 4.5.5).

51. Cic. *Fam.* 4.6.1 (= 249 SB), discussed by Wilcox (2005b).

52. Coleman-Norton (1939), pp. 224–226.

53. My discussion relies especially on Erskine (1997); Altman (2009) offers a different, but interesting, perspective.

54. Cic. *Tusc.* 3.62. Cicero engages critically with Epicurean views at *Tusc.* 3.32–54.

55. Cic. *Tusc.* 3.76.

56. Cic. *Tusc.* 3.82.

57. On slave readers (often women), see Treggiari (1976), p. 90.

58. Wistrand (1976), pp. 72–75.

59. Wistrand (1976), pp. 70–71 citing Sen. *Ad Marciam* 5.2. The argument is also used in *Consolatio ad Liviam* 265–270. For understanding the Roman obsession with *fama*, Flower (1996) and Flower (2006) are very useful.

60. *On Glory*: Coleman-Norton (1939), p. 223. Childhood goal: *Q. fr.* 3.5.4 (= 25 SB), slightly misquoting this Homeric line (*Il.* 11.784, also *Il.* 6.208).

61. Hom. *Il.* 7.89–90, 91, discussed by Griffin (1980), pp. 81–102.

62. Cic. *Sen.* 12. Quotation of Hector's lines in *On Glory*: Gell. *NA* 15.6.

63. Quoted by Lactant. *Div. Inst.* 1.15.19–20.

64. Shackleton Bailey (1965–1970), vol. 5, pp. 404–413.

65. Claridge (2010), pp. 204–207. See also below, p. 135.

Chapter 6

1. Hope (2009), pp. 65–66, 93. My account of Roman funerals in this chapter is much indebted to Hope (2009), pp. 65–96, and also draws on Toynbee (1971), pp. 43–64; Flower (1996); Richlin (2001); and Šterbenc Erker (2011).

2. Hope (2007), pp. 85–127 gives a good selection of textual material with helpful explanations.

3. Toynbee (1971), pp. 44 with note, p. 119 gives a full description. Compare the similar scene on a sarcophagus from Rome, housed in the British Museum, discussed by Hope

(2009), pp. 52–53; Noy (2011), p. 1–3. On *conclamatio* iconography in general: Huskinson (1996), pp. 13–15.

4. See above, p. 87.

5. Hope (2009), p. 43.

6. See especially Richlin (2001); Šterbenc Erker (2011).

7. On the dirge (*nenia*), see also Dutsch (2008).

8. Toynbee (1971), pp. 44–45; Flower (1996), pp. 93–95; and Hope (2009), p. 73 give briefer discussions; for a full description, see Sinn and Freyberger (1996), pp. 45–51.

9. Toynbee (1971), pp. 43–48; Flower (1996), pp. 97–114; Hope (2009), pp. 74–75.

10. Toynbee (1971), pp. 46–47; Flower (1996), pp. 98–99; and Hope (2009), pp. 74–75 offer brief treatments. Hughes (2005) is a fuller discussion.

11. For what follows see Toynbee (1971), pp. 39–55; Noy (2000); Hope (2009), pp. 77, 80–88.

12. For what follows see Toynbee (1971), p. 51, 61–64; Hope (2009), pp. 98–102.

13. Toynbee (1971), pp. 37–39, 52–54, 132–143; Hope (2009), p. 101.

14. Lattimore (1962), pp. 67–72.

15. In addition to the helpful commentary of Durry (1950), see *OCD* s.v. *manes* for an overview.

16. Catull. 101, superbly discussed by Feldherr (2000), which informs my account.

17. Durry (1950) commences his edition of the *Laudatio Turiae* with an excellent discussion of the *laudatio* (at pp. xi–xliii), which I have found very useful. Also important are Vollmer (1892); Kierdorf (1980); North (1983); Flower (1996), pp. 128–158.

18. Loraux (1986) gives a discussion.

19. Kierdorf (1980), pp. 94–105; Cf. North (1983), p. 170.

20. Durry (1950), pp. xxxv–xliii; with qualifications by Kierdorf (1980), pp. 58–93; and Flower (1996), pp. 133–136.

21. Flower (1996), pp. 136–145 accessibly discusses surviving quotations of *laudationes*.

22. Plin. *NH* 7.139, also discussed above, p. 66.

23. Flower (1996), p. 139.

24. Gronewald (1983).

25. E.g., Durry (1950), pp. xx–xxi.

26. Durry (1950), pp. xxii, lxxvii–lxxix. An example of such a graveside *laudatio* might be Atticus' remarks at his mother's funeral in 42 BC, in which Atticus managed to praise himself too (Nep. *Att.* 17.1–2).

27. Cf. North (1983), p. 170.

28. Cic. *De Or.* 2.44, but see Hillard (2001).

29. Suet. *Iul.* 6.1 (*laudavit…pro rostris*); Plut. *Caes.* 5.1–5.

30. Suet. *Iul.* 6.1.

31. *Laudatio* for grandmother Julia: Nic. Dam. *Vit. Aug.* 4; Quint. *Inst.* 12.6.1; Suet. *Aug.* 8.1. *Laudatio* for Octavia: Dio 54.35.5. I thank the anonymous reader for this point.

32. *CIL* 6.10230 = *ILS* 8394. Lindsay (2004) is the most helpful discussion, and see also Horsfall (1988); Saller (2001), p. 104.

33. Lindsay (2004), p. 97 writes that Murdia's son should "see her as a lady who has choices and who exercises them in a highly creditable manner"; Cf. Lindsay (2009) for the *Laudatio Turiae*.

34. Hemelrijk (2004), p. 194.

35. Cutolo (1983–1984), pp. 33–38 offers further remarks on the rhetoric of the husband's speech.

36. Kierdorf (1980), pp. 96–104; Flower (1996), p. 142.

37. Flower (1996), p. 42; Lindsay (2009), p. 183.

38. Prop. 1.6.25–26.

39. Prop. 1.17.19–24.

40. Prop. 2.25.36–37.

41. Prop. 1.6.13–14.

42. Prop. 1.8.31–32.

43. Prop. 3.12.38.

44. Prop. 4.3.69–70.

45. Prop. 4.11.46.

46. Wedding torches: Treggiari (1991), pp. 166, 168.

47. Williams (1958).

48. Prop. 2.15.36; 2.20.15–18, 34.

49. Cf. Williams (1958), p. 25.

50. Catull. 109. Wiseman (1985), pp. 101–107 contextualizes Catullus' tendency to see personal relations, including love, as solemn obligations.

51. Griffin (1985), pp. 142–162 discusses the interrelationship between love and death in the love poets, and also makes a strong case that love poetry and verse epitaphs were mutually enriching. Cutolo (1983–1984), pp. 38–47 argues for the influence of the elegiac poets, especially Propertius, on the husband's *laudatio*.

52. Val. Max. 4.6.3.

53. I discuss the "publication" of the *laudatio*, in monumental form, more fully below, pp. 139–145.

Chapter 7

1. On the missing pieces, see, e.g., Durry (1950), p. lxxxi. For the discovery of what survives, see above, pp. 3–7.

2. Mommsen (1863), pp. 477–478. Some other major discussions: Warde Fowler (1905); Durry (1950), pp. liv–lxiv; Horsfall (1983), pp. 91–92; Flach (1991), pp. 1–8; Lindsay (2009), pp. 185–189. My discussion here supersedes that in Osgood (2006), pp. 76–77.

3. 1.16, 47; 2.9. On his identity, see, e.g., Durry (1950), p. lv; Horsfall (1983), p. 98 note, 69; Lindsay (2009), p. 188.

4. Dio 52.42.4.

5. Cic. *Fam.* 13.7 (= 320 SB).

6. *RRC* 476.

7. Cf. Wistrand (1976), p. 32.

8. Cic. *Fam.* 13.56 (= 131 SB), hinting that Pompey may have been the true creditor; *Att.* 6.2.3 (= 116 SB), 13.46.2 (= 338 SB).

9. Reported in the edition of Orelli (1828) vol. 2, p. 352.

10. Val. Max. 6.7.2.

11. App. *B Civ.* 4.44.

12. Dio 54.10.1–2; cf. Aug. *RG* 11, 12.1. On his career, see Birley (2000).

13. Birley (2000), pp. 713–714. Ban lifted: Dio 41.18.2; Plut. *Caes.* 37.2; etc.

14. Caes. *BC* 3.7.1; cf. App. *B Civ.* 2.54.

15. Durry (1950), pp. lxi–lxii gives a clear statement of these.

16. Cf. Lindsay (2009), pp. 186–187.

17. Wistrand (1976), pp. 9–10.

18. Horsfall (1983), p. 91. Ramage (1994) gives a full discussion of the speaker's rhetorical abilities.

19. Millar (1988), in an excellent overview of Nepos' *Atticus*, specifically compares this biography to the *Laudatio Turiae* ("the closest parallel," p. 41); see also my earlier discussion, Osgood (2006), pp. 67–74. Horsfall (1989) gives a most useful commentary on *Atticus*, and his translation has informed mine.

20. Nep. *Att.* 2.3, 4.3–4.5.

21. Nep. *Att.* 13.1–2.

22. Nep. *Att.* 5.1–2, 13.6, 14.2–3. Uncle Caecilius' usury: Sen. *Ep.* 118.2. See also above, p. 42.

23. Nep. *Att.* 6.2.

24. Nep. *Att.* 6.4. Nepos states that Atticus did accept the title, but on a purely honorific basis; Jones (1999) has suggested an inscription from Ephesus attests Atticus holding such a prefectship.

25. Nep. *Att.* 6.5.

26. Nep. *Att.* 7.1.

27. Nep. *Att.* 8.6, 11–12. See above, p. 51.

28. Nep. *Att.* 10.3, 11.3–4.

29. Nep. *Att.* 17.1.

30. Nep. *Att.* 17.3.

31. Thus I join those scholars who have denied Mommsen's identification (e.g., Durry [1950], pp. liv–lxiv; Horsfall [1983], pp. 91–92; Flach [1991], pp. 1–8). Wiseman (1985), pp. 101–107 is a good discussion of a financial attitude not untypical of equestrians; see also Wiseman (1971), pp. 65–89.

32. As did Caesar in Gaul, and then the triumvirs in their various wars (better-documented phenomena): on prefects, see Nicolet (1966–1974), pp. 434–439; for equestrians in the triumviral period: Demougin (1983); Demougin (1988), pp. 19–69. One of Pompey's best-known prefects is the historian Velleius Paterculus' grandfather, who also had very close ties with Livia's first husband, Ti. Claudius Nero (Vell. Pat. 2.76.1).

33. Nep. *Att.* 7.2. Recall here Cicero's comment (*Att.* 8.13.2 [= 163 SB]) on the wealthy townspeople of Italy at the outbreak of civil war, quoted above, p. 14.

34. Nep. *Att.* 12.4 ("proscription of the equestrians").

35. See especially Millar (1988), building on Wiseman (1971), as well as works cited above, p. 191, n. 32.

36. Vedius Pollio: see above, p. 81. Marius of Urbinum: Val. Max. 7.8.6; *CIL* 11.6058, with Osgood (2006), pp. 272–273.

37. As is shown by the women of Atticus' family and their marriages: Millar (1988), pp. 46–47. More broadly, see Wiseman (1971), pp. 53–64.

38. I have discussed this briefly in Osgood (2006), pp. 267–273.

39. Welch (2009) is an outstanding discussion, and I draw on it here, of the writing of memoirs by one-time opponents or victims of Augustus after his victory.

40. Welch (2009), p. 196 notes the universal exoneration of Augustus. On this literature, see also above, pp. 54–55.

41. Cf. Welch (2009), p. 196.

42. Nep. *Att.* 10.4.

43. Nep. *Att.* 12.3.

44. Nep. *Att.* 10.4, 12.3, 10.2. This is not to say that he entirely embraced the victory of Augustus; for those who knew Cicero, Nepos' comment at *Att.* 16.4 could suggest otherwise.

45. See Osgood (2006), pp. 74–76, citing literary evidence for two other funerary monuments commemorating those who saved the proscribed.

46. Tanusia: Dio 47.7.4–5. Sulpicia: Val. Max. 6.7.3; App. *B Civ.* 4.39. Wife of Acilius: App. *B Civ.* 4.39.

47. Vell. Pat. 2.67.2.

48. Dio 44.13.1; cf. Plut. *Brut.* 13, *Cat. Min.* 73.4. Bibulus' work: Plut. *Brut.* 13.3.

49. Plut. *Brut.* 13.4–11 (quotation from 13.7); Dio 44.13.3–14.1; cf. Val. Max. 3.2.15 for a variant.

50. Plut. *Brut.* 23.2–6 (quotation from 23.6).

51. Octavia features in standard treatments of the triumviral period (above, p. 179, n. 45), as well as in scholarship on Livia (above, p. 183, n. 41). Two specific discussions are Singer (1947) and Bauman (1992), pp. 91–98.

52. Plut. *Ant.* 31; App. *B Civ.* 5.64, 66, 76; Dio 48.31.3.

53. Plut. *Ant.* 35; App. *B Civ.* 5.93, 5.95; Dio 48.54.3–5.

54. Plut. *Ant.* 35.3.

55. See above, pp. 57–59.

56. See above, pp. 75–76.

57. Plut. *Ant.* 54.1.

58. Plut. *Ant.* 54.2.

59. Plut. *Ant.* 57.3 (source of following quotation); cf. Plut. *Ant.* 87.1; Dio 51.15.7.

60. See above, pp. 62–64.

61. Welch (2010), pp. 314–317. Cf. Purcell (1986), pp. 86–88, 92. Sabine women: Liv. 1.13; another version in Dion. Hal. *Rom. Ant.* 2.45–47.

62. See above, p. 75.

63. Suet. *Aug.* 64.2, 73 (cf. Dio 54.16.4–5). This is discussed by Milnor (2005), pp. 83–85.

64. Dio 54.35.4–5.

65. Dio 47.7.4–5.

66. Bauman (1992), pp. 99–104 focuses on women and the rise of monarchy, as does Severy (2003) in a rich discussion of Augustus and family life. Milnor (2005) relates the Augustan emphasis on "private life" (including women) to the political needs of post-civil war Rome. In emphasizing continuity between the period of the civil wars and what followed, I follow Welch (2010). See also Kleiner (1996) and Kleiner (2005) for the 40s and 30s BC as foundational.

67. I owe this key point to Rawson (2005), who cites the significance of the sort of funerary monuments I discuss, for understanding the recognition of women and the family in Augustan Rome.

68. *CIL* 6.9499 = *ILS* 7472. Koortbojian (2006) is a full and excellent discussion of the monument (favoring an approximate date of 75–50 BC).

69. Davies (1985) discusses the iconography of clasped hands.

70. Kleiner (1990) and Kleiner and Matheson (1996), pp. 199–200.

71. Kleiner (1977) and Kockel (1993) are essential collections of the evidence with discussion; I also recommend Mouritsen (2005), an important study based on epigraphy.

72. Treggiari (1991), pp. 229–261; Dixon (1991) is also an important discussion.

73. Treggiari (1991), p. 231.

74. Treggiari (1991), pp. 248–249, 261.

75. Shaw (1987); Saller (1987); Saller (1994), pp. 25–41.

76. Suet. *Aug.* 62.2. Barrett (2002), pp. 115–145 gives an excellent discussion of Livia's role as the wife of Augustus.

77. Treggiari (2005) is a good overview of the recognition of women in Augustan Rome.

78. Flory (1984), Purcell (1986), Barrett (2002), and Welch (2010) are essential reading, and see also the other works mentioned above, p. 183, n. 41.

79. Dio 55.2.4.

80. Dio 54.23.6, 55.8.2; Suet. *Aug.* 29.4; Ov. *Fast.* 6.637–648; Flory (1984). On Pollio, see above, p. 81.

81. Ov. *Ars. am.* 1.71; Plin. *NH* 14.11.

82. Ov. *Fast.* 6.637–38.

83. Dio 55.2.5.

84. Dio 55.2.6–7, 56.10.2.

85. Milnor (2005), pp. 12–16.

86. Purcell (1986), pp. 85–86; Cf. Barrett (2002), pp. 174–185.

87. Guardianship: Dio 49.38.1.

88. Dio 56.32.1, 56.10.2.

89. Tac. *Ann.* 1.8.1; Suet. *Aug.* 101.1–3; Dio 56.32.1.

90. See esp. Suet. *Aug.* 100.4; Dio 56.46.1–2; full details in Barrett (2002), pp. 159–162.

91. Undowered girls: Dio 58.2.3. Fire victims: Dio 57.16.2. Firefighting: Suet. *Tib.* 50.3.

92. Shrines: e.g., Ov. *Fast.* 5.157–158, 6.637–638; Plin. *NH* 12.94; Dio 55.8.2, 56.46.3; *CIL* 6.883; full details in Barrett (2002), pp. 199–205. Dedication to Jupiter: Plin. *NH* 37.27.

93. A few examples: Suet. *Oth.* 1.1; Tac. *Ann.* 3.17.1–2, 5.2.2; Dio 58.2.2–3; Reynolds (1982), no. 13; full details in Barrett (2002), pp. 186–198.

94. Ehrenberg and Jones (1955), no. 102; Tac. *Ann.* 1.14.1–3, 3.71.1, 4.37–38; 5.2.1–2; Suet. *Tib.* 50.2–3; Dio 57.12.1–6, 58.2.1–6.

95. Dio 58.2.1–6.

96. Purcell (1986) is the major statement of such an argument; see also Kleiner (1986), and more broadly Fejfer (2008), pp. 331–369 on visual evidence and Welch (2010).

97. See Hemelrijk (2012), and for the situation in Rome, Eck (1984) is important.

98. Hemelrijk (2012) offers a splendid panorama, building on her earlier detailed studies, and is essential reading. Woodhull (2004) is a valuable case study (discussed immediately below).

99. My discussion relies on the study of Woodhull (2004).

Chapter 8

1. Discussions of the Augustan transformation of Rome are manifold; Purcell (1996) and Favro (2005) are helpful orientations, while Claridge (2010) is an invaluable guide to individual structures. See also the works cited below, p. 194, n. 9. *Maxima Roma*: e.g., Prop. 4.1.1.

2. Suet. *Aug.* 31.5. Geiger (2008) is a full study of this very important "hall of fame" (as he calls it). Note that prior to the building of this Forum, a gallery of distinguished Romans in the old Forum may have been created ca. 15 BC: see the epigraphic evidence gathered at *CIL* 6.40912–40928.

3. Brief account with further references in Claridge (2010), pp. 204–207.

4. Cooley (2009) is a splendid introduction to this text (preserved only in provincial copies) and its monumental display.

5. Suet. *Claud.* 1.5.

6. The source for this is so-called *Tabula Siarensis* (fr. 2. col. A 5–7); see p. 195, n. 16 below and Cooley (2009), p. 5.

7. Ehrenberg and Jones (1955), no. 69; translation in Cooley (2003), pp. 221–223.

8. See esp. Dio 55.10a.1–8.

9. On the epigraphic revolution in the lifetime of Augustus, see Eck (1984), Wallace-Hadrill (1990), Alföldy (1991), Elsner (1996), and Woolf (1996). This last paper has been especially helpful to me in writing this chapter. Güven (1998) is an interesting analysis of the monumental display of the text of the *Res Gestae*. Hope (2009), pp. 151–181 gives an overview of the development of funerary monuments, including epitaphs.

10. Gordon and Gordon (1957), pp. 80–82; Gordon (1983), pp. 5–7, 38–39; Bodel (2001), pp. 7–8.

11. *CIL* 6.32323; *AE* 1988.20–21. A good translation of the inscribed texts pertaining to this festival can be found in Cooley (2003), pp. 271–276. For a discussion of the festival, see Beard, et al. (1998), vol. 1, pp. 201–206.

12. See Woolf (1996) on this aspect of Roman monuments.

13. Gordon (1983), pp. 100–101.

14. Aug. *RG* 8.5.

15. Quoted by Suet. *Aug.* 31.5.

16. This is recorded in the so-called *Tabula Siarensis* fr. 2. col a 5–7: text and translation can be found conveniently in Lott (2012), pp. 79–100.

17. Geiger (2008), pp. 112–115 argues for statues of the women in the Forum of Augustus, but there is no firm evidence. The new Portico of Octavia included a statue of at least one exemplary woman, Cornelia, mother of the Gracchi: see Plin. *NH* 34.31 with Hemelrijk (1999), pp. 66–67.

18. *CIL* 6.40356–57. On her funeral, see above, p. 128.

19. Prop. 4.11. Hallett (1985) is an outstanding discussion that I draw on here.

20. Prop. 4.11.35–36.

21. Hallett (1985); Cf. Hemelrijk (2004).

22. Prop. 4.11.11–12.

23. Prop. 4.11.50.

24. Prop. 4.11.44.

25. Prop. 4.11.67.

26. Hutchinson (2006), pp. 1–21 gives a good overview of Propertius' fourth and last book of poetry, emphasizing elements of "discontinuity."

27. Prop. 4.11.71–72.

28. Prop. 4.11.57–60.

29. Prop. 4.11.61.

30. On the *laudatio Murdiae*, see above, pp. 109–112.

31. On the appearance of the laudatio, see, among other discussions, Gordon (1950); Wistrand (1976), pp. 11–16; Horsfall (1983), pp. 85–89; Gordon (1983), pp. 103–104.

32. Keegan (2008) makes some suggestions that inform this paragraph.

33. Brief account with further references in Claridge (2010), pp. 430–431. On the inscription on the monument, see Gordon (1983), pp. 99–100.

34. Flower (1996), p. 182 suggests that Caecilia's very simple epitaph may have been a "conscious archaism," in keeping with her family's long and glorious history.

35. On Cicero's plans for a shrine, see above, p. 99.

36. *CIL* 6.15345 = *ILS* 8403. Text, translation, and commentary in Courtney (1995), pp. 46–47, 234–236.

37. Wistrand (1976), pp. 14–15.

38. Horsfall (1983), p. 89.

39. Horsfall (1983), p. 89. Reading of *laudationes:* Dio 56.34.4, 56.42.1.

40. *CIL* 9.3158 = *ILS* 2682. Translation in Cooley (2003), p. 388.

41. See above, pp. 83–86.

42. Suet. *Aug.* 89.2; Liv. *Per.* 59.

43. Quoted at Gell. *NA* 1.6.2.

44. Williams (1996), pp. 131–137 is a brilliant discussion.

45. Ulp. *Reg.* 14; cf. Suet. *Aug.* 34.

46. Val. Max. 7.7.4.

47. The dislike is shown by efforts to "evade" the law, as Treggiari (1991), pp. 79, 297 rightly puts it. A colorful example, the Senatorial Vistilia who registered as a prostitute so that she could have extramarital sex, caught the eye of Tacitus (*Ann.* 2.85.2). Fantham (2006) discusses the complicated problem of Julia's (alleged) adulteries.

48. See above, pp. 85–86.

49. *CIL* 6.15345 = *ILS* 8403.

50. Dixon (1991) brings out new public expressions of the view in the early imperial period. The outstanding exception to this trend is Juvenal's enormous sixth satire, well discussed by Braund (1992), who relates it to some more positive statements about marriage as well as standard rhetorical exercises on the theme of whether or not a man should marry—background not irrelevant for understanding the *laudatio*.

51. Prop. 4.11.79–84. Did the husband of the *laudatio* have such a painting to offer him solace?

52. For a fuller understanding of this opening up of the domestic, consult Milnor (2005).

53. Evans Grubbs (2006), pp. 316–320 is a brief sketch of Pliny's family life. Walsh (2006) is an excellent translation of all of Pliny's letters with a helpful introduction. Syme (1958) is the classic study of this new ruling class.

54. Stat. *Silv.* 5.1.43–44.

55. Stat. *Silv.* 5.1.47.

56. Stat. *Silv.* 3.5.22–24.

57. Plin. *Ep.* 6.4, 6.7, 7.5.

58. Plin. *Ep.* 8.5.

59. Tac. *Agr.* 6.1.

60. Suet. *Tib.* 7.2–3.

61. The good old days: Val. Max. 2.1.5b, 6.3.9–10. "Marital love": Val. Max. 4.6.

62. Val. Max. 4.3.3.

63. I draw on Marshall (1975) and Barrett (2006), as well as Dixon (1991), pp. 100–101.

64. Caecilia Metella: Plut. *Sull.* 6.12, etc. Cornelia: Plut. *Pomp.* 66.3, 74–76.1, etc.

65. Full details in Marshall (1975) and Barrett (2006). For a detailed discussion of Julia's travels in the East with Agrippa, see Fantham (2006), pp. 61–67.

66. Helvia: Sen. *Consolatio ad Helviam* 19.6. Tacitus' wife: *Agr.* 45.4–5. Calpurnia: Plin. *Ep.* 10.120–121.

67. Tac. *Ann.* 3.33–35.1.

68. Tac. *Ann.* 3.33.1.

69. Tac. *Ann.* 3.34.6. She was later accused of adultery (Tac. *Ann.* 4.3.2–5, 4.10.2, 4.39–40, 6.2.1, 6.29.4).

70. See esp. Tac. *Ann.* 4.19–20; *Dig.* 1.16.4.2 (Ulpian).

71. Plin. *Ep.* 3.9.

72. Here I disagree with Riess (2012), pp. 495–497, who writes of the *laudatio*: "…the text really does not depict her individual personality, but rather a type, even in its most detailed *encomium*." As I see it, the wife is exemplary, but also individual.

Appendix 1

1. See above, pp. 55–56.

2. On the auction of Milo's property, see above, p. 37.

3. See above, p. 38.

4. Kierdorf (1980), pp. 35–42; Flach (1991), p. 5–6.

5. Lacking the Portuense fragment, Mommsen (1863), p. 466 still dated events of 1.1–26 to the outbreak of the war between Pompey and Caesar, on the grounds that the husband, with his wealth and standing, must have taken a stand in the civil war, and it would have been on the Pompeian side. As I would see it, the discovery of the Portuense fragment spectacularly vindicated Mommsen's intuition.

6. It is, of course, possible that the mother's house was separate from that of her son (see above, p. 37), but regardless, taking care of the mother fits well into the context of the civil war.

7. Horsfall (1983), p. 93.

Bibliography

Alföldy, G. (1991). "Augustus und die Inschriften: Tradition und Innovation. Die Geburt der imperialen Epigraphik." *Gymnasium* 98:289–324.

Altman, W. H. F. (2009). "Womanly Humanism in Cicero's *Tusculan Disputations*." *TAPA* 139:407–441.

Anderson, R. D., Parsons, P. J., and Nisbet, R. G. M. (1979). "Elegiacs by Gallus from Qaṣr Ibrîm." *JRS* 69:125–155.

Badian, E. (1985). "A Phantom Marriage Law." *Philologus* 129:82–98.

Badian, E. (2009). "From the Iulii to Caesar." In Griffin, M., ed., *A Companion to Julius Caesar*, 11–22. Malden.

Barrett, A. A. (2002). *Livia: First Lady of Imperial Rome*. New Haven.

Barrett, A. A. (2006). "Augustus and the Governors' Wives." *RhMus* 149:129–147.

Bartman, E. (1999). *Portraits of Livia: Imaging the Imperial Woman in Augustan Rome*. Cambridge.

Bauman, R. A. (1992). *Women and Politics in Ancient Rome*. London and New York.

Beard, M., North, J., and Price, S. (1998). *Religions of Rome*. 2 vols. Cambridge.

Berry, D. H. (2000). *Cicero: Defence Speeches*. Oxford.

Birley, A. R. (2000). "Q. Lucretius Vespillo (*cos. ord.* 19)." *Chiron* 30:711–748.

Bodel, J., ed. (2001). *Epigraphic Evidence: Ancient History from Inscriptions*. London.

Bongaarts, J., and Potter, R. G. (1983). *Fertility, Biology, and Behavior: An Analysis of the Proximate Determinants*. New York and London.

Bonner, C. (1950). *Studies in Magical Amulets, Chiefly Graeco-Egyptian*. Ann Arbor.

Bowman, A. K., Champlin, E., and Lintott, A., eds. (1994). *The Cambridge Ancient History*. 2nd ed. Vol. 10, *The Augustan Empire, 43 B.C.–A.D. 69*. Cambridge.

Bradley, K. (1994). *Slavery and Society at Rome*. Cambridge.

Braund, D. C. (1985). *From Augustus to Nero: A Sourcebook on Roman History 31 BC–AD 68*. London.

Braund, S. H. (1992). "Juvenal—Misogynist or Misogamist?" *JRS* 82:71–86.

Brennan, T. C. (2012). "Perceptions of Women's Power in the Late Republic: Terentia, Fulvia, and the Generation of 63 BCE." In James, S. L., and Dillon, S., eds., *A Companion to Women in the Ancient World*, 354–366. Malden.

Brown, R. D. (1987). *Lucretius on Love and Sex: A Commentary on* De rerum natura IV, *1030–1287 with Prolegomena, Text, and Translation*. Leiden.

Brunt, P. A. (1971). *Italian Manpower,* 225 B.C.–A.D. 14. Oxford.

Buckland, W. W. (1908). *The Roman Law of Slavery*. Cambridge.

Carroll, M. (2006). *Spirits of the Dead: Roman Funerary Commemoration in Western Europe*. Oxford.

Castor, H. (2006). *Blood and Roses: One Family's Struggle and Triumph during England's Tumultuous Wars of the Roses*. New York.

Champlin, E. (1991). *Final Judgments: Duty and Emotion in Roman Wills,* 200 BC–AD 250. Berkeley.

Claassen, J.-M. (1996). "Documents of a Crumbling Marriage: The Case of Cicero and Terentia." *Phoenix* 50:208–232.

Claridge, A. (2010). *Rome: An Oxford Archaeological Guide*. Oxford.

Clarke, J. (2005). "Augustan Domestic Interiors: Propaganda or Fashion?" In Galinsky, K., ed., *The Cambridge Companion to the Age of Augustus*, 264–278. Cambridge.

Cluett, R. G. (1998). "Roman Women and Triumviral Politics, 43–37 B.C." *EMC* 42:67–84.

Coleman-Norton, P. R. (1939). "The Fragmentary Philosophical Treatises of Cicero." *CJ* 34:213–228.

Colley, L. (1992). *Britons: Forging the Nation, 1707–1837*. New Haven.

Cooley, A. E. (2009). Res Gestae Divi Augusti: *Text, Translation, and Commentary*. Cambridge.

Cooley, M. G. K. (2003). *The Age of Augustus*. London.

Corbeill, A. (2004). *Nature Embodied: Gesture in Ancient Rome*. Princeton.

Courtney, E. (1995). Musa lapidaria: *a Selection of Latin Verse Inscriptions*. Oxford.

Crook, J. A. (1986). "Woman in Roman Succession." In Rawson, B., ed., *The Family in Ancient Rome: New Perspectives*, 58–82. Ithaca.

Crook, J. A. (1990). " 'His and Hers': What Degree of Financial Responsibility Did Husband and Wife Have for the Matrimonial Home and Their Life in Common, in a Roman Marriage?" In Andreau, J., and Bruhns, H., eds., *Parenté et stratégies familales dans l'antiquité romaine*, 153–172. Rome.

Crook, J. A., Lintott, A., and Rawson, E., eds. (1994). *The Cambridge Ancient History*. 2nd ed. Vol. 9, *The Last Age of the Roman Republic, 146–43 BC*. Cambridge.

Crook, J. A. (1996). "Political History, 30 B.C. to A.D. 14." In Bowman, A. K., et al., eds., *The Cambridge Ancient History*. 2nd ed. Vol. 10, 70–112. Cambridge.

Cutolo, P. (1983–1984). "Sugli aspetti letterari poetici e culturali della cosiddetta *Laudatio Turiae*." *Annali della facoltà di lettere e filosofia dell'Università di Napoli* 26:33–65.

D'Ambra, E. (2007). *Roman Women*. Cambridge.

Daube, D. (1964). "Dodges and Rackets in Roman Law." *Proceedings of the Classical Association* 61:28–30.

Daube, D. (1972). *Civil Disobedience in Antiquity*. Edinburgh.

Daube, D. (1977). *The Duty of Procreation*. Edinburgh.

Daube, D. (1986). "Fraud No. 3." In MacCormick, N., and Birks, P., eds., *The Legal Mind: Essays for Tony Honoré*, 1–17. Oxford.

Daube, D. (2003). *Biblical Law and Literature: Collected Works of David Daube*. Volume 3. Carmichael, C., ed. Berkeley.

Davies, G. (1985). "The Significance of the Handshake Motif in Classical Funerary Art." *AJA* 89:627–640.

Demougin, S. (1983). "Notables municipaux et l'ordre équestre à l'époque des dernières guerres civiles." In *Les bourgeoisies municipales italiennes aux IIᵉ et Iᵉʳ siècles av. JC.* 279–298. Paris.

Demougin, S. (1988). *L'ordre équestre sous les julio-claudiens*. Collection de l'Ecole française de Rome 108. Paris.

de Rossi, J.-B. (1856). "Relazioni dei lavori fatti dal sottoscritto per il *Corpus Inscriptionum Latinarum* dal Novembre 1855 all'Ottobre 1856." *Monatsberichte der Königlichen Preussische Akademie der Wissenschaften zu Berlin* 1856:562–568.

Dixon, S. (1983). "A Family Business: Women's Role in Patronage and Politics at Rome 80–44 BC." *C&M* 34:91–112.

Dixon, S. (1985). "Breaking the Law to Do the Right Thing: The Gradual Erosion of the Voconian Law in Ancient Rome." *Adelaide Law Review* 9:519–534.

Dixon, S. (1986). "Family Finances: Terentia and Tullia." In Rawson, B., ed., *The Family in Ancient Rome: New Perspectives*, 93–120. Ithaca.

Dixon, S. (1991). "The Sentimental Ideal of the Roman Family." In Rawson, B., ed., *Marriage, Divorce, and Children in Ancient Rome*, 99–113. Oxford.

Dolansky, F. (2011). "Reconsidering the Matronalia and Women's Rites." *CW* 104:191–209.

Dunbabin, K. M. D. (2002). *Mosaics of the Greek and Roman World*. Cambridge.

Durry, M. (1950). *Éloge funèbre d'une matrone romaine (éloge dit de Turia)*. Paris.

Dutsch, D. (2008). "*Nenia*: Gender, Genre, and Lament in Ancient Rome." In Suter, A., ed., *Lament: Studies in the Ancient Mediterranean and Beyond*, 258–279. Oxford.

Dyck, A. (2003). "Evidence and Rhetoric in Cicero's *Pro Roscio Amerino*: The Case against Sex. Roscius." *CQ* 53:235–246.

Dyson, S. L. (1992). *Community and Society in Roman Italy*. Baltimore.

Eck, W. (1984). "Senatorial Self-Representation: Developments in the Augustan Period." In Millar, F., and Segal, E., eds., *Caesar Augustus: Seven Aspects*, 129–167. Oxford.

Eck, W., Caballos, A., and Fernández, F. (1996). *Das senatus consultum de Cn. Pisone patre*. Munich.

Edwards, C. (2007). *Death in Ancient Rome*. New Haven.

Ehrenberg, V., and Jones, A. H. M. (1955). *Documents Illustrating the Reigns of Augustus and Tiberius*. 2nd ed. Oxford.

Elsner, J. (1996). "Inventing *imperium*: Texts and the Propaganda of Monuments in Augustan Rome." In Elsner, J., ed., *Art and Text in Roman Culture*, 32–53. Cambridge.

Erskine, A. (1997). "Cicero and the Expression of Grief." In Braund, S. M., and Gill, C., eds., *The Passions in Roman Thought and Literature*, 36–47. Cambridge.

Evans Grubbs, J. (1995). *Law and Family in Late Antiquity: The Emperor Constantine's Marriage Legislation*. Oxford.

Evans Grubbs, J. (2002). *Women and the Law in the Roman Empire: A Sourcebook on Marriage, Divorce, and Widowhood*. London.

Evans Grubbs, J. (2006). "The Family." In Potter, D., ed., *A Companion to the Roman Empire*, 312–326. Malden.

Fantham, E. (2006). *Julia Augusti: The Emperor's Daughter*. London and New York.

Fantham, E., Foley, H. P., Kampen, N. B., Pomeroy, S. B., and Shapiro, H. A. (1995). *Women in the Classical World*. Oxford.

Favro, D. (2005). "Making Rome a World City." In Galinsky, K., ed., *The Cambridge Companion to the Age of Augustus*, 234–263. Cambridge.

Fejfer, J. (2008). *Roman Portraits in Context*. Berlin and New York.

Feldherr, A. (2000). "*Non inter nota sepulcra*: Catullus 101 and Roman Funerary Ritual." *CA* 19:209–231.

Flach, D. (1991). *Die sogenannte Laudatio Turiae: Einleitung, Text, Übersetzung und Kommentar*. Texte zur Forschung 58. Darmstadt.

Flemming, R. (2000). *Medicine and the Making of Roman Women: Gender, Nature, and Authority from Celsus to Galen*. Oxford.

Flory, M. B. (1984). "*Sic exempla parantur*: Livia's Shrine to Concordia and the Porticus Liviae." *Historia* 33:309–330.

Flory, M. B. (1988). "*Abducta Neroni uxor*: The Historiographical Tradition on the Marriage of Octavian and Livia." *TAPA* 118:343–359.

Flory, M. B. (1989). "Octavian and the Omen of the *gallina alba*." *CJ* 84:343–356.

Flory, M. B. (1993). "Livia and the History of Public Honorific Statues for Women in Rome." *TAPA* 123:287–308.

Flory, M. B. (1995). "The Symbolism of Laurel in Cameo Portraits of Livia." *MAAR* 40:43–68.

Flower, H. I. (1996). *Ancestor Masks and Aristocratic Power in Roman Culture*. Oxford.

Flower, H. I. (2006). *The Art of Forgetting: Disgrace and Oblivion in Roman Political Culture*. Chapel Hill.

Frederiksen, M. (1966). "Caesar, Cicero and the Problem of Debt." *JRS* 56:128–141.

Frier, B. (1985). *The Rise of the Roman Jurists: Studies in Cicero's Pro Caecina*. Princeton.

Frier, B. (1994). "Natural Fertility and Family Limitation in Roman Marriage." *CP* 89:318–333.

Galinsky, K. (1996). *Augustan Culture: An Interpretive Introduction*. Princeton.

Galinsky, K. (2012). *Augustus: Introduction to the Life of an Emperor*. Cambridge.

Gardner, J. F. (1986). *Women in Roman Law and Society*. London.

Gardner, J. F. (1993). *Being a Roman Citizen*. London.

Gardner, J. F. (1998). *Family and Familia in Roman Law and Life*. Oxford.

Gaughan, J. E. (2010). *Murder Was Not a Crime: Homicide and Power in the Roman Republic*. Austin.

Geiger, J. (1973). "The Last Servilii Caepiones of the Republic." *Anc. Soc.* 4:143–156.

Geiger, J. (2008). *The First Hall of Fame: A Study of the Statues in the Forum Augustum*. Leiden.

Goold, G. P. (1990). *Propertius: Elegies*. Cambridge, Mass.

Gordon, A. E. (1950). "A New Fragment of the *Laudatio Turiae*." *AJA* 54:223–226.

Gordon, A. E. (1983). *Illustrated Introduction to Latin Epigraphy*. Berkeley.

Gordon, A. E., and Gordon, J. S. (1957). *Contributions to the Palaeography of Latin Inscriptions.* Berkeley.

Gourevitch, D. (1984). *Le mal d'être femme: La femme et la medicine à Rome.* Paris.

Gowing, A. M. (1992). "Lepidus, the Proscriptions, and the *Laudatio Turiae*." *Historia* 41:283–296.

Graham, E.-J. (2011). "Memory and Materiality: Re-embodying the Roman Funeral." In Hope, V. M., and Huskinson, J., eds., *Memory and Mourning: Studies on Roman Death*, 21–39. Oxford and Oakville, Conn.

Grant, M. (1975). *Cicero: Murder Trials.* London.

Griffin, J. (1980). *Homer on Life and Death.* Oxford.

Griffin, J. (1985). *Latin Poets and Roman Life.* London.

Gronewald, M. (1983). "Ein Neues Fragment der Laudatio Funebris des Augustus auf Agrippa." *ZPE* 52:61–62.

Güven, S. (1998). "Displaying the *Res Gestae* of Augustus: A Monument of Imperial Image for All." *JSAH* 57:30–45.

Hallett, J. (1977). "Perusinae Glandes and the Changing Image of Augustus." *AJAH* 2:151–171.

Hallett, J. (1985). "Queens, *princeps*, and Women of the Augustan Elite: Propertius' Cornelia-Elegy and the *Res Gestae Divi Augusti*." In Winkes, R., ed., *The Age of Augustus*, 73–88. Providence.

Hanson, A. E. (1987). "The Eight Months' Child and the Etiquette of Birth: *obsit omen!*" *Bulletin of the History of Medicine* 61:589–602.

Hanson, A. E. (1995). "Uterine Amulets and Greek Uterine Medicine." *Medicina nei secoli* 7:281–299.

Harris, W. V. (2006). "A Revisionist View of Roman Money." *JRS* 96:1–24.

Hemelrijk, E. A. (1987). "Women's Demonstrations in Republican Rome." In Blok, J., and Mason, P., *Sexual Asymmetry: Studies in Ancient Society*, 217–240. Amsterdam.

Hemelrijk, E. A. (1999). Matrona docta: *Educated Women in the Roman Elite from Cornelia to Julia Domna.* London and New York.

Hemelrijk, E. A. (2004). "Masculinity and Femininity in the *Laudatio Turiae*." *CQ* 54:185–197.

Hemelrijk, E. A. (2012). "Public Roles for Women in the Cities of the Latin West." In James, S. L., and Dillon, S., eds., *A Companion to Women in the Ancient World*, 478–490. Malden.

Heyworth, S. J. (2007). *Sexti Properti Elegos.* Oxford.

Hillard, T. W. (2001). "Popilia and *laudationes funebres* for Women." *Antichthon* 35:45–63.

Hin, S. (2011). "Family Matters: Fertility and Its Constraints in Roman Italy." In Holleran, C., and Pusdey, A., eds., *Demography and the Graeco-Roman World: New Insights and Approaches*, 99–116. Cambridge and New York.

Hinard, F. (1985). *Les proscriptions de la Rome républicaine.* Rome.

Hope, V. M. (2007). *Death in Ancient Rome: A Sourcebook.* London and New York.

Hope, V. M. (2009). *Roman Death: The Dying and the Dead in Ancient Rome.* London.

Hope, V. M., and Huskinson, J., eds. (2011). *Memory and Mourning: Studies on Roman Death.* Oxford and Oakville, Conn.

Hopkins, K. (1983). *Death and Renewal*. Cambridge.

Hopwood, B. *(forthcoming)*. "Hortensia Speaks: An Authentic Voice of Resistance." In Welch, K., ed., *Appian's* Rhomaika: *Empire and Civil War*. Swansea.

Horsfall, N. (1983). "Some Problems in the 'Laudatio Turiae.'" *BICS* 30:85–98.

Horsfall, N. (1988). "Stylistic Observations on Two Neglected Subliterary Prose Texts." In Horsfall, N., ed., Vir bonus discendi peritus: *Studies in Celebration of Otto Skutsch's Eightieth Birthday*, 53–56. London.

Horsfall, N. (1989). *Cornelius Nepos: A Selection, Including the Lives of Cato and Atticus*. Oxford.

Hubbard, M. (1974). *Propertius*. London.

Hughes, L. A. (2005). "Centurions at Amiternum: Notes on the Apisius Family." *Phoenix* 59:77–91.

Huskinson, J. (1996). *Roman Children's Sarcophagi: Their Decoration and Its Social Significance*. Oxford.

Hutchinson, G. (2006). *Propertius: Elegies, Book IV*. Cambridge.

James, S. L., and Dillon, S., eds. (2012). *A Companion to Women in the Ancient World*. Malden.

Jones, C. P. (1999). "Atticus in Ephesus." *ZPE* 124:89–94.

Keegan, P. (2008). "Turia, Lepidus, and Rome's Epigraphic Environment." *Studia Humaniora Tartuensia* 9:1–7.

Keith, A. M. (2008). *Propertius: Poet of Love and Leisure*. London.

Kenney, E. J. (1971). *Lucretius: De rerum natura Book III*. Cambridge.

Keppie, L. (1991). *Understanding Roman Inscriptions*. Baltimore.

Kierdorf, W. (1980). *Laudatio funebris: Interpretationen und Untersuchungen zur Entwicklung der Römischen Leichendrede*. Meisenheim am Glam.

Kleiner, D. E. E. (1977). *Roman Group Portraiture: The Funerary Reliefs of the Late Republic and Early Empire*. New York.

Kleiner, D. E. E. (1986). "Private Portraiture in the Age of Augustus." In Winkes, R., ed., *The Age of Augustus*, 107–135. Providence.

Kleiner, D. E. E. (1990). "Social Status, Marriage, and Male Heirs in the Age of Augustus: A Roman Funerary Relief." *North Carolina Museum of Art Bulletin* 14:20–28.

Kleiner, D. E. E. (1992). *Roman Sculpture*. New Haven.

Kleiner, D. E. E. (1996). "Imperial Women as Patrons of the Arts in the Early Empire." In Kleiner, D. E. E., and Matheson, S. B., eds., *I, Claudia: Women in Ancient Rome*, 28–41. Austin.

Kleiner, D. E. E. (2005). *Cleopatra and Rome*. Cambridge, Mass.

Kleiner, D. E. E., and Matheson, S. B., eds. (1996). *I, Claudia: Women in Ancient Rome*. Austin.

Klynne, A. (2004). "The Laurel Grove of the Caesars: Looking In and Looking Out." In Santillo Frizell, B., and Klynne, A., eds., *Roman Villas around the* Urbs: *Interaction with Landscape and Environment*, 1–9. Rome.

Kockel, V. (1993). *Porträtsreliefs stadtrömischer Grabbauten*. Mainz.

Koortbojian, M. (2006). "The Freedman's Voice: The Funerary Monument of Aurelius Hermia and Aurelia Philematio." In D'Ambra, E., and Métraux, G., eds., *The Art of Citizens, Soldiers and Freedmen in the Roman World*, 91–99. Oxford.

Kruschwitz, P. (1999). "Zu 'Laudatio Turiae' 2, 6a." *ZPE* 126:88–90.

Lange, C. H. (2009). Res publica constituta: *Actium, Apollo, and the Accomplishment of the Triumviral Assignment*. Leiden.

Langlands, R. (2006). *Sexual Morality in Ancient Rome*. Cambridge.

Lattimore, R. (1962). *Themes in Greek and Latin Epitaphs*. Urbana.

Leach, E. W. (1982). "Patrons, Painters, and Patterns: The Anonymity of Romano-Campanian Painting and the Transition from the Second to the Third Style." In Gold, B. K., ed., *Literary and Artistic Patronage in Ancient Rome*, 135–173. Austin.

Lendon, J. E. (2011). "Roman Honor." In Peachin, M., ed., *The Oxford Handbook of Social Relations in the Roman World*, 377–403. Oxford.

Levick, B. (2010). *Augustus: Image and Substance*. Harlow.

Lindsay, H. (2004). "The *laudatio Murdiae*: Its Content and Significance." *Latomus* 63:88–97.

Lindsay, H. (2009). "The Man in Turia's Life, with a Consideration of Inheritance Issues, Infertility, and Virtues in Marriage in the 1st c. B.C." *JRA* 22:183–198.

Lintott, A. W. (1968). *Violence in Republican Rome*. Oxford.

Lintott, A. W. (2009). "The Assassination." In Griffin, M., ed., *A Companion to Julius Caesar*, 72–82. Malden.

Loraux, N. (1986). *The Invention of Athens: The Funeral Oration in the Classical Greek City*. Cambridge, Mass.

Lott, J. B. (2012). *Death and Dynasty in Early Imperial Rome: Key Sources, with Text, Translation, and Commentary*. Cambridge.

Lyne, R. O. A. M. (1980). *The Latin Love Poets: From Catullus to Horace*. Oxford.

MacMullen, R. (1974). *Roman Social Relations*, 50 B.C.–A.D., 284. New Haven.

Manning, C. E. (1981). *On Seneca's "Ad Marciam."* Leiden.

Marshall, A. J. (1975). "Tacitus and the Governor's Lady: A Note on Annals iii.33–4." *G&R* 22:11–18.

McGinn, T. A. J. (1998). *Prostitution, Sexuality, and the Law in Ancient Rome*. New York.

Millar, F. (1988). "Cornelius Nepos, 'Atticus,' and the Roman Revolution." *G&R* 35:40–55.

Milnor, K. (2005). *Gender, Domesticity and the Age of Augustus: Inventing Private Life*. Oxford.

Mommsen, T. (1863). "Zwei Sepulcralreden aus der Zeit Augusts und Hadrians." *Abhandlungen der Königlichen Akademie der Wissenschaften zu Berlin* 1863: 455–489.

Mouritsen, H. (2005). "Freedmen and Decurions: Epitaphs and Social History in Imperial Italy." *JRS* 95:38–63.

Münzer, F. (1999). *Roman Aristocratic Parties and Families*. Ridley, T., trans. Baltimore.

Mustakallio, K. (2005). "Roman Funerals: Identity, Gender and Participation." In Mustakallio, K., et al., eds., *Hoping for Continuity: Childhood, Education and Death in Antiquity and the Middle Ages*, 179–190. Rome.

Nicolet, C. (1966–1974). *L'Ordre équestre à l'époque républicaine (312–43 av. J.-C.)*. 2 vols. Paris.

North, J. A. (1983). "These He Cannot Take." *JRS* 73:169–174.

North, J. A. (2008). "Caesar at the Lupercalia." *JRS* 98:144–160.

Noy, D. (1988). "The Senatusconsultum Gaetulicianum: *manus* and Inheritance." *Tijdschrift voor Rechtgeschiednis* 56:299–304.

Noy, D. (2000). "Building a Roman Funeral Pyre." *Antichthon* 34:30–45.

Noy, D. (2011). "'Goodbye Livia': Dying in the Roman Home." In Hope, V. M., and Huskinson, J., eds., *Memory and Mourning: Studies on Roman Death*, 1–20. Oxford and Oakville, Conn.

Oliver, D. (2000). "Jewelry for the Unmarried." In Kleiner, D. E. E., and Matheson, S. B., eds., *I, Claudia II: Women in Roman Art and Society*, 115–124. Austin.

Orelli, J. K. (1828). *Inscriptionum latinarum...collectio.* 2 vols. Rome.

Osgood, J. (2006). *Caesar's Legacy: Civil War and the Emergence of the Roman Empire.* Cambridge, UK.

Parkin, T. G. (1992). *Demography and Roman Society.* Baltimore.

Patterson, J. R. (1992). "The City of Rome: From Republic to Empire." *JRS* 82:186–215.

Pearce, T. E. (1974). "The Role of the Wife as *custos* in Ancient Rome." *Eranos* 72:16–33.

Pelling, C. B. R. P. (1996). "The Triumviral Period." In Crook, J. A., et al., eds., *The Cambridge Ancient History.* 2nd ed. Vol. 10, 1–69.

Pomeroy, S. B. (1975). *Goddesses, Whores, Wives, and Slaves: Women in Classical Antiquity.* New York.

Powell, A. (2008). *Virgil the Partisan: A Study in the Re-integration of Classics.* Swansea.

Powell, A. (2009). "Augustus' Age of Apology: An Analysis of the Memoirs—and an Argument for Two Further Fragments." In Smith, C., and Powell, A., eds., *The Lost Memoirs of Augustus*, 173–194. Swansea.

Purcell, N. (1986). "Livia and the Womanhood of Rome." *PCPS* 32:78–105.

Purcell, N. (1996). "Rome and Its Development under Augustus and His Successors." In Bowman, A. K., et al., eds., *The Cambridge Ancient History.* 2nd ed. Vol. 10, 782–811. Cambridge, UK.

Ramage, E. S. (1994). "The So-called *Laudatio Turiae* as Panegyric." *Athenaeum* 82: 341–370.

Ramsey, J. T. (2001). "Did Mark Antony Contemplate an Alliance with His Political Enemies?" *CP* 96:255–270.

Ramsey, J. T. (2004). "Did Julius Caesar Temporarily Banish Mark Antony from His Inner Circle?" *CQ* 54:161–173.

Rawson, E. (1994a). "Caesar: Civil War and Dictatorship." In Crook, J. A., et al., eds., *The Cambridge Ancient History.* 2nd ed. Vol. 9, 424–459. Cambridge, UK.

Rawson, E. (1994b). "The Aftermath of the Ides." In Crook, J. A., et al., eds., *The Cambridge Ancient History.* 2nd ed. Vol. 9, 468–490. Cambridge, UK.

Rawson, B. (2005). Review of Severy, *Augustus and the Family at the Birth of the Roman Empire. Bryn Mawr Classical Review* 2005.05.15 (online).

Reynolds, J. (1982). *Aphrodisias and Rome.* London.

Rice Holmes, T. (1923). *The Roman Republic and the Founder of the Empire.* 3 vols. Oxford.

Rice Holmes, T. (1928). *The Architect of the Roman Empire.* 2 vols. Oxford.

Rich, J. W., and Williams, J. H. C. (1999). "*Leges et iura p. R. restituit*: A New Aureus of Octavian and the Settlement of 28–27 BC." *NC* 159:169–213.

Richlin, A. (1981). "Approaches to the Sources on Adultery at Rome." *Women's Studies* 8:225–250.

Richlin, A. (1997). "Pliny's Brassiere." In Hallett, J. P., and Skinner, M. B., eds., *Roman Sexualities*, 197–220. Princeton.

Richlin, A. (2001). "Emotional Work: Lamenting the Roman Dead." In Tylawsky, E., and Weiss, C., eds., *Essays in Honor of Gordon Williams*, 229–248. New Haven, Conn.

Riess, W. (2012). "*Rari exempli femina*: Female Virtues on Roman Funerary Inscriptions." In James, S. L., and Dillon, S., eds., *A Companion to Women in the Ancient World*, 491–501. Malden.

Roller, D. W. (2010). *Cleopatra: A Biography*. Oxford.

Saller, R. P. (1987). "Men's Age at Marriage and Its Consequences in the Roman Family." *CP* 82:21–34.

Saller, R. (1994). *Patriarchy, Property, and Death in the Roman Family*. Cambridge, UK.

Saller, R. (2001). "The Family and Society." In Bodel, J., ed., *Epigraphic Evidence: Ancient History from Inscriptions*, 95–117. London and New York.

Saller, R. (2007). "Household and Gender." In Scheidel, W., Morris, I., and Saller, R., eds., *The Cambridge Economic History of the Greco-Roman World*, 87–112. Cambridge, Mass.

Scheidel, W. (2001). "Progress and Problems in Roman Demography." In Scheidel, W., ed., *Debating Roman Demography*, 1–82. Leiden.

Schulz, C. E. (2006). *Women's Religious Activity in the Roman Republic*. Chapel Hill.

Scullard, H. H. (1982). *From the Gracchi to Nero: A History of Rome* 133 B.C. to A.D. 68. 5th ed. London.

Severy, B. (2003). *Augustus and the Family at the Birth of the Roman Empire*. New York and London.

Shackleton Bailey, D. R. (1965–1970). *Cicero: Letters to Atticus*. 7 vols. Cambridge, Mass.

Shackleton Bailey, D. R. (1971). *Cicero*. London.

Shackleton Bailey, D. R. (1976). *Two Studies in Roman Nomenclature*. Philadelphia.

Shackleton Bailey, D. R. (1977). *Cicero: Epistulae ad familiares*. 2 vols. Cambridge, Mass.

Shackleton Bailey, D. R. (2001). *Cicero: Letters to Friends*. 3 vols. Cambridge, Mass.

Shackleton Bailey, D. R. (2002). *Cicero: Letters to Quintus and Brutus; Letter Fragments; Letter to Octavian; Invective; Handbook of Electioneering*. Cambridge, Mass.

Shaw, B. D. (1987). "The Age of Roman Girls at Marriage: Some Reconsiderations." *JRS* 77:30–46.

Singer, M. W. (1947). "Octavia's Mediation at Tarentum." *CJ* 43:173–178.

Sinn, F., and Freyberger, K. S. (1996). *Vatikanische Museen: Museo Gregoriano Profano ex Lateranense; Die Grabdenkmäler 2; Die Ausstatung des Hateriergrabes*. Mainz.

Skinner, M. B. (2011). *Clodia Metelli: The Tribune's Sister*. Oxford.

Spagnuolo Vigorita, T. (2010). *Casta domus: Un seminario sulla legislazione matrimoniale augustea*. Naples.

Šterbenc Erker, D. (2011). "Gender and Roman Funeral Ritual." In Hope, V. M., and Huskinson, J., eds., *Memory and Mourning: Studies on Roman Death*, 40–60. Oxford and Oakville, Conn.

Stevenson, J. (2005). *Women Latin Poets: Language, Gender, and Authority, from Antiquity to the Eighteenth Century*. Oxford.

Stone, L. (1977). *The Family, Sex and Marriage in England, 1500–1800*. New York.

Storoni Mazzolani, L. (1982). *Una moglie*. Rome.

Sumi, G. S. (2004). "Civil War, Women and Spectacle in the Triumviral Period." *Ancient World* 35:196–206.

Syme, R. (1939). *The Roman Revolution*. Oxford.

Syme, R. (1958). *Tacitus*. 2 vols. Oxford.

Syme, R. (1961). "Who Was Vedius Pollio?" *JRS* 51:23–30.

Syme, R. (1986). *The Augustan Aristocracy*. Oxford.

Temkin, O. (1956). *Soranus' Gynecology*. Baltimore.

Toher, M. (2006). "The Earliest Depiction of Caesar and the Later Tradition." In Wyke, M., ed., *Julius Caesar in Western Culture*, 29–44. Malden.

Toynbee, J. M. C. (1971). *Death and Burial in the Roman World*. London.

Traina, G. (2001). "Lycoris the Mime." In Fraschetti, A., ed., *Roman Women*, 82–99. Chicago.

Treggiari, S. (1973). "Domestic Staff in the Julio-Claudian Period." *Histoire sociale* 6: 241–255.

Treggiari, S. (1975). "Jobs in the Household of Livia." *PBSR* 43:48–77.

Treggiari, S. (1976). "Jobs for Women." *AJAH* 1:76–104.

Treggiari, S. (1991). *Roman Marriage: Iusti coniuges from the Time of Cicero to the Time of Ulpian*. Oxford.

Treggiari, S. (1998). "Home and Forum: Cicero between 'Public' and 'Private.'" *TAPA* 128:1–23.

Treggiari, S. (2005). "Women in the Time of Augustus." In Galinsky, K., ed., *The Cambridge Companion to the Age of Augustus*, 130–147. Cambridge, UK.

Treggiari, S. (2007). *Terentia, Tullia and Publilia: The Women of Cicero's Family*. London and New York.

Vaglieri, D. (1898). "Di un nuovo frammento del così detto elogio di Turia, rinvenuto sulla via Portuense." *Not. Scav.* 1898:412–418.

Vollmer, F. (1892). "Laudationum funebrium romanorum historia et reliquiarum editio." Fleckeisens Jahrbuch für class. Phil. Suppl. 18, 445–528. Leipzig.

Wallace-Hadrill, A. (1981). "Family and Inheritance in the Augustan Marriage Laws." *PCPS* 27:58–80.

Wallace-Hadrill, A. (1990). "Roman Arches and Greek Honours: The Language of Power at Rome." *PCPS* 36:143–181.

Wallace-Hadrill, A. (2008). *Rome's Cultural Revolution*. Cambridge, UK.

Walsh, P. G. (2006). *Pliny the Younger: Complete Letters*. Oxford.

Warde Fowler, W. (1905). "On the New Fragment of the So-Called Laudatio Turiae." *CR* 19:261–266.

Watson, A. (1965). "The Divorce of Carvilius Ruga." *Tijdschrift voor Rechtgeschiednis* 33:38–50.

Watson, A. (1967). *The Law of Persons in the Later Roman Republic.* Oxford.

Watson, A. (1971). *The Law of Succession in the Later Roman Republic.* Oxford.

Welch, K. E. (1995). "Antony, Fulvia, and the Ghost of Clodius in 47 B.C." *G&R* 42:182–201.

Welch, K. E. (1996). "T. Pomponius Atticus: A Banker in Politics?" *Historia* 45:450–471.

Welch, K. E. (2006). "*Maiestas regia* and the Donations of Alexandria." *Mediterranean Archaeology* 19–20:181–192.

Welch, K. E. (2009). "Alternative Memoirs: Tales from the 'Other Side' of the Civil War." In Smith, C., and Powell, A., eds., *The Lost Memoirs of Augustus*, 195–224. Swansea.

Welch, K. E. (2010). "Velleius and Livia: Reflecting History." In Cowan, E., ed., *Velleius Paterculus: Making History*, 309–334. Swansea.

Welch, K. E. (2012). *Magnus Pius: Sextus Pompeius and the Transformation of the Roman Republic.* Swansea.

Wilcox, A. (2005a). "Sympathetic Rivals: Consolation in Cicero's Letters." *AJP* 126:237–255.

Wilcox, A. (2005b). "Paternal Grief and the Public Eye: Cicero *ad Familiares* 4.6." *Phoenix* 59:267–287.

Williams, G. (1958). "Some Aspects of Roman Marriage Ceremonies and Ideals." *JRS* 48:16–29.

Williams, G. (1962). "Poetry in the Moral Climate of Augustan Rome." *JRS* 52:28–46.

Williams, G. (1996). "Representations of Roman Women in Literature." In Kleiner, D. E. E., and Matheson, S. B., eds., *I, Claudia: Women in Ancient Rome*, 126–138. Austin.

Wiseman, T. P. (1971). *New Men in the Roman Senate*, 139 B.C.–A.D. 14. London.

Wiseman, T. P. (1985). *Catullus and His World: A Reappraisal.* Cambridge, Mass.

Wiseman, T. P. (2009). "The House of Augustus and the Lupercal." *JRA* 22:527–545.

Wistrand, E. (1976). *The So-Called* Laudatio Turiae. Studia Graeca et Latina Gothoburgensia 34. Göteborg.

Wood, S. E. (1999). *Imperial Women: A Study in Public Images,* 40 B.C.–A.D. 68. Leiden.

Woodhull, M. (2004). "Matronly Patrons in the Early Roman Empire: The Case of Salvia Postuma." In McHardy, F., and Marshall, E., eds., *Women's Influence on Classical Civilization*, 75–91. London and New York.

Woolf, G. (1996). "Monumental Writing and the Expansion of Roman Society in the Early Empire." *JRS* 86:22–39.

Wyke, M. (1987). "Written Women: Propertius' *scripta puella.*" *JRS* 77:47–61.

Zanker, P. (1988). *The Power of Images in the Age of Augustus.* Shapiro, A., trans. Ann Arbor.

Index

discovery of its fragments, 3–7, 27, 121, 151
gaps in, 11, 39, 117–118
identity of its characters, 5, 117–124
reconstruction of its appearance, 3–7, 139–140, 142
rhetoric in, 111, 121
See also husband in *LT*; wife in *LT*
laudationes, 97, 105, 107–112, 122, 139, 142
Lepidus. *See* Aemilius Lepidus, M.
lex Voconia, 22–23, 85, 88, 132
Licinia, Cicero's neighbor, 26
Livia Drusilla, 35
 as builder, 131–132, 135
 father of, 72
 honored publicly, 75, 82, 131–132
 marriage to Augustus, 73–75, 85, 131, 147, 148
 marriage to Ti. Claudius Nero, 71–74
 as mother, 68, 90, 94
 and philosophy, 90
 refugee during civil wars, 8
Lucretius, poet, 68
Lucretius Vespillo, Q., sometimes identifies as husband in *LT*, 5, 117–124
Lupercalia, 69

mandata, 23, 88
manus. *See* marriage, Roman, with *manus*
marriage, Roman
 ages at, 69, 92, 130
 changing evaluations of, 128–131, 145–149
 with *manus*, 19, 20, 23, 40, 85, 88
 property in, 40–43, 59, 84–85, 109–110, 131–132, 144 (*see also* Terentia)
 purpose of, 66, 80, 86, 143
 traditional ideals of, 85–86, 112–115, 138, 143
 See also Augustus, legislation on marriage and adultery
Milo. *See* Annius Milo, T.
Murdia. *See* Laudatio Murdiae

Octavia, wife of Mark Antony
 divorced by Antony, 76, 127
 funeral of, 109, 128, 138
 honored publicly, 75, 82, 127
 marriage to Antony, 63, 75, 126, 147

as mother, 83, 90, 94, 127
as peacemaker, 126–127
Octavian. *See* Augustus
Orestilla, wife of Plautius, 114, 146

pearls. *See* jewelry, women's
pietas, 20, 24, 82
Pliny the Elder, 69
Pliny the Younger, 68, 145, 146–147, 148, 152
Pompey the Great (C. Pompeius Magnus), 23, 28, 49, 122, 123
 See also civil war
Pompey, Sextus, 54, 57, 62–63, 71–74
Pomponius Atticus, T.
 biography of, by Cornelius Nepos, 42, 121–122, 125
 as equestrian, 42, 121–123
 finances of, 42, 50, 122
 friend of Servilia, 50, 51
 helps friends during civil war, 51, 122, 125
 money-manager for friends, 34, 99
 relationship with Cicero, 95–96
Popilia, mother of Q. Lutatius Catulus, 109
Porcia, wife of Brutus, 49, 125–126, 127
Priscilla, wife of Abascantus, 90, 145–146
Propertius
 and death, 88, 112–114
 elegy for Cornelia, 90, 113, 138–139, 145
 love poetry of, 27, 78–80, 138
 on marriage legislation, 83–86, 114
proscriptions, triumviral, 52–60
 memories of, 53, 54, 124–128
pudicitia, 19, 25–27, 31, 36, 39, 66, 84, 110, 150

Rome, city of
 during Caesarian civil war, 11–12, 27–30, 32–39, 61
 during triumviral period, 56, 71, 74, 76, 125
 after final victory of Augustus, 77–78, 132–134, 135–138

Salvia Postuma, of Pula, 8, 118, 134
Scribonia, wife of Augustus, 73, 138–139
self-help, at Rome, 18
Seneca the Younger, 90, 98, 147
Septicia, wife of Publicius, 144

Printed in the USA
CPSIA information can be obtained
at www.ICGtesting.com
CBHW032002071223
2464CB00003B/99